BIRNBAUM'S
Disneyland®
RESORT
THE OFFICIAL VACATION GUIDE 2025-2026

Wendy Lefkon Editorial Director

Jessica Ward Editor

Disney Editions Design Team Designer

Alexandra Mayes Birnbaum Consulting Editor

Stephen Birnbaum Founding Editor

Disney
EDITIONS

LOS ANGELES · NEW YORK

For Steve, who merely made all this possible.

ISBN: 978-1-368-10496-8
FAC-023274-25205
First Edition, October 2025
10 9 8 7 6 5 4 3 2 1

Printed in the United States of America

Other 2025 Birnbaum's Official Disney Guides:
Walt Disney World
Walt Disney World for Kids

THE OFFICIAL
D𝒾𝓈𝓃𝑒𝓎 FAN CLUB

CONTENTS

115 GOOD MEALS, GREAT TIMES

Whether it's a simple snack or a multi-course feast, the Disneyland Resort offers something for nearly every palate and pocketbook. Our dining and entertainment section reflects Disneyland Resort's extensive range of possibilities, from the spirited nightspots in the Downtown Disney District to theme park dinner shows, birthday celebrations, and the ever-popular meals hosted by Disney characters.

141 SPORTS & RECREATION

Perhaps you dream of catching the perfect wave, hiking along cliffs above the Pacific coast, polishing your tennis serve, or taking in a spectator sport. It's a cinch to fulfill your fondest athletic fantasies in the land of sun and surf.

WHAT'S NEW?

To spotlight the various attractions, shows, shops, and restaurants making their debut, some listings are marked with the "new" icon shown here. Look for it throughout this book. Here are a few highlights:

A Word from The Editors

Walt Disney, the man who pioneered the realm of family entertainment, was at once an artist, entrepreneur, and creative visionary. He was also a dad. And, like many of the folks who visit Disneyland each year, Walt treasured the time he spent with his kids. In fact, while his two daughters were growing up, Walt would accompany them to carnivals, zoos, and local amusement parks. It was something of a Saturday tradition for the Disney family. During these outings he'd often make the same observation: The youngsters were happily entertained, but the adults didn't have much to do. It didn't seem right that he'd be stuck sitting on a bench while the kids had all the fun. To his way of thinking, a park should appeal to the sense of wonder and exploration in guests of all ages. His bold vision became a reality on July 17, 1955, when Disneyland had its opening day in Anaheim, California.

Now, over 70 magical years later, Disneyland is in the midst of a celebration. The Disneyland 70th Anniversary party began in late spring 2025 and will continue through summer 2026. A vacation during this wonderful time means special entertainment, new additions to classic attractions, and a slew of unique surprises. As if we needed extra convincing to visit the "Happiest Place on Earth"! Walt's original park is as beloved as ever—and it continues to grow and evolve. Disneyland park has an exciting new attraction in Bayou Country—Tiana's Bayou Adventure! The splashy crowd-pleaser—inspired by the beloved Disney animated feature *The Princess and the Frog*—offers joyous thrills and enchanting original music in a one-of-a-kind Mardi Gras celebration. Of course, Disneyland park continues to delight park-goers of all ages with new favorites such as Mickey & Minnie's Runaway Railway, Star Wars: Rise of the Resistance, and a refreshed Fantasmic!, plus cherished classics, including "it's a small world", Pirates of the Caribbean, Haunted Mansion, Peter Pan's Flight, and the Magic Happens afternoon parade.

Set across from Disneyland, Disney California Adventure is firing on all cylinders. Attractions such as Soarin' Around the World, Guardians of the Galaxy—Mission: BREAKOUT!, and Radiator Springs Racers helped put this place on the map, but they're just the tip of the iceberg. In addition to a super land dubbed Avengers Campus, guests are treated to an array of attractions and entertainment bearing that distinctive Disney Parks stamp. Among them are Toy Story Midway Mania!, Incredicoaster, and the vibrant (wildly popular) nighttime spectacle, World of Color.

While we have traditionally published a meticulously revised edition each year, as founder Steve Birnbaum did, we have decided upon a bold change. We now live in an age of instant access to information, which enables anyone with a smartphone to look up the nearest location of a Mickey waffle. Magical! That syrupy golden treat can be tickling your taste buds all the sooner. So where does a book like ours fit into the equation? Well, we can suggest the best attractions to ride—and to avoid!—after enjoying said Mickey waffle, and explain *why*. We realize that the firsthand experiences gathered by our editors are what make this guide truly unique. Owing to this, and due to the fact that Disneyland news breaks so often and the most up-to-date information is always available on *disneyland.com*, we have elected to move to a biannual publication schedule, with large-scale updates every two years and smaller updates in between. This new schedule should give us ample time to accrue more firsthand experiences, which, accumulated over the years, make this book the most authoritative guide to the Disneyland Resort. Those experiences (where we leave no attraction untested, no snack or meal untasted, no hotel untried) are what fuel the thoughtful details in the guide's updates. Our expertise, however, was not achieved by being escorted through back doors of attractions. Instead, we have waited in lines with everyone else, always hoping to have a Disney experience like any other guest.

Of course, there's so much more to the Disneyland Resort than the theme parks. There's also a dynamic dining, shopping, and entertainment zone known as the Downtown Disney District—which is experiencing a renaissance with new restaurants, shops, and entertainment, and three Disney hotels (with one having received an exciting Pixar makeover). It all adds up to a total that is truly greater than the sum of its parts. And, though it has seven decades of history under its belt, this is still just the beginning—as per its founder's wishes: "Disneyland will never be completed. It will continue to grow as long as there is imagination left in the world."

TAKE OUR ADVICE

In creating this book, we've considered every possible aspect of your trip, from planning it to plotting day-by-day activities. We realize that even the most meticulous vacation planner needs detailed, accurate, and objective information to prepare a successful itinerary. To achieve that lofty goal, we encourage the submission of factual information and insight from Disneyland staffers—but the decision to use such information is entirely at the discretion of the editor.

We have also packaged handy bits of advice in the form of "Hot Tips" throughout the book. These helpful hints come directly from the copious notes we have taken during our countless trips to the Disneyland Resort and the surrounding Anaheim area. We have also used our "Birnbaum's Best" stamp of approval wherever we deemed it appropriate, highlighting our favorite attractions, shows, and restaurants—the crowd-pleasers we feel stand head, shoulders, and ears above the rest.

You, the reader, benefit from the combination of our decades of experience and access to inside information from the Disneyland staff—that makes this guide unique. We like to think it's indispensable, but you be the judge of that 150 pages from now.

DON'T FORGET TO WRITE!

No contribution is of greater value to us in preparing the next edition of this book than your comments on its usefulness and your own experiences at the Disneyland Resort. We encourage you to send us an email at **WDI.Birnbaum.Guides@disney.com**, or drop us a note at the address below. Thank you!

Attn: Birnbaum Guides
7 Hudson Square
New York, NY 10013

CREDIT WHERE CREDIT IS DUE

Enormous thanks to the amazing teams of dedicated, detail-conscious Disneyland Resort cast members from Guest Communications, the Disney Resort Reservation Center, Food & Beverage, Merchandise, Resort Operations, Attractions Operations, Disney Vacation Club, Marketing, Disney Parks Synergy, and more for helping us ensure the factual accuracy of *Birnbaum's Official Guide to Disneyland Resort 2025–2026*.

Immeasurable gratitude to our incredible predecessor Jill Safro, for being the most magical mentor. Kudos to copy editor extraordinaire Warren Meislin. We'd also like to tip our hats to Jerry Gonzalez, Jennifer Eastwood, Winnie Ho, Monica Vasquez, Jennifer Thornton, Kinden Sevorwell, Joksan Alcala, Julie Rose, Lindsay Swantek, Matt Stroshane, Mathew James, Valerie Lee, Chris Ostrander, Flossie Gillen, Alyce Diamandis, Dan Kunkel, Jilly Bean Kunkel, and Christina Fontana for their editorial support and production panache.

Of course, no list of acknowledgments would be complete without mentioning our founding editor, Steve Birnbaum, whose spirit, wisdom, and humor still infuse these pages, as well as Alexandra Mayes Birnbaum, who continues to be a guiding light—to say nothing of a careful reader of every word.

THE LAST WORD

Finally, it's important to remember that every worthwhile travel guide is a living enterprise; the book you hold in your hands is our best effort at explaining how to enjoy the Disneyland Resort at the moment, but its text is not etched in stone. Details change often—especially these days! Disneyland is always charging and growing, and in each edition we refine and expand our material to better serve your needs. Just before the grand opening of Disneyland, Walt Disney remarked that the main attraction was still missing: people. That's where you come in.

Have a wonderful time!

—The Editors

GETTING READY TO GO

To all who come to this happy place: Welcome. Disneyland is your land. So said Walt Disney on July 17, 1955. Fast-forward 70 fun-filled years, and the "Happiest Place on Earth" is as welcoming as ever, hosting millions of visitors from around the globe year in and year out. The beloved 500-acre Disneyland Resort has evolved quite a bit over time, but Walt's original theme park, Disneyland, is still at its heart. Besides this magical kingdom, guests will discover Disney California Adventure park; Downtown Disney District, a trio of elaborately themed on-site resort hotels: Disney's Grand Californian Hotel & Spa, Pixar Place Hotel, and the Disneyland Hotel; and dozens of decidedly Disney dining and shopping destinations.

Of course, you will want to do and see it all, but where should you start? When should you go? And then there are the all important questions of how to get there and where to stay. Maybe you'd like to extend your California vacation—perhaps you will even include a visit to (or a stay at) the beach or one of the other nearby attractions.

That's a lot to think about. But don't worry: By the time you've read this chapter, you will have the information you need to make smart decisions. So read on, and remember—a little advance planning can go a very long way. Note that details are subject to change. For updates, visit *disneyland.com*.

When to Go

When you weigh the best times to visit the Disneyland Resort, the most obvious possibilities often seem to be weekends, Christmas, Easter, and summer vacation—particularly if there are children in the family. But there are a few good reasons to avoid these periods—the major one being that almost everybody else wants to go then, too. (While foot traffic at Disney California Adventure [aka DCA] is often lighter than it is over at Disneyland park, DCA is a whole lot busier than it was in years past.)

If you can only visit during one of these busy times and worry that the crowds might spoil your fun, there are some tactics for making optimal use of every minute and avoiding the longest of lines—notably, go to the park early to get a jump on the day (and on the crowds), use Lightning Lane service if budget allows, and remember that Disney keeps the parks open later during busy seasons. Note that "early admission" (aka "Early Entry") to Disneyland park or Disney California Adventure park is available 7 days a week for guests registered at one of the three Disneyland Resort hotels (The Disneyland hotel, the new Pixar Place Hotel, and Disney's Grand Californian Resort & Spa; refer to pages 42–46 of the *Accommodations* chapter for hotel specifics). For updates and additional information, use the Disneyland mobile app or visit *disneyland.com*.

On the other hand, choosing to visit when the parks are least crowded may mean that you miss some special events—a treasured fireworks show or parade might not be listed on the entertainment schedule, and certain shows and attractions may be closed for annual refurbishment.

A lovely time to visit is the kickoff to the holiday season, starting in mid-November. That's when the Christmas parade takes place and carolers add festive music to the mix. Other good times to visit are the periods after the busy summer months—September through early October—and after New Year's Day.

When Not to Go: If crowds make you queasy, keep in mind that Saturday is traditionally the busiest day of the week year-round. In summer, Sunday, Monday, and Friday tend to be the next busiest. If you decide to visit Disneyland park during a weekend, opt for Sunday (it gets less busy as the day wears on). And remember that the week before Christmas through New Year's Day, Easter week, and the period from early July through Labor Day are usually packed.

DISNEYLAND RESORT CROWD PATTERNS

LEAST CROWDED

- Second week in January to Presidents' week

- Two weeks after Easter Sunday until Memorial Day week

- End of Labor Day week to Columbus Day

- The last two weeks of August

AVERAGE CROWDS

- Period just after Presidents' week until about two weeks before Easter Sunday

- Sundays in spring, autumn, and winter, except holiday weekends

- Memorial Day week to beginning of summer vacation

- Week after Labor Day weekend

- Early November to week before Thanksgiving

MOST CROWDED

- Any Saturday, year-round

- Sundays throughout the summer and during holiday weekends

- Presidents' week

- Weeks before through weeks after Easter Sunday

- Beginning of summer through Labor Day weekend

- Thanksgiving weekend (Thursday through Sunday)

- Week before Christmas through first week of January

Keeping Disney Hours

Operating hours tend to fluctuate based on the date and the season. For updates, call 714-781-4636, visit *disneyland.com*, or use the Disneyland Resort mobile app. All details are subject to change.

DISNEYLAND PARK: This park is typically open from about 8 A.M. to about 10 P.M. Monday through Thursday, 8 A.M. to midnight on Friday and Saturday, and 8 A.M. to 11 P.M. on Sunday. Hours are often extended in the summer months, during holiday seasons, and for other special occasions. A benefit known as "Early Entry" allows guests registered at one of the three Disneyland Resort Hotels to enter a park 30 minutes before it officially opens on select days (valid hotel stay, theme park admission, and park reservation are required). For updates, use the Disneyland app, or visit *disneyland.com*.

DISNEY CALIFORNIA ADVENTURE PARK: The theme park generally opens at about 8 or 9 A.M. and closes at 9 or 10 P.M., sometimes later. Early Entry allows guests staying at one of the three Disneyland Resort Hotels to enter the park 30 minutes before it officially opens on select days (valid hotel stay, theme park admission, and park reservation are required). For updates, use the Disneyland mobile app, or visit *disneyland.com*.

DOWNTOWN DISNEY DISTRICT: Many of the spots in Disneyland Resort's shopping, dining, and entertainment district open when the parks do, but some may open as early as 7 A.M. and most close by 10 P.M. Sunday through Thursday (often later on Friday and Saturday nights and during peak times of year).

TRANSPORTATION: The Disneyland Monorail begins making its 2.5-mile loop about the time Disneyland park opens (including "Early Entry") and runs until about 15 minutes before the park closes. Trams transporting guests between parking lots and the parks begin picking up guests about an hour before the first theme park opens, and continue transporting guests back to parking areas until about an hour or so after the last park closes. If you miss the last tram, ask about alternate transportation to the Mickey and Friends parking structure (it's usually in the form of a van).

ANAHEIM WEATHER

If dry, sunny weather is your ideal, Anaheim may seem like a dream come true. Rainy days are few and far between and generally occur between the months of November and April, which is also the coolest time of year. During this season, Santa Ana winds sometimes produce short periods of dry, warm desert weather and sparkling-clear skies that unveil distant mountains usually hidden by smog. In summer, thin, low morning clouds make it logical to plan expeditions to the beach for the afternoon, when the haze burns off and the mercury rises. Mornings and nights are generally cool. The average daytime year-round temperature is about 76 degrees.

	TEMPERATURE AVERAGE		RAINFALL AVERAGE
	HIGH	LOW	
JANUARY	69	47	1.8
FEBRUARY	69	48	2.2
MARCH	71	52	1.0
APRIL	74	54	0.5
MAY	75	59	0.2
JUNE	79	62	0.3
JULY	84	66	0.4
AUGUST	87	66	0.0
SEPTEMBER	85	64	0.2
OCTOBER	80	59	0.5
NOVEMBER	74	51	0.6
DECEMBER	68	46	1.7

Holidays & Special Events

Disneyland Resort hosts special events all year long. For additional information, use the Disneyland mobile app, visit *disneyland.com*, or call 714-781-7290. Here are a few highlights to consider:

JANUARY–FEBRUARY

Three Kings Day—Día de los Reyes: Celebrate the 12th day of Christmas and some of the Latin American traditions associated with the Epiphany as part of Disney California Adventure's Festival of Holidays.

Lunar New Year: Disney California Adventure welcomes the Lunar New Year with time-honored traditions celebrating Chinese, Korean, and Vietnamese cultures. Guests may follow a young lantern's quest to reunite with his family and celebrate good fortune in Hurry Home—a special 6-minute show presented before World of Color.

Valentine's Day: Sweethearts will certainly swoon over the romantic backdrop that Disneyland Park provides on this lovestruck holiday.

MARCH–MAY

Disney California Adventure Food and Wine Festival: Enjoy savory sips and nibbles at this popular annual event featuring culinary demonstrations, spirit seminars, appearances by well-known chefs, and more. Cheers!

Easter: The parks stay open late the week before and the week after Easter (it's a very busy time to visit). Eggstravaganzas are held across the Disneyland resort—scavenger hunts for giant Easter eggs. (Maps, which may come with a character keepsake, are offered for a fee.)

Season of the Force: From late March to early May, Star Wars fans can enjoy special nighttime shows, galactic treats, and after-hours parties (for which separate tickets are required).

JUNE–AUGUST

Fourth of July: This is one of the busiest days of the year—and one to avoid if you're easily overwhelmed by crowds. The more-patriotic-than-usual day features exceptionally festive fireworks at Disneyland Park.

EARLY SEPTEMBER–OCTOBER

Halloween Festivities: At Disneyland Park, Halloween Time lets guests celebrate in many not-so-scary ways. In addition to fall color decor, the Disneyland Band and Dapper Dans celebrate with seasonal tunes. The Haunted Mansion attraction's holiday transformation gives this spot a *Tim Burton's The Nightmare Before Christmas* motif. Main Street, U.S.A., features hundreds of hand-carved jack-o'-lanterns. And Disney characters celebrate the holiday by donning Halloween costumes. (For current policies regarding guest costumes, visit *disneyland.com*.) Disney California Adventure park gets into the spirit with Oogie Boogie Bash—a special-ticket party. Expect lots of spooky touches such as a "frightfully fun parade" and treat trails with Disney villains. Paradise Gardens hosts a tribute to Día de los Muertos during this time.

NOVEMBER–DECEMBER

Thanksgiving Weekend: The four days of this holiday weekend are filled with musical entertainment and the early installments of Disneyland's A Christmas Fantasy Parade and It's a Small World Holiday, and the holiday transformations of Cars Land and Buena Vista Street, all of which kick off in mid-November. The parks usually observe extended hours.

Holiday Festivities: By early November, Disneyland's Main Street is festooned with greenery and poinsettias, while more than a million lights create a wonderland that glistens from the Town Square Christmas Tree to Sleeping Beauty's Winter Castle. On two festive evenings in December, a massive choir walks down Main Street in a Candlelight Ceremony. It features a live orchestra and guest narrator who reads the story of the Nativity. There's also a holiday-themed fireworks show, "Believe . . . In Holiday Magic." It's presented throughout the holiday season. It is not to be missed.

It's a Small World is transformed into a wondrous world of holiday magic. A Christmas Fantasy Parade also takes place. Haunted Mansion Holiday extends through holiday season. Disney California Adventure has the Festival of the Holidays. The celebration includes Christmas, Navidad, Hanukkah, Diwali, Kwanzaa, and Three Kings' Day, and features a holiday World of Color, and Viva Navidad!, an energetic street party hosted by the Three Caballeros.

The entire Disneyland Resort celebrates New Year's Eve in exceptionally festive fashion, too. Happy holidays!

MAGICAL MILESTONES

Walt Disney once said, "Disneyland will never be completed. It will continue to grow as long as there is imagination left in the world." Truer words were never spoken. Here's a sampling of major milestones and important dates in Disney history.

1901
Walter Elias Disney is born on December 5 in Chicago, Illinois. He spends part of his childhood in Marceline, Missouri.

1922
Walt and collaborator Ub Iwerks start Laugh-O-Gram Films, an animation studio located in Kansas City, Missouri. (The business lasts one year.)

1923
Walt and his brother Roy open the Disney Bros. Studio in Hollywood, California.

1928
The Disney studio introduces the world to the immortal Mickey Mouse with *Steamboat Willie*, the first cartoon with a synchronized soundtrack. (Walt Disney provides the voice for Mickey.)

1932
Flowers and Trees wins the Disney Studio its first Academy Award.

1937
Disney releases *Snow White and the Seven Dwarfs*, the world's first feature-length animated movie.

1940
Disney animation meets great classical music with the release of *Fantasia*.

1955
Disneyland opens its doors in Anaheim, while television's original *Mickey Mouse Club* begins a four-year run.

1967
Disneyland debuts Pirates of the Caribbean—one of the most popular and beloved attractions of all time.

1971
Walt Disney World debuts in Central Florida. It has one theme park—the Magic Kingdom—and two themed resort hotels: Contemporary and Polynesian Village.

1989
Disney animation experiences a renaissance of sorts with the release of the Studio's 28th animated feature film, *The Little Mermaid*.

2001
For the first time since its opening, the Disneyland Resort gets a new theme park: Disney California Adventure.

2003
The Many Adventures of Winnie the Pooh attraction makes its debut in Critter Country inside Disneyland park.

2004
Turtle Talk with Crush opens at Disney California Adventure park. Like, totally awesome, dude.

2006
Captain Jack Sparrow joins the merry marauders in Pirates of the Caribbean.

2012
Cars Land races onto the scene with new fan favorites, including Radiator Springs Racers and Mater's Junkyard Jamboree.

2019-2020
The Force awakens at Disneyland Park in Star Wars: Galaxy's Edge. There, guests fly in Han Solo's ship at *Millennium Falcon: Smugglers Run*, ride out an epic battle between the First Order and the Resistance, customize a lightsaber, and wet their whistles at Oga's Cantina.

2023
Mickey & Minnie's Runaway Railway chugs into a newly re-imagined Mickey's Toontown. The cheerful neighborhood unveils a charming new nature zone: CenTOONial Park—an inspirational spot where you can dream like Walt.

2024
A re-imagined resort welcomes its first guests: Pixar Place Hotel!

WEDDINGS & CELEBRATIONS

Disney's Fairy Tale Weddings & Honeymoons program at the Disneyland Resort lets brides and grooms create an affair to remember in the parks or at one of the three Disneyland Resort hotels—either indoors or out. Couples may go the traditional route or plan a themed event with invitations, decorations, souvenirs, napkins, and thank-you notes emblazoned with favorite Disney characters, including Cinderella and Prince Charming, and Mickey Mouse and Minnie Mouse.

One special spot for tying the knot is the Rose Court Garden at the Disneyland Hotel, in a picturesque natural setting where the bride, groom, or couple may arrive in Cinderella's platinum coach. Another setting choice is the courtyard area at Disney's Grand Californian Hotel & Spa. A fantasy reception may follow (in either of the aforementioned hotels), at which the fanfare of trumpets greets the happy couple. Mickey Mouse and Minnie

Mouse may even arrive to help the newlyweds with the cake-cutting moment.

A trusty Disney wedding coordinator assists with the arrangements for the wedding and reception—everything, that is, except providing the guest's very own Prince or Princess Charming.

The bridal salon (at the Disneyland Resort Center, between the Disneyland Hotel and Disney's Pixar Place Hotel) helps guests through the planning and prep stages, and even through those pre-ceremony jitters.

For information about creating a happy occasion in a happy location, contact Disney's Fairy Tale Weddings at Disneyland. The department coordinates all wedding and vow renewal events at Disneyland Resort hotels and parks: *disneyweddings.com;* 321-939-4610. For details about Disneyland honeymoons, visit *disneyweddings.com*, or call Disneyland Resort Travel Sales at 800-854-3104.

Quinceañeras

Along with its popular wedding program, Disneyland Resort also offers customized quinceañera celebrations for young women who are coming of age. These popular family-oriented milestone events invite the birthday girl to become a "princess for a day" and step into magical realms such as *Beauty and the Beast, Cinderella,* or *Encanto.* Offered in a spacious ballroom, the celebrations feature dinner, dancing, and time-honored quinceañera traditions. For additional information, visit *disneyland.disney.go.com/events-tours/ quinceaneras,* or call 714-520-7072.

Planning Ahead

Collect as much information as you can about the area attractions you're interested in from the sources listed below (and this book, of course). Then consider all the possibilities before making definite travel plans.

INFORMATION

For up-to-the-minute information about special events and performance times, ticket prices, theme park hours, attractions under refurbishment, and other specifics, use the Disneyland app and/or contact:

Disneyland Resort Guest Services; Call 714-781-4565, or visit *disneyland.com*. Or send a question via *disneyland.disney.go.com/en-ca/help/email*.

If you are staying at one of the Disneyland Resort hotels (see *Accommodations*), contact Guest Services

MAGICBAND+

MagicBand+ is an interactive wristband that can link theme park tickets, Lightning Lane selections, PhotoPass photos, and more with a Disney account. It can also interact with certain aspects of the theme parks via nifty lighting and other technology. The rechargeable bands are sold at Disneyland Resort shops and *disneystore.com*. The price ranges from about $35 to $70, depending on the design. For details, including how to activate and link a MagicBand+ and how to create a Disney account, visit *disneyland.com*, or go to a Guest Relations location at the Disneyland Resort.

KNOW BEFORE YOU GO

The information in this chapter is tailored to help you plan, book, and seamlessly modify your Disney vacation dreams. And we've done our best to ensure that it and all other content within this edition of *Birnbaum's Official Guide to Disneyland Resort* is as useful, comprehensive, and current as possible. That said, procedures and policies do change now and then — especially these days. So before you begin your trip, check on the latest procedural changes and updates by visiting *disneyland.disney.go.com/experience-updates*.

Finally, Disneyland Resort asks all who come to this happy place to treat others with respect, kindness, and compassion. To help everyone have a safe and enjoyable experience, Disneyland Resort Rules are updated often. For details, visit *disneyland.com*.

at the hotel for help in planning your visit to the Disney parks and the surrounding area.

Inside the Disneyland Resort: Cast members (the friendly folks who work at Disneyland) can answer questions. Information stations in Disneyland Park include City Hall in Town Square and the Information Board near Central Plaza, on Main Street. In Disney California Adventure, the Chamber of Commerce is on the east side of the Entry Plaza and the Information Board is on Buena Vista Street. At any Disneyland Resort hotel, visit the lobby for assistance.

For other Anaheim area information, contact these bureaus of tourism:

Visit Anaheim; Call 714-765-2800 during business hours to reach a rep, or go to *www.visitanaheim.org*. You can visit in person at 2099 S. State College Blvd., Suite 600, Anaheim, CA 92806. (They have a travel guide and a map, but no other brochures at this time.)

Long Beach Area Convention & Visitors Bureau; 301 E. Ocean Blvd., Suite 1900, Long Beach, CA 90802; *www.visitlongbeach.com*, 562-436-3645, or 800-452-7829.

Los Angeles Convention & Visitors Bureau; There were no walk-in visitor centers at press time; For more information, visit *www.discoverlosangeles.com*.

RESORT RESERVATIONS

Given the popularity of the Disneyland Resort, advance planning is essential. To get your choice of accommodations, especially for visits during the busy spring and summer seasons, make lodging reservations as far in advance as possible—at least six months ahead, if you can, since area hotels fill up rather quickly during these months. For visits at other times of the year, check with Visit Anaheim or the Anaheim/Orange County Visitor & Convention Bureau (714-765-2800), to see if conventions are scheduled when you want to travel. Some of these events can crowd facilities enough to warrant altering travel plans. To book a room at a Disneyland Resort hotel, visit *disneyland.com*, or call 714-956-6425.

TRAVEL PACKAGES

The biggest advantage to purchasing a travel package is that it almost always saves you money over what you would pay separately for the individual elements of your vacation, or it offers special options not available if you simply buy a one-day ticket. This is especially true the longer you stay. And there is the convenience of having all the details arranged in advance by someone else.

Finding the best package means deciding what sort of vacation you want and studying what's available. Do not choose a package that includes elements that don't interest you—remember, you're paying for them. And if it's Disney theming and "extras" you want, consider a Walt Disney Travel Company package.

The Walt Disney Travel Company offers packages that include a stay at a Disney hotel and a theme park ticket. It's possible to add extras, such as Lightning Lane Multi Pass and Disneyland VIP Tours.

Besides booking guests into official Disneyland Resort hotels, the Walt Disney Travel Company also works closely with Good Neighbor hotels and motels (see pages 47–52), and they are included in its packages as well. To book a Disneyland Resort package, go to *disneyland.disney.go .com/vacation-packages*, contact a travel agent, or call the Walt Disney Travel Company at 714-520-5060.

The Disneyland Resort is also featured in a variety of non-Disney-run package tours, including those sponsored by individual hotels and airlines (Alaska Airlines, Southwest Vacations, and jetBlue Vacations offer packages, to name a few). AAA Vacations (800-922-8228 ext. 3; *www .aaa.com*) offers packages to the traveling public, too.

This book's selective guide to Anaheim-area hotels and motels can help you decide initially which property best suits your party's travel style, needs, and budget (refer to the *Accommodations* chapter for guidance). Pick one, then contact a travel agent or the hotel itself to make a reservation or book a Disneyland Resort package. Be sure to inquire about deposit requirements, cancellation policies, and trip insurance (we recommend opting for insurance). Happy hunting!

WHAT TO PACK

Southern California isn't so laid-back that you only need to pack shorts, T-shirts, and sneakers. Nor is it a place that demands formal attire. Casual wear will suffice in all but the fanciest restaurants, and, even there, men can usually wear sports jackets without ties. Bathing suits are an obvious must if you plan to take advantage of your hotel's swimming pool or go for a walk on a long, surf-pounded Pacific beach. It's also a good idea to bring along a bathing suit cover-up and sunglasses (and do not forget the all-important sunscreen). Tennis togs or golf gear may be necessary if you plan to hit the courts or the course. The weather in summer can be quite warm, but because Southern California air-conditioning can be exceptionally robust, you should take a lightweight sweater or jacket to wear indoors.

In winter, warm clothing is a must for evening; during nighttime visits to the parks, a heavy jacket may be a godsend. We like having hats and gloves, too. Whatever the time of year you decide to visit, always come prepared for the unexpected: Pack a lightweight shirt *and* a warm sweater or jacket—just in case.

Finally, we highly recommend packing hand sanitizer, plus a lightweight power pack (or two) and an extra charger for your mobile phone.

Making a Budget

Vacation expenses tend to fall into five major categories: (1) transportation (which may include costs for airfare, airport transfers, train tickets, car rental, gas, parking, and taxi service); (2) lodging; (3) theme park tickets; (4) meals; and (5) miscellaneous (recreational activities, souvenirs, toiletries, forgotten items, and expenses such as pet boarding, etc.).

When budgeting, first consider what level of service suits your needs. Some prefer to spend fewer days at the Disneyland Resort, but stay at a deluxe hotel like the Grand Californian or dine at pricier restaurants. Others may want a longer vacation with a value-priced Good Neighbor hotel and less expensive meals. The choice is up to you. (Having said that, we do feel that a great deal of the Disney experience comes from staying on Disneyland Resort property and recommend accommodations at one of the three Disneyland Resort hotels if your budget allows.)

Once you have established your spending priorities, it's time to determine your price limit. Then make sure you don't exceed it when approximating your expenses—without a ballpark figure to work around, it's easy to get carried away.

SAMPLE BUDGET

Disneyland Hotel: $631 per night (x 4 nights)

Lodging total = $2,524

THEME PARK TICKETS:

Adult 4-day Park Hopper ticket: $569 (x 2 people)
Child 4-day Park Hopper ticket: $539 (x 2 people)

Tickets total = $2,216

MEALS:

(two inexpensive and one moderate meal per day, plus one snack)
Average adult: $100 (x 5 days) (x 2 people)
Average child: $70 (x 5 days) (x 2 people)

Meals total = $1,700

MISCELLANEOUS*:

Average adult: $50 (x 5 days) (x 2 people)
Average child: $35 (x 5 days) (x 2 people)

Miscellaneous total = $850

DISNEYLAND RESORT VACATION TOTAL = $7,290

If you'd like a lower hotel rate, consider a stay at one of Disney's Good Neighbor hotel partners. Room rates may start under $200.

Don't forget: To enter a Disneyland Resort theme park, you'll need a valid ticket and a park reservation, (For details, see page 17 and visit *disneyland.com*).

Even if you plan to stick to fast food, expect to spend at least $75 (per adult) and $40 (per child) per day.

Careful packing should help cut down on miscellaneous expenses, which include forgotten toiletries such as toothpaste, hand sanitizer, and the all-important sunscreen.

This is an example of a budget for a family of four (two adults and two kids staying at the Disneyland Hotel for four nights and five days during "off-peak" dates), excluding transportation costs. Theme park admission prices are likely to increase in 2026. (They always do.)

*Does not include airfare, airport transfers, or other transportation fees. See page 25 for details. Be sure to include all transportation costs (which vary widely) in your travel budget.

Money-Saving Strategies

COST-CUTTING TIPS

LODGING: The most important rule is not to pay for more than you need. Budget chains don't offer many frills, but they are usually clean and provide the essentials; many even have a swimming pool, albeit a small one. (Bigger isn't always better!)

You can also save by checking the cutoff age at which kids can no longer share their parents' room for free. Many hotels and motels allow children under age 18 to stay free. A few places have a cutoff age of 15 or 17, so it is best to investigate *before* making a reservation. And ask about special rates or discounts, especially if you are a California resident, Disney Vacation Club member, AARP member, or are in the military.

Hostels and Recreational Vehicle (RV) parks also offer lower-priced lodging alternatives. Contact Visit Anaheim at 714-765-2800 for a listing of those areas closest to the Disneyland Resort.

FOOD: The budget-minded (and who isn't?) should plan to have meals in coffee shops or fast-food restaurants, or save your splurges for buffets and family-style eateries to get your fill and your money's worth. If you want to try an upscale place, go for lunch; the entrées are often the same as those at dinner time, but may cost a little less.

Pack a picnic and enjoy meals outside. There's a small picnic area just to the left of Disneyland Park's entrance. (It's surrounded by trees—so it's easy to miss.) Snacks may be brought into the parks, but not glass bottles, knives, or beverages containing alcohol. Refillable plastic or metal cups and bottles are permitted. Coolers are allowed, but must be no larger than 24 inches long, 15 inches wide, and 18 inches high. Loose and dry ice are not permitted. Reusable ice packs are recommended. You can also save on meals by choosing lodging with kitchen facilities and opting to eat in some of the time. Don't forget to pack snack items, too—especially if you're traveling with kids.

In the Anaheim area, a number of spots offer refrigerators or kitchen facilities (look for suite hotels); some may even provide breakfast.

TRANSPORTATION: When calculating the cost of driving from your home to the Disneyland Resort, consider your car's gas mileage, the price of gasoline, and the expense of the accommodations and food along the way. If you're planning to fly, don't forget about the cost of getting from home to the airport and later to the hotel. Also factor in the cost of renting a car at your destination, if that's part of your plan. Remember to ask what your hotel charges for parking (rates tend to vary) or shuttle transportation to the Disneyland Resort—these daily charges can tack quite a bit onto a family's total vacation cost.

DISNEY DISCOUNTS

MAGIC KEY PASSES: Bearers of Magic Key annual passes net savings at select Disneyland Resort restaurants and retail locations throughout the parks, Disneyland hotels, and at Downtown Disney. Inspire Key Passholders may enjoy up to 20 percent discounts on select merchandise at many Disneyland Resort shops, and up to 15 percent at select eateries, plus free standard theme park parking. Believe Key and Enchant Key Passholders get up to 10 percent off at select restaurants and merchandise spots. Believe Key–bearers also net a 50 percent savings on standard theme park parking. Enchant Key–holders get 25 percent off standard parking (blockout dates may apply). All Magic Key passes net bearers a 25 percent discount on Lightning Lane Multi Pass (see page 22). Magic Key passes are subject to availability, may sell out, and sales and renewals may be suspended at any time.

DISNEY VISA® CARDS: Cardmembers who pay with their Disney Visa Card may enjoy savings on merchandise, dining, and guided tours. Note that all details are subject to change. For additional information, visit *DisneyRewards.com* or *DisneyDebit.com*.

AUTOMOBILE ASSOCIATION OF AMERICA (AAA): You don't have to be a member of the Auto Club to order a vacation package through AAA (though you won't net all the membership discounts). Contact your regional AAA office for additional information.

BIRNBAUM COUPONS: The coupons at the back of this book will net you savings at several spots in the Downtown Disney District. You're welcome!

THEME PARK RESERVATIONS

To enter a Disneyland Resort theme park, you need a valid ticket *and* a valid park reservation. It's crucial to check for reservation availability prior to purchasing tickets. If your desired dates are open, buy the ticket and make reservations right way. All details are subject to change. For updates, visit *disneyland.com*.

Theme Park Tickets

TICKET OPTIONS

One- to Five-Day Tickets allow admission to one theme park per day, while One- to Five-Day Park Hopper tickets allow admission to both parks and allow you to "hop" between parks. Tickets generally expire 13 days after first use. Theme park reservations are required and should be made in advance with the Disneyland app or via *disneyland.com*. If you plan to park-hop, you must visit your first park before entering the second. At press time, guests could hop between theme parks starting at 11 A.M., but that may change at any time.

The main types of "Magic Key" annual passes are Inspire Key, Believe Key, and Enchant Key versions. All afford the bearer shopping and dining discounts, as well as park-hopping (visiting both theme parks in one day) with theme park reservations. Two notable differences between Magic Key pass types—all of which are valid for one year after activation—are blockout dates (select dates when the passholder may not enter the Disney parks) and the number of theme park reservations that may be held at any given time.

Inspire Key pass has no blockout dates and lets the bearer hold up to 6 theme park reservations on a rolling basis. Believe Key has blockout dates and allows up to 6 theme park reservations on a rolling basis. Enchant Key pass has blockout dates and allows for up to 4 theme park reservations to be held on a rolling basis. Inspire Key passholders get free standard theme park parking, Believe Key bearers get half off select parking, and Enchant Key holders get 25 percent off select parking.

There may be special passes for California residents. For Magic Key program updates, call 714-781-4565 or go to *disneyland.disney.go.com/magic-key*. Sales of Magic Key passes are limited and may be suspended at any time.

PURCHASING TICKETS

How to Buy Tickets: While tickets may be purchased at Disneyland Resort ticket booths, it is best to get them in advance via *disneyland.com*, or the Disneyland app. This will ensure that you get a park reservation for the date you plan to attend a Disneyland theme park. (You can print tickets, store on a smartphone, have them mailed, or pick them up at Will Call. The latter two options come with a fee. Electronic tickets may be scanned for admission, but must be displayed on an Internet-accessible handheld device.) To recap: Buy your theme park tickets in advance via *disneyland.com* or by using the Disneyland mobile app. Before you make the purchase, check for reservation availability on the date(s) you have selected. If park reservations are available, buy the tickets and book theme park reservations immediately. Having a valid ticket does not guarantee admission to a Disneyland Resort park—you need a valid park reservation, too. Theme park reservation details are subject to change.

Tickets by Mail: Send a check or money order and ticket request (plus a $10 fee for all orders over $200) to Disneyland Ticket Mail Order Services, Box 61061, Anaheim, CA 92803. It's also possible to order by calling Ticketing & Reservations at 714-781-4400 (up to 30 days ahead). Allow at least 10 business days for processing.

Tickets by Phone: Allow at least 7 to 10 business days for delivery: 714-781-4565.

TICKET PRICES

Although prices[†] will likely increase, the following should give an idea of what you will pay for tickets in 2025/2026. Note that 1-Day tickets purchased in 2026 must be used by 12/30/26. The first day of use of multi-day tickets must be on or before 12/30/26. Multi-day tickets must be used within 13 days of first use or by January 12, 2027, whichever occurs first. For updates, use the Disneyland app or visit *disneyland.com*. All details are subject to change.

	ADULTS	CHILDREN*
1-Day Ticket (1 park)	$104/206	$98/196
1-Day Ticket (hopper)**	$169/281	$163/271
2-Day Ticket	$330	$310
2-Day Ticket (hopper)**	$415	$395
3-Day Ticket	$415	$390
3-Day Ticket (hopper)**	$505	$480
4-Day Ticket	$474	$444
4-Day Ticket (hopper)**	$569	$539
5-Day Ticket	$511	$476
5-Day Ticket (hopper)**	$616	$581
Enchant Key pass		$974
Believe Key pass		$1,374
Inspire Key pass		$1,749

† One-day prices represent the range in which you can expect to pay. Prices may be higher. Prices vary by date. For dates, visit *disneyland.com*.
* 3 through 9 years of age; children under 3 free
** Guests with Park Hopper tickets and valid park reservations must enter the park as designated in their park reservation, and may hop between parks on the same day starting at 11 A.M. (subject to availability). After 11 A.M., guests with Park Hopper tickets who have a reservation for Disneyland park or Disney California Adventure, but have not yet entered that park, may enter either theme park (subject to availability).

There is a single price (for adults and children) for Enchant Key, Believe Key, and Inspire Key passes.

Customized Travel Tips

TRAVELING WITH CHILDREN

When you tell your kids that a Disneyland vacation is in the works, the challenge is keeping them relatively calm until you actually arrive at the House of Mouse.

PLANNING: Get kids involved in plotting a Disneyland trip from the outset, putting each of the kids in charge of a small part of vacation preparation—such as visiting *disneyland.com*, choosing which attractions to see and in what order to see them, and investigating which other activities you may want to include during your Southern California sojourn.

EN ROUTE: Certain resources can stave off the "Are we there yet?" chorus, such as travel games, tablets (and chargers), books, and snacks to quiet rumbling stomachs. If you drive, take plenty of breaks along the way. If you plan to fly, try to book your departure and return flight times for off-peak hours and during the off-season, when chances are better that an empty seat or two will be available (prices should be a bit cheaper, too). During takeoffs and landings, encourage toddlers to suck on bottles or pacifiers to keep ears clear, and supply older kids with chewing gum, a lollipop, or water. And don't forget toys to keep the wee ones occupied.

IN THE HOTELS: Several Anaheim-area hotels offer kids' programs. Some offer babysitting services or babysitting referrals year-round (fees apply).

IN THE THEME PARKS: The smiles that light up your kids' faces as they enter a Disney theme park should repay you a thousandfold for any fuss en route. No place in the world is more aware of the needs of little ones—or their parents—than this one.

Favorite Attractions: Fantasyland and Mickey's Toon-town in Disneyland Park are great places to start with small kids, who delight in the bright colors and familiar characters. In DCA, Cars Land, Disney Junior Mickey Mouse Clubhouse Live!, and Monsters, Inc. Mike and Sulley to the Rescue! have big kid appeal. If you have kids of different ages in your party, you may have to do some juggling or split the group up for a few hours so that older kids won't have to spend their whole visit waiting in line for Dumbo. Some rides, like Pinocchio's Daring Journey, may be too intense for some youngsters.

Strollers: They can be rented for $18 ($36 for a double) at the Stroller Shop, located to the right of the entrance to Disneyland Park. This is the only place to rent a stroller for either park. If you leave the parks but plan to return later that day, keep the receipt and get another stroller at no additional charge.

Baby Care: Baby Care Centers feature toddler-size toilets that are quite cute—and completely functional. In addition, there are changing tables, a limited selection of formulas, baby foods, and diapers for sale, plus facilities for warming baby bottles (you can wash out your bottles here, too). A special room with comfy chairs is available for nursing mothers. The decor is soothing, and a stop here for a diaper change or feeding is a tranquil break for parent and child alike. The Baby Care Centers are located in Central Plaza, at the Castle end of Main Street, U.S.A. in Disneyland Park, and near Ghirardelli Soda Fountain & Chocolate Shop in Disney California Adventure.

Changing tables and diaper vending machines are also available in many restrooms.

Note: Parents of toddlers should pack a supply of swim diapers. They are required for children who want to spend time frolicking in hotel pools.

Where to Buy Baby Care Items: Disposable diapers, baby bottles, formula, etc., are sold at Baby Care Centers in the parks. Pack as much of your own as possible—prices can be steep and the selection is small.

HEIGHT HO!

At attractions with age and/or height restrictions, a parent who waits with a child too young or too small to ride while the other parent goes on the attraction will have expedited boarding as soon as the first parent comes off. This is known as the "rider switch" policy, and if lines are long, it can save a great deal of time. The cast member at the attraction entrance can explain what to do.

HOT TIP

Pack kid-friendly snacks, such as fruit, cereal, crackers, breakfast bars, and water. Snack stands are plentiful at Disneyland Resort, but not always handy or cost-efficient.

Lost Children: Youngsters should carry the mobile phone number for the parent or guardian who accompanies them to the parks. But even without it, when a child gets separated from their family or fails to show up on time, cast members (Disney employees) and Disneyland Resort's security force follow specific procedures when they encounter a lost child. Please report a lost child to a cast member, and Disneyland Resort security personnel will assist you.

Kids age 3 and younger will be escorted (by a Disney cast member) to the park's Baby Care Center, while a parent or guardian is contacted via mobile phone or otherwise directed to the Baby Care location. Kids older than 13 will be taken to City Hall in Disneyland park or the Chamber of Commerce just inside the entrance area of Disney California Adventure. Lost children found in the Downtown Disney District are taken to either the Disneyland Hotel or the Baby Care Center/Lost Children location inside Disneyland Park (near the Plaza Inn on Main Street, U.S.A.)

TRAVELING WITHOUT CHILDREN

Disneyland Resort is as enjoyable for solo travelers and couples as it is for families for several reasons: Its ambience encourages interaction, and the attractions are naturally shared events.

PLANNING: Read Disneyland Resort planning literature carefully before you arrive to familiarize yourself with the area's layout and activities. Also, search for information about other places in Southern California that you intend to visit.

Food for Thought: Sightseeing takes lots of energy, and only healthy meals can provide it at a consistent level. Don't attempt to save money by skipping meals. Prices at the parks and nearby "off-property" eateries are relatively reasonable, and there are some healthy options, even in the fast-food restaurants. Pack nutritious snacks. And remember to stay hydrated—running around theme parks all day is a lot of work.

Health Matters: If you visit in summer, avoid getting overheated. Protect yourself from the sun with a hat and plenty of sunscreen, rest in the shade often, and beat the mid-afternoon heat with a cold drink or a snack in an air-conditioned spot.

If you are injured or feel ill, speak to a Disney cast member or go to First Aid to see the nurse. In case of emergency, call 911. Above all, heed attraction warnings. If you have a back problem, heart condition, or other physical ailment, suffer from motion sickness, or are pregnant, skip rough rides. Restrictions are noted at attraction entrances, as well as on park guidemaps.

Lost Companions: Traveling companions can get separated. If someone in your party wanders off or fails to show up at an appointed meeting spot and cell phone communication is thwarted, head for City Hall in Disneyland park or Chamber of Commerce in Disney California Adventure park. Guests can leave and receive messages for one another during the day.

TRAVELING WITH DISABILITIES

The Disneyland Resort is remarkably accessible to guests with disabilities, and, as a result, it makes a solid choice as a vacation destination. But advance planning is still essential.

GETTING TO ANAHEIM

Probably the most effective means of ensuring a smooth trip is to make as many advance contacts as possible for every phase of your journey. It's important to make phone calls regarding transportation well before your departure date to arrange for any special facilities or services you may need en route.

The Society for Accessible Travel & Hospitality (SATH), *www.sath.org;* 212-447-7284) has member travel agents who book trips for travelers with disabilities, keeping special needs in mind. The non-profit organization has different levels of membership fees.

The following agencies specialize in booking trips for travelers with physical disabilities: TravelAble (855-500-3440; *travelablevacations.com*) and Wheel the World, (*www.wheeltheworld.com*; 628-900-7778).

Note that the aforementioned agencies are neither run by nor endorsed by The Walt Disney Company.

Hertz (800-654-3131), Alamo (800-651-1223), and National (888-273-5262) rent hand-controlled cars at Southern California airports. Order your car at least 72 hours in advance and confirm before arrival.

Though less direct, it is also possible to access the area by public transportation. Anaheim Resort Transportation (aka ART, the official Disneyland Resort Shuttle Bus) routes provide access to the Disneyland Resort through the Main Transportation Center (visit *www.rideart.org,* or call

888-364-2787). The same is true for many of the routes covered by the Orange County Transportation Authority, the public bus company that serves Orange County (*www.octa.net*, or 714-560-6282). All ART and OCTA buses have lifts for travelers using wheelchairs.

Scootaround rents standard and electric wheelchairs, as well as motorized scooters. Visit *www.scootaround.com*, or call 888-441-7575. Wheelchair Getaways of California rents wheelchair-accessible vans and offers pick-up and delivery options for most area hotels. Call 866-224-1750, or visit *www.wheelchairgetaways.com*.

LODGING

Most hotels and motels in Orange County have rooms equipped for guests with disabilities, with extra-wide doorways, grab bars in the bathroom for shower or bath and toilet, and sinks at wheelchair height, along with ramps at curbs and steps to allow wheelchair access. Unless otherwise indicated, all the lodging described in the Accommodations chapter (page 41) provide guest-rooms for travelers with disabilities.

INSIDE THE DISNEYLAND RESORT

Cars displaying a "disability" placard will be directed to a section of each Disney parking lot, next to the tram pick-up and drop-off area.

Wheelchairs and Electric Conveyance Vehicles (ECVs) can be rented at the Stroller Shop outside the entrance to Disneyland Park. This is the only rental location for both theme parks. The price is $15 per day for wheelchairs, and $60 for ECVs, plus tax and a refundable $20 deposit. Quantities are limited.

ScooterBug, a private mobility rental company in the local area, offers strollers, ECVs, and wheelchair rentals for Disneyland Resort hotel guests. For information or to make a reservation, visit *ScooterBug.com/Anaheim* or

call 800-726-8284. Of course, you're welcome to use your own mobility device throughout the Disneyland Resort.

Most waiting areas are accessible, but some attractions offer auxiliary entrances for guests who use wheelchairs or other mobility devices; guests may be accompanied by up to five party members using the special entry point. The Main Street train station is not wheelchair accessible. However, guests using wheelchairs have easy access to the Disneyland Railroad in New Orleans Square, Mickey's Toontown, or Tomorrowland.

Accessibility information is provided in special brochures (see Park Resources, below). In all cases, guests with mobility disabilities should be escorted by someone in their party who can assist as needed.

In some theme park attractions, guests may remain in their wheelchair or Electric Conveyance Vehicle; in others, they must be able to transfer in and out of their wheelchair or ECV. In a few attractions, guests must leave their wheelchair or ECV and remain ambulatory during the majority of the attraction experience.

For Guests with Visual Disabilities: An audio tour and the Braille Guidebook are available upon request at City Hall in Disneyland Park and at Chamber of Commerce in Disney California Adventure. Both are free to use but require a $25 refundable deposit. A portable handheld device containing several services, including audio description, is available from Guest Relations at each theme park (a refundable deposit is required).

Trained service animals are permitted in most locations. Animals may not be permitted to ride some attractions. They may wait with a non-riding member of their party or in a portable kennel. For additional information, visit *disneyland.disney.go.com/guest-services/service-animals*.

For Guests with Hearing Disabilities: Reflective captioning is available in the pre-show areas of select

PARK RESOURCES

Contact Disney Disability Services by telephone (407-560-2547) or via email (send email inquiries to disability.services@disneyland.com) for details on Services for Guests with Visual Disabilities and Hearing Disabilities; Services for Guests with Service Animals; and Attraction Access for Guests Using Wheelchairs and Electric Conveyance Vehicles (ECVs), or use the (free) Disneyland Resort mobile app or visit *disneyland.com*. Information is also available at City Hall in Disneyland and at Chamber of Commerce in Disney California Adventure.

theme park shows and attractions—inquire at the show or attraction entrance or visit *disneyland.disney.go .com/guest-services/hearing-disabilities*.

Dozens of attractions provide handheld captioning service. The system uses a wireless handheld receiver to display text in locations where fixed captioning systems are impractical, such as moving attractions. Receivers are available through Guest Relations and require a $25 refundable deposit. For details, visit the website referenced in the previous paragraph or check at City Hall in Disneyland Park or Chamber of Commerce inside Disney California Adventure.

Text typewriters (TTYs) are available to borrow from all three of the Disneyland Resort hotels. Ask about them when you check in.

Sign Language interpretation is available by request for select special events with at least 14 days advance notice. Call 714-781-4636 (select option 1, and then option 0). Guests under age 18 must have the permission of parent or guardian to call.

A portable device containing several services, including handheld captioning, may be borrowed at City Hall in Disneyland Park or Chamber of Commerce in Disney California Adventure (with a $25 refundable deposit).

DISNEYLAND RESORT TOURS

Guided tours provide guests with a chance to explore Disneyland and Disney California Adventure parks in entertaining and informative ways. Most guided tours may be reserved up to 60 days in advance. Availability is limited and, until further notice, tour reservations are available online only (via *disneyland.com* or the [free] Disneyland app). Valid theme park admission and valid theme park reservations are required (but not included) for all guided tours. Guests must check in up to fifteen minutes ahead of their reservation time at Tour Gardens on Main Street. (Late arrivals may not be able to join a tour-in-progress.) At check-in, you will present your reservation confirmation, photo ID, and the credit card provided at booking. For additional information and

to make reservations, use the Disneyland app, or visit *disneyland.com*. All details are subject to change.

• ***Cultivating the Magic:*** From the moment guests enter Disneyland Park, they begin their journey into its living storybook and discover the part plants and flowers play in Disney storytelling. The walking tour includes a ride on the Jungle Cruise and a special keepsake. For details and pricing, *visit disneyland.com*.

• ***Disneyland Railroad Guided Tour:*** All aboard! Get a behind-the-scenes view into Walt Disney's lifelong love of trains and the impact it had on the Disneyland Resort. One highlight of the 2-hour walking tour is a ride in the Presidential Car on the *Liberty Belle* steam train (weather permitting). The tour includes a sweet treat and a keepsake. For details, including pricing, visit *disneyland.com*.

• ***Walt's Main Street Story Tour*** (8 A.M., noon, and 2 P.M. daily, plus 10 A.M. Friday through Sunday): Led by a knowledgeable guide, the intimate tour covers hidden details and behind-the-scenes stories about Disneyland's Main Street, U.S.A. and the links between it and Walt Disney's childhood town of Marceline, Missouri. The tour culminates with a visit to Walt's legendary apartment atop the Disneyland Fire Station in Town Square (which includes refreshments on the patio). In addition to your theme park ticket, expect to pay about $160 (per person, for all guests ages 3 and up) for the 90-minute tour. The price includes the aforementioned refreshments, plus a commemorative lanyard and PhotoPass pictures of your party (with free digital downloads). The tour is open to folks of all ages, but guests younger than age 14 must be accompanied by an adult age 18 or older.

• ***Holiday Time at the Disneyland Resort*** (Seasonal): This tour shares the history of Disneyland's holiday traditions and enchanting tales of holidays from around the world, includes visits to attractions that have had holiday makeovers, and offers special seating for the holiday parade, A Christmas Fantasy. The cost is at least $110 per person and includes a special pin, a warm beverage, and a gingerbread cookie. Each tour lasts about 2½ hours. There is a 24-hour cancellation policy— full price will be charged if canceled within one day or if a guest does not show up for the tour.

• ***VIP Tour Services:*** A dedicated team is available to customize and guide your Disneyland Resort vacation. Ranging from $500 to $700 per hour (plus gratuity), you and up to 9 other guests can enjoy a customizable VIP Tour, with a minimum of 7 hours and a maximum of 10 hours. Reservations are required and can be made by calling 714-300-7710, or by sending an email to DisneylandVIPTours@disney.com.

Lightning Lane Entrances

Every theme park attraction at the Disneyland Resort has a traditional "standby" line that's included with park admission. A subset of those diversions offers something called Lightning Lane, too. The fee-based alternative to the traditional standby line offers quicker access to many popular theme park attractions.

A Lightning Lane may be accessed by one of the following methods: by using Lightning Lane Multi Pass (for a daily fee) or by purchasing a Lightning Lane Single Pass for a limited number of extremely popular attractions. It is important to note that the attractions designated for Lightning Lane Single Pass are different than those included under Lightning Lane Multi Pass. However, it is possible to utilize both types of passes if desired (and budget allows).

LIGHTNING LANE MULTI PASS

Lightning Lane Multi Pass lets guests enter select theme park attractions up to once per day via "Lightning Lane" entrances rather than using the standby queues. How does it work? First, you need to purchase the service. That can be done as an add-on to your ticket or vacation package via disneyland.com (prior to arrival), or via the Disneyland app once you've entered a park for the day (pending availability). Note that if you pre-purchase Multi

LEARN THE LINGO

disneyland.com: A hub for planning and managing your Disneyland Resort visit. It's also one place to add Multi Pass service to a park ticket purchase (the other is the Disneyland Resort mobile app).

Disneyland Resort mobile app: The official app for the Disneyland Resort has planning tools, park updates, exclusive content, and more. The app lets you use (complimentary) Disney Genie service, buy Multi Pass, and pay for Lightning Lane Single Passes while inside a Disney theme park. Be sure to download the app before you start your Disneyland theme park visit.

Disney Genie: A complimentary service that is intended to "create your best Disney day based on your interests." It's available as a feature within the official Disneyland Resort mobile app.

Lightning Lane Entrances: A fee-based alternative to traditional standby entrances, Lightning Lane Entrances are designed to offer expedited wait times at select theme park attractions. A Lightning Lane may be accessed by one of two ways: Lightning Lane Multi Pass or Lightning Lane Single Pass. Fees apply for both categories.

Lightning Lane Multi Pass: Multi Pass lets park guests select the next available arrival window for a Lightning Lane entrance at select attractions throughout the day, one at a time. A flat fee (which varies) covers Multi Pass for the day.

Lightning Lane Single Pass: Lightning Lane Single Pass is offered for the most highly demanded theme park attractions at the Disneyland Resort. At press time there was a limit of two attractions per person, per day. Fees vary.

HOT TIP

The purchase of Lightning Lane Multi Pass does not guarantee attraction access. In fact, popular rides run out of availability early in the day. That said, some folks do cancel their selections, so keep checking for availability.

Pass, it will be added to each day of a multi-day ticket. Same-day purchases can be done one day at a time. (All details are subject to change.) The cost of Multi Pass service varies, starting at about $32+ per ticket, per day, and it includes PhotoPass (see page 87 for PhotoPass details). If you have questions or need help with your in-park purchase of Multi Pass, head to a Guest Relations location. They'll know what to do.

Next up? Enter the park for which you have a ticket and reservation. Now it's time to make the first Lightning Lane selection of the day. Once you have redeemed your initial selection (or 120 minutes have passed), you can use the Disney Genie Tip Board to view available attractions and see when to make the next selection. Note that Multi Pass selections can be made throughout the day—one at a time—until regular park closing time. All Lightning Lane selections are subject to availability and are limited to one per attraction, per day.

When your first arrival window kicks in, you can head to the attraction's Lightning Lane entrance, flash your ticket, MagicBand+, or smartphone (so the bar code may be scanned), and zip on into the Lightning Lane. You can make your next Multi Pass selection after your current selection has been redeemed. You can also make an additional selection if you are holding a selection with an arrival window that's more than two hours away—provided there is availability. Feeling a bit of information overload? Not to worry. The Disneyland mobile app is an efficient way to keep track of it all. And Disney's Guest Relations team is always happy to help.

LIGHTNING LANE SINGLE PASS

Lightning Lane access to a small number of Disneyland Resort's most popular "E-ticket" attractions may be purchased on an à la carte basis. They're limited to two purchases per person, per day and can range quite a bit in price. (Prices vary based on date and attraction.) Be sure to check the Disneyland app on the day of your visit for current prices and attraction availability.

You can purchase up to two Lightning Lane Single Passes upon entering a Disneyland Resort theme park. Remember: Lightning Lane entry for these attractions is only available to purchase individually and not included with Multi Pass. Both types of Lightning Lane passes may be purchased on the same day; they are not mutually exclusive. For details, use the Disneyland mobile app, or visit *disneyland.com*.

HOT TIP

At press time, theme park attractions with Lightning Lane Single Pass status included Disneyland Park's Star Wars: Rise of the Resistance and Disney California Adventure Park's Radiator Springs Racers. Single Pass status can change at any time. For updates, visit *disneyland.com*.

LIGHTNING LANE PREMIER PASS

Granting onetime access to each Lightning Lane attraction in both parks (a Park Hopper ticket would be required to use it fully), Lighting Lane Premier Pass is available in very limited quantities. Using it is quite simple as arrival times do not need to be selected; simply enter the Lightning Lane queue at any time and scan your ticket or MagicBand. But remember, it can be used only once at each eligible attraction. Premier Pass can be purchased up to 7 days in advance of your visit.

MULTI PASS ATTRACTIONS*

The following theme park attractions were included with Multi Pass as this book went to press (details are subject to change):

DISNEYLAND PARK
- Autopia
- Big Thunder Mountain Railroad
- Buzz Lightyear Astro Blasters
- Haunted Mansion
- Indiana Jones Adventure
- It's a Small World
- Matterhorn Bobsleds
- Mickey & Minnie's Runaway Railway
- *Millennium Falcon:* Smugglers Run
- Roger Rabbit's Car Toon Spin
- Space Mountain
- Star Tours—The Adventures Continue
- Tiana's Bayou Adventure

DISNEY CALIFORNIA ADVENTURE
- Goofy's Sky School
- Grizzly River Run
- Guardians of the Galaxy— Mission: BREAKOUT!
- Incredicoaster
- The Little Mermaid— Ariel's Undersea Adventure
- Monsters, Inc. Mike & Sulley to the Rescue!
- Soarin' Around the World
- Toy Story Midway Mania!
- WEB SLINGERS: A Spider-Man Adventure

* Attractions and shows may be added or removed from Lightning Lane Service at any time. For updates, visit *disneyland.com* or check the Disneyland mobile app.

How to Get There

Most visitors to Disneyland Resort arrive by car. Many who live nearby own Magic Key passes and often drive there to spend a day or weekend at the resort. But for those traveling any significant distance, it tends to cost less to fly than to drive, and can save time. During your days at Disneyland Resort, you won't need a vehicle. Rent a car only for the days you plan to venture off Disneyland property, or rely on local tours to see the area sights. If you prefer to leave the driving to someone else, traveling to Disneyland by bus or train are alternatives.

BY CAR

SOUTHERN CALIFORNIA FREEWAYS: Driving just about anywhere in Orange County, or farther afield, requires negotiating a number of freeways and surface streets. But once you familiarize yourself with a few names and numbers, navigating through California becomes much more manageable.

The freeways are well marked and relatively fast, barring (common) traffic snags. That said, they can be rather frenetic. Major thoroughfares may merge with little or no notice. Monstrous traffic jams are common during morning and evening rush hours. And proper names of most roads change, depending on where you are. I-5, for instance, is called the Santa Ana Freeway in Orange County; in the Los Angeles area, it becomes the Golden State Freeway; to the south, it's the San Diego Freeway. It's a good idea to learn both the name and the route number of any freeway on which you plan to

travel. Exit signs list a route number and either a direction or city name (but not always both).

Even with GPS, it's always good to have an idea of the layout of the freeways. Several run parallel to the Pacific coast and are intersected by others running east and west. While this scheme is fairly straightforward, it is complicated by a couple of freeways that squiggle across the map.

CALIFORNIA DRIVING LAWS: Under state law, seat belts are required for all passengers; right turns at red lights are legal unless otherwise posted, as are U-turns at intersections; and pedestrians have the right-of-way at all crosswalks. By law, kids must be in car or booster seats until they reach the age of 8 or a height of 4 feet, 9 inches. And keep your hands off your phone—it's illegal to use it while driving in California.

AUTOMOBILE CLUBS: Any one of the nation's leading automobile clubs will come to your aid in the event of a breakdown en route (be sure to bring your membership card with you), as well as provide insurance covering accidents, arrest, bail bond, lawyers' fees for defense of contested traffic cases, and personal injury. They also offer trip-planning services—not merely advice, but also free maps and route-mapping assistance.

MAPS/GPS: If you don't have a GPS app on your smartphone, know that some car rental agencies provide GPS systems and maps. Of course, it's still wise to familiarize yourself with the route beforehand. Said route can be plotted via *www.bing.com/maps; www.mapquest.com;* or *maps.google.com.*

BY AIR

Anaheim lies approximately 45 to 120 minutes southeast of Los Angeles by car. Most Disneyland Resort guests who arrive by plane disembark at Los Angeles International Airport (LAX), one of the busiest in the world. It handles approximately 1,600 departures and arrivals daily of more than 71 commercial airlines. Major carriers serving Los Angeles include JetBlue, American, Delta, and United Airlines.

Much closer to Anaheim, Orange County's John Wayne Airport is about a half-hour drive from Disney and is served by 12 commercial airlines and more than 300 flights a day. It is sometimes possible to find the same fare to John Wayne/Orange County Airport (SNA) as to LAX, and if it's

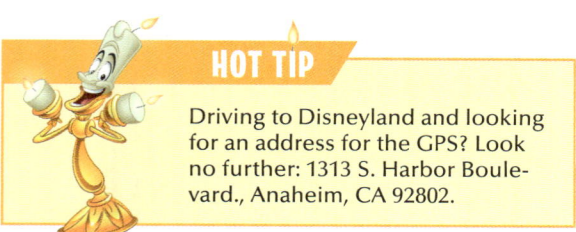

HOT TIP

Driving to Disneyland and looking for an address for the GPS? Look no further: 1313 S. Harbor Boulevard., Anaheim, CA 92802.

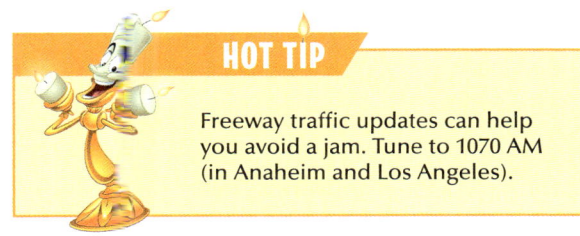

a nonstop flight, so much the better. There are not as many direct flights available, but given the proximity to the Disneyland Resort area, it's worth considering. Another airport vying for attention is the Long Beach Airport (LGB). The lovely, little airport is relatively close to Anaheim, but few airlines serve it on a nonstop basis.

HOW TO GET THE BEST AIRFARE: Airfares seem to be forever in flux, changing often. That makes it very important to shop around—or have your travel agent do so. It pays to keep these suggestions in mind:

• Check out all airlines serving your destination. See if you can get a lower fare by slightly altering the dates of your trip, the hour of departure, or the duration of your stay—or, if you live halfway between two airports, by leaving from one rather than the other or by flying into a different area airport.

• Weekend flights tend to bring higher prices. Fly midweek whenever possible. (Tuesdays and Wednesdays are usually best.)

• Purchase your tickets online. Airlines often offer lower fares or waive transaction fees when customers use their websites.

• Keep an eye on airline websites, social media sites, and newspapers for ads announcing special fares.

AIRPORT TRANSPORTATION: There are a number of shuttles and limousines available to transfer you from area airports to the Disneyland Resort.

At Los Angeles International Airport (LAX), limos, shuttles, and car services pick up passengers on the Lower/Arrival Level islands in front of each terminal on the middle island curb under the white sign marked "Passenger Pickup." For additional information about transportation to and from LAX, visit *flylax.com*.

Those who fly into John Wayne Airport, 14 miles from Disneyland, have an easier time of it. The ride into town takes half the time than from LAX. From baggage claim, head to the Ground Transportation Center. This is the spot to meet prearranged transportation, connect with Karmel Shuttle, and get a taxi. Look for coordinators who can assist you with your ground transportation needs. And be sure to inquire about a flat rate for a one-way trip to the Disneyland Resort. For more details about John Wayne Airport's ground transportation, visit *ocair.com*.

Karmel Shuttle (*karmel.com*; 714-670-3480) serves most area airports. At Los Angeles International Airport, claim luggage and call 714-670-3480 Extension 2 for pickup. Or, if you've provided a cell phone number and received a text alert upon landing, tap the "Ready to Go" link in the text from Karmel Shuttle. You will be provided with both a vehicle number and a license plate number. Be sure to match these numbers with the vehicle sent to pick you up. Then head on over to the

TO THE DISNEYLAND RESORT FROM THE AIRPORT*

	Yellow Cab	Karmel Shuttle**
Los Angeles International Airport (LAX)	Expect to pay at least $115 (plus a tip for the driver), depending on traffic.	$135.50 (plus tip) per car (up to 5 passengers)
John Wayne Airport (SNA)	Expect to pay at least $58 (plus tip).	$74 (plus tip) per car (up to 5 passengers)
Long Beach Airport (LGB)	Expect to pay at least $52 (plus tip).	$103 (plus tip) per car (up to 9 passengers)

* For updates and/or more information on transfers between the Disneyland Resort and area airports, visit *disneyland.disney.go.com/guest-services/getting-here/by-plane*. Prices quoted are for one-way trips.

** Price paid per person varies based on the number of passengers in the car. Solo riders pay the full price. For shared rides, the "car total" is divided evenly among passengers. Shared-ride service is available for pick-ups between 6 A.M. and 7 P.M. Private service is available 24/7. For details, visit *karmel.com*, or call 714-670-3480.

Rideshare services such as Lyft and Uber are authorized to transport guests to and from the Disneyland Resort, too. The companies listed on this page are not owned or endorsed by The Walt Disney Company.

Lower/Arrival Level islands in front of each terminal on the middle island curb under the white sign indicating "Passenger Pickup." Follow the same procedures for John Wayne and Long Beach airport, where the pickup areas are at the airports' respective Ground Transportation Centers. (Long Beach Airport's pickup center is the island next to the covered parking structure across Douglas Drive.) Karmel offers private and shared rides.

CAR RENTALS: Several major car rental agencies have locations at LAX, John Wayne, and Long Beach airports; in Union Station; at many hotels; and elsewhere in the Anaheim area. Expect to pay somewhere between $501 and $780 a week for an intermediate car (plus tax and insurance fees), and $282 to $682 for a 3-day weekend, with unlimited mileage. Some rental companies to choose from are Avis (800-331-1212), Budget (800-527-0700), Dollar (800-800-4000), Hertz (800-654-3131), Alamo (800-651-1223), and National (888-273-5262).

It pays to call agencies and check websites to get the best available deals. Be sure to ask about any special promotions or discounts. Loss Damage Waiver (LDW) coverage is essential for your protection in case of an accident, but it can add a lot to your bill (usually at least $25 a day). Most packages that include a rental car do not include LDW. If you have your own car insurance, check with your carrier to see what is covered.

An increasing number of major credit card companies offer free collision damage coverage for charging the rental to their card, and some may provide primary coverage. That means your credit card company may deal with the rental company directly in the event of an accident, rather than compensate you after your insurance has kicked in. It's worth a call to find out.

If you are renting a car at Los Angeles International Airport (LAX), the drive to the Disneyland Resort is only 31 miles, but it'll take at least 45 minutes with light traffic, or up to two hours if the roads are congested. From John Wayne Airport (SNA), the drive takes about 25 minutes (without traffic). Expect a drive of about a half hour from Long Beach Airport (LGB)—again, that estimate does not factor in the wild card known as Southern California traffic.

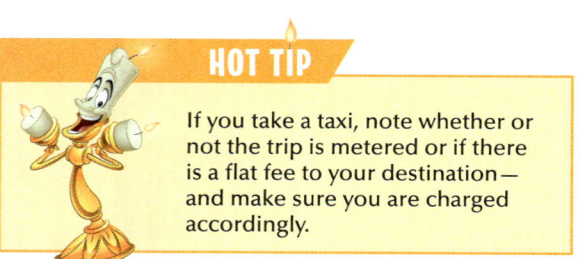

HOT TIP

If you take a taxi, note whether or not the trip is metered or if there is a flat fee to your destination— and make sure you are charged accordingly.

If a car rental is needed once at the Disneyland Resort or you need a location to drop a one-way Enterprise rental, go to Disney's Pixar Place Hotel. To confirm that this service will be offered during your visit, call 888-826-6893.

BY TRAIN

It's possible to get to Anaheim by rail from Union Station in Los Angeles by using Amtrak's Pacific Surfliner train (*www.pacificsurfliner.com*; 800-872-7245) or L A.'s Metrolink Orange County light-rail (*www.metrolinktrains.com*; 800-371-5465). Union Station is in downtown L.A. and is served by trains from all over the country.

You can get to Union Station from Los Angeles International Airport (LAX) by cab, by bus (LAX FlyAway Bus; *www.flylax.com/flyaway*; 866-435-9529), or by L.A.'s Metro subway (323-466-3876; *www.metro.net*; the system also serves Long Beach Airport). Avis, Budget, and Hertz rental car agencies have counters at Union Station; call companies directly for rates and hours.

The Anaheim train station is adjacent to Angel Stadium in Anaheim, which is approximately two miles from the Disneyland Resort. Yellow Cabs can be summoned from the train station (714-444-4444).

BY BUS

Buses make sense if you're traveling a short distance, if you have plenty of time to spend in transit, if there are only two or three people in your party, and/or if cost-control is key.

Buses make the journey from Los Angeles and San Diego, though they usually make a few stops along the way. Travel from most other destinations usually requires a change of vehicle in Los Angeles. Transfers are usually made at 1716 E. 7th St. at Alameda in downtown L.A.

The Anaheim Greyhound bus terminal is at 2626 E. Katella Ave.; *www.greyhound.com*; 800-231-2222. Yellow Cabs can get you to Disneyland from the bus terminal for about $20; 714-444-4444.

Southern California

Miles
0 5 10 15 20

To Palm Springs →

San Bernardino

Riverside

San Bernardino Fwy.

Riverside Fwy.

To Santa Barbara

Pasadena

Burbank

Hollywood

Los Angeles

Beverly Hills

Santa Monica Fwy.

Santa Monica

Venice Beach

Los Angeles International Airport

Manhattan Beach

Redondo Beach

Santa Ana Fwy.

Long Beach Airport

Long Beach

Palos Verdes Peninsula

Buena Park

Fullerton

Anaheim

Disneyland RESORT

Orange

Santa Ana

Garden Grove

Garden Grove Fwy.

Fountain Valley

Costa Mesa

Newport Beach

Balboa Peninsula

Huntington Beach

Irvine

John Wayne (Orange County) Airport

Laguna Beach

San Juan Capistrano

Dana Point

San Clemente

San Diego Fwy.

To San Diego →

PACIFIC OCEAN

CATALINA ISLAND

Avalon

Getting Oriented

Southern California's patchwork of small communities has undeniably blurred borders. The Disneyland Resort is in Anaheim, but you might not know if you were in that city or one of its immediate neighbors except for the signs. Buena Park lies to the northwest, Garden Grove to the south, Santa Ana to the southeast, and Orange to the east.

Farther south—in Huntington Beach, Newport Beach, Laguna Beach, and San Juan Capistrano—there's a bit more breathing room between communities. Heading northwest from Anaheim, you'll come to Los Angeles International Airport.

Continuing northwest into L.A., you will find Santa Monica to the west, and, to the east, Beverly Hills, West Hollywood, and Hollywood. On the beach farther north and west is Malibu, and inland to the east are Burbank (home of the Walt Disney Studios) and Glendale. The San Fernando Valley lies farther north and a bit inland from Los Angeles proper, while Santa Barbara, Southern California's northern boundary, is on the coast, about two hours to the north.

North–South Freeways: There are two north-south thoroughfares: I-5 (the Santa Ana Freeway in the Anaheim area) runs from Vancouver, Canada, to San Diego, and is the main inland route in Southern California, linking Los Angeles and San Diego; I-405 (the San Diego Freeway) sprouts from I-5 north of Hollywood, veers south toward the coast, then rejoins I-5 at Irvine, a bit south of Anaheim.

East–West Freeways: Of the roads that intersect the two principal north-south arteries, one of the closest to the Disneyland Resort is Route 22, also known as the Garden Grove Freeway; it begins near the ocean in Long Beach and runs beyond the southern border of Anaheim. Route 91, called the Artesia Freeway on the west side of I-5 and the Riverside Freeway on the east, lies about eight miles north of Route 22.

Farther north you will reach I-10, called the Santa Monica Freeway from its beginning point near the Pacific shore in Santa Monica to just east of downtown Los Angeles. At this juncture, it jogs north and then turns east again, becoming the San Bernardino Freeway. The I-10 thoroughfare is located approximately twelve miles north of Route 91.

North of I-10 (anywhere from two to eight miles, depending on your location) is U.S. 101, which heads south from Ventura and then due east, crossing I-405. It is known as the Ventura Freeway until a few miles

TRAVEL TIMES

To/From the Resort	Approx. Distance	Drive Time
Balboa	20 miles	40 min.
Buena Park	7 miles	12 min.
Carlsbad	60 miles	60 min.
Costa Mesa	15 miles	30 min.
Dana Point	30 miles	40 min.
Garden Grove	5 miles	10 min.
Huntington Beach	20 miles	30 min.
John Wayne Airport	16 miles	25 min.
Laguna Beach	30 miles	45 min.
Las Vegas	280 miles	5–6 hrs.
Long Beach	26 miles	30 min.
Los Angeles (downtown and airport)	31 miles	45–90 min.
Newport Beach	20 miles	30 min.
Palm Springs	100 miles	2–3 hrs.
San Diego	95 miles	90 min.
San Juan Capistrano	32 miles	45 min.
San Simeon	270 miles	5–6 hrs.
Santa Ana	7 miles	15 min.
Santa Barbara	120 miles	2–3 hrs.

east of I-405, at which point the road angles to the south and becomes the Hollywood Freeway, and eventually merges into I-5.

HOW TO GET THERE: Disneyland Resort is on Harbor Boulevard between Katella Avenue, Disneyland Drive, and Ball Road, 31 miles south of downtown Los Angeles and 87 miles north of San Diego. Many visitors drive to Disneyland from elsewhere in Southern California, while those who come from farther away fly into one of the area airports, rent a car, and drive from there. Once at their hotel, guests may prefer to use the hotel's shuttle or Anaheim Resort Transportation (ART) to and from the Disneyland Resort (rather than their own vehicle).

Southbound I-5 Exit: To get to Disneyland, southbound I-5 (the Santa Ana Freeway) travelers should exit at Disneyland Drive, turn left, cross Ball Road, and follow signs to the most convenient parking area.

Northbound I-5 Exit: Northbound travelers should exit I-5 at Katella Avenue, proceed straight to Disney Way, and then follow signs to the most convenient parking area.

From John Wayne/Orange County Airport: Take I-405 north to CA-55 north to I-5 north. Watch carefully for highway signs once out of the airport. Exit at Katella Avenue, head straight to Disney Way, then follow signs to the most convenient parking area.

From Los Angeles International Airport: Take I-105 east to I-605 north to I-5 south. Take Disneyland Drive exit toward Ball Road. Merge onto Disneyland Drive, and proceed to the most convenient parking zone (the Mickey & Friends parking structure or the Toy Story parking area).

Exit off Orange Freeway: Travelers on the 57 freeway should exit on Katella Avenue and proceed west. Turn right on Harbor Boulevard, and follow signs to the parking area.

ANAHEIM SURFACE STREETS: The Disneyland Resort is in the center of the Anaheim Resort, a 1,100-acre district. Disneyland Resort is bounded by Harbor Boulevard on the east, Disneyland Drive (a segment of West Street) on the west, Ball Road on the north, and Katella Avenue on the south.

Harbor Boulevard, near Ball Road, is the most convenient place to pick up I-5 (Santa Ana Freeway) going north to Los Angeles. Katella Avenue, past Anaheim Boulevard, is the most convenient entrance to southbound I-5 going to Newport Beach and points south.

Note: Parking rules are strictly enforced in Anaheim. Be sure to park in a designated lot, feed the parking meter often, and heed all signs.

LOCAL TRANSPORTATION: The Orange County Transportation Authority (OCTA; *www.octa.net*; 714-560-5282) provides daily bus service throughout the area, with limited service on the weekend. Several different lines stop at the Disneyland Resort, but note that public transportation, while cost-efficient, may involve considerable waiting and transferring. Tickets must be purchased at a Metrolink vending machine at any station or through the Metrolink app. Los Angeles' Union Station has ticket windows, too.

Anaheim Resort Transportation, also known as ART (*www.rideart.org*; 888-364-2787), is a multi-route guest transit system serving the Anaheim Resort area. ART Passes may be purchased online and from many area hotels, public sales outlets, and various kiosk locations. Drivers do not sell passes. Adult fares are $6 for a one-day pass, $16 for three days, and $25 for a five-day pass. Kids ages 3 to 9 pay $2.50 for one day, $3.50 for three days, and $5.50 for five-day passes. There is no charge for baby passengers.

The Metro serves L.A. County and the major attractions of Orange County (*www.metro.net*; 323-466-3876). Cost is about $1.75 each way (75 cents for seniors). A refillable TAP (Transit Access Pass) card is required.

TAXIS: The only licensed taxi company that's officially authorized to serve Disneyland Resort is the Anaheim Yellow Cab Company (*www.californiayellowcab.com*; 714-444-4444). The fare to John Wayne Airport from the Disneyland Hotel generally runs about $58, plus tip; if you are going to LAX, figure at least $115 (or more, depending on the traffic). The fare to and from Long Beach Airport runs approximately $52, plus gratuity. Prices for town cars are usually slightly higher. Taxis can be called to pick you up at train and bus stations. Lyft and Uber car-sharing services are also authorized to pick up and drop off guests—see the Hot Tip below for more information.

HOT TIP

There are two areas for Disneyland Resort park guests to get picked up or dropped off by car (including taxis and car-sharing services). One is off Harbor Boulevard and the other is at Downtown Disney District.

For Downtown Disney District, take Magic Way from Disneyland Drive, then turn left at Downtown Drive. Follow the signs to the drop-off area. There's a 15-minute grace period—after that, standard parking rates apply. (The first hour costs $10. For more rate specifics, visit *disneyland.com*.)

For Harbor Boulevard, enter the drop-off area from the right southbound lane on South Harbor Boulevard. This spot is located between South Manchester Avenue and Disney Way.

Planning Your Itinerary

For those lucky enough to live in the Los Angeles/Orange County area, the Disneyland Resort offers the opportunity to return frequently. Seasoned visitors and first-timers alike will do well to plan each step of their visit far in advance—make the travel arrangements as soon as vacation dates are set (refer to the Trip Planning Timeline below to make sure you don't miss any crucial steps), and then study the following chapters of this book to decide how you'd like to spend each day of the trip.

How many days should you spend with the Mouse and his pals? Well, that's up to you, but to experience the Disneyland Resort at its best, we recommend a stay of at least four full days—you will have enough time to see quite a few theme park attractions, parades, and shows (plus revisit all of your favorites), lounge beside your hotel's pool, enjoy a meal with favorite Disney characters, shop for souvenirs, and enjoy a rejuvenating spa treatment. If you'd like to visit other area attractions, add on one day for each excursion. But don't try to cram too much into one visit; this is your vacation, after all.

Once you've decided how many days you're going to dedicate to Disney, it's time to decide how you'll split up your time on Disney property. We suggest starting with a day at Disneyland Park (for the original and quintessential Disney experience), followed by a visit to Disney California Adventure. On day three, return to Disneyland and hit the park's highlights, plus any attractions you missed, and save time for souvenir shopping. Day four should be focused on your preferred park and some downtime by the pool or in the Downtown Disney District. Evenings can be spent in a park, if it's open late, or in Downtown Disney's lively restaurants, lounges, and play zones. The options are plentiful.

On the following pages, we have provided full-day schedules to guide you through four days in the parks (with tips for families with young children and priorities for days when the lines are at their longest). The schedules are meant to be flexible and fun (not Disney boot camp), so take them at your own pace and plan breaks to relax: Have a Mickey Mouse ice cream bar, browse through the shops, smell the flowers, or just pick a bench and watch the crowds pass by. Details are subject to change. Visit *disneyland.com,* or use the Disneyland mobile app for updates.

TRIP PLANNING TIMELINE

FIRST THINGS FIRST
● Check for hotel availability as far ahead as possible. Go to *disneyland.com,* or call 714-520-5050 to book Disney hotel accommodations; remember that a deposit must be paid within 21 days of the reservation.

6 MONTHS
● Unless you opted for a vacation package that includes theme park admission, it's time to buy park tickets and make park reservations. Check for theme park reservation availability *before* you buy park tickets! Link all tickets to your *disneyland.com* account as soon as possible. (For details about park reservations, see page 17 and visit *disneyland.com*). Be sure to arrange for transportation to/from the Disneyland Resort, too.

UP TO 2 MONTHS
● Find out theme park hours, attraction refurbishment schedule, and details on any special events by visiting *disneyland.com,* using the Disneyland Resort mobile app, or calling 714-781-4565.
● Make dining reservations (they're necessary at most table-service eateries at the Disneyland Resort and can be made up to 60 days ahead; use the Disneyland app,

visit *disneyland.com,* or call 714-781-3463. Refer to the *Good Meals, Great Times* chapter for information about Disneyland Resort dining spots.) Now's the time to book Disneyland backstage tours, too.

1 WEEK
● Confirm all reservations and finalize your day-by-day vacation schedule. We recommend making printouts of all reservations, just in case. And double-check theme park operating hours (they change often).
● Jot down—on paper—important telephone numbers (doctors, family members, house sitter, etc.) in case something happens to your mobile phone during your travels.

5 DAYS
● If you're booked at one of the 3 Disneyland Resort hotels, it's time to complete Online Check-In via the Disneyland app or *disneyland.com* to simplify your arrival.

1 DAY
● Place printouts of any tickets you have purchased (and a valid, government-issued photo ID) in a day-bag or carry-on bag.

DISNEYLAND PARK
One-Day Schedule

🔴 Disneyland's breakfast options have expanded of late. If you don't nosh at the hotel, consider having a bite at Red Rose Taverne, Plaza Inn, or Carnation Cafe.

🔴 Take in the sights as you walk down Main Street, but don't stop to shop now (you'll have time for that later). Instead, head straight to Adventureland's Jungle Cruise and Indiana Jones Adventure* before making your way to the Pirates of the Caribbean and—if you don't mind getting wet this early—Tiana's Bayou Adventure* in Bayou Country followed by The Many Adventures of Winnie the Pooh. (If you want to dine at the Blue Bayou restaurant, make a reservation up to 60 days in advance via the Disneyland app or disneyland.com, or by calling 714-781-3463.)

🔴 Experience the out-of-this-world land known as Star Wars: Galaxy's Edge. Highlights include *Millennium Falcon: Smugglers Run** and Star Wars: Rise of the Resistance.**

🔴 Backtrack to New Orleans Square, and pay a visit to the Haunted Mansion* and Pirates of the Caribbean (if you haven't hit it yet) before breaking for a bite to eat.

🔴 Check a schedule and be sure to catch the Magic Happens parade. Then tackle Big Thunder Mountain Railroad* in Frontierland. (Don't ride on a full stomach!)

🔴 Explore Fantasy Faire. Then walk through the castle into Fantasyland and visit Snow White, Pinocchio, Peter Pan, and Mr. Toad. Be sure to see Alice, the Mad Tea Party, the Matterhorn,* and It's a Small World,* too.

🔴 Head over to Mickey's Toontown, making the delightful Mickey & Minnie's Runaway Railway* a priority. Let little ones frolic in Goofy's How-to-Play Yard and Donald's Duck Pond. Have a bite at Cafe Daisy or Good Boy! Grocers.

(Continued on page 32)

DISNEYLAND DELIGHTS

These attractions combine to form the quintessential Disneyland park experience:

- **Tiana's Bayou Adventure**
- **Indiana Jones Adventure**
- **Pirates of the Caribbean**
- **Haunted Mansion**
- **Big Thunder Mountain Railroad**
- **Peter Pan's Flight**
- **Matterhorn Bobsleds**
- **Mickey & Minnie's Runaway Railway**
- **It's a Small World**
- **Star Tours—The Adventures Continue**
- **Jungle Cruise**
- **The Many Adventures of Winnie the Pooh**
- **Buzz Lightyear Astro Blasters**
- **Space Mountain**
- **Fantasmic!**
- **Mr. Toad's Wild Ride**
- **Star Wars: Rise of the Resistance**

LINE BUSTERS

When the park is packed, the following attractions may have shorter waits: The Disneyland Railroad, Enchanted Tiki Room, Pirates Lair on Tom Sawyer Island, The Many Adventures of Winnie the Pooh, *Mark Twain* riverboat, and Main Street Opera House, Presenting Walt Disney — A Magical Life.

IF YOU HAVE YOUNG CHILDREN

- First, go to Fantasyland and visit each area attraction (note that some are scary for young kids) before visiting the delightfully kid-friendly Mickey's Toontown. Then head to Bayou Country to enjoy The Many Adventures of Winnie the Pooh.
- Take tykes to King Arthur Carrousel and It's a Small World (the latter is an absolute must!).
- Ride the Jungle Cruise, then sing with the Tiki Birds in Adventureland, or enjoy a frozen treat at Tropical Hideaway before returning to your favorite rides.
- Scope out a spot on a Main Street curb up to an hour before the Magic Happens parade. For smaller crowds, watch from the viewing area near It's a Small World.

DISNEYLAND PARK One-Day Schedule

(Continued from page 31)

🔴 If you haven't experienced Tiana's Bayou Adventure yet, it's time to take the plunge. Try to fit an afternoon show or parade into your schedule, too.

🔴 Hop aboard the Disneyland Railroad and disembark in Tomorrowland. Enjoy the Finding Nemo Submarine Voyage, Space Mountain,* and Buzz Lightyear Astro Blasters* before heading to dinner.

Note: If the park is open late, you can board the monorail in Tomorrowland and dine in the Downtown Disney District before returning to the park.

🔴 After dinner, take the wheel of a hot rod at Autopia,* then take flight at Star Tours—The Adventures Continue,* and/or Astro Orbitor.

🔴 Take youngsters back to Fantasyland to hit any attractions you may have missed earlier in the day or to repeat a favorite. This land tends to get a bit less congested as the evening hours kick in.

🔴 On nights when Fantasmic! is presented, make a point of getting to New Orleans Square and the Rivers of America in plenty of time to see it. (Check a park Tip Board, the Disneyland app, or *disneyland.com* for the schedule.)

🔴 Stroll back to Main Street, U.S.A. Shop, stop for dessert; see the Main Street Opera House, Presenting Walt Disney — A Magical Life; and watch the fireworks light up the sky above Sleeping Beauty Castle.

🔴 If there's time, go back for seconds of your favorite shows and attractions.

SEE THE CHARACTERS

There are lots of places to see Disney characters in this park. Some of the better spots include Mickey's Toontown (Mickey, Minnie, Daisy, Donald, Goofy, Clarabelle, and Pete), Bayou Country (Pooh and pals), Fantasyland's Fantasy Faire (princesses), Star Wars: Galaxy's Edge, and around Town Square on Main Street, U.S.A. Details are subject to change. For character appearance schedules, check a park Tip Board, the Disneyland Resort mobile app, or *disneyland.com*. And don't forget your camera!

TOP SHOPS

Whether you're browsing or buying, Disneyland is a shopper's paradise. Here are a few of the spots where wallets get a workout:

Candy Palace
Disneyana
Emporium
Eudora's Chic Boutique
Main Street Magic Shop
Pieces of Eight
Pioneer Mercantile
Port Royal Curios & Curiosities
The Star Trader

HOT TIP

Single Rider service lets groups split up and enter attractions individually—usually resulting in a reduced wait time. The following attractions may offer Single Rider service: *Millennium Falcon:* Smugglers Run, Matterhorn Bobsleds, and Space Mountain (at Disneyland park); Incredicoaster, Radiator Springs Racers, Goofy's Sky School, WEB SLINGERS: A Spider-Man Adventure, and Grizzly River Run (at Disney California Adventure). Enjoy.

* *Lightning Lane Multi Pass is available for this attraction. Details are subject to change.*
** *Lightning Lane Single Pass is available for this attraction. Details are subject to change. Fees apply for Multi Pass and Single Pass. To learn about how to use Lightning Lane Passes, see page 22.*

DISNEY CALIFORNIA ADVENTURE
One-Day Schedule

🔷 Begin your California adventure with an early-as-possible visit to Cars Land. Do not miss Radiator Springs Racers.** If possible, enjoy Mater's Junkyard Jamboree before moving on to Avengers Campus. Enjoy a thrilling adventure at popular Guardians of the Galaxy—Mission: BREAKOUT!* and wrangle spider-bots at WEB SLINGERS: A Spider-Man Adventure.*

🔷 Mosey through Hollywood Land, taking in Monsters, Inc. Mike & Sulley to the Rescue!,* Mickey's PhilharMagic, and visit Disney Animation (be sure to say hello to Anna and Elsa and see an amazing interactive show called Turtle Talk with Crush). Take little ones to the energetic Disney Junior Mickey Mouse Clubhouse Live!

🔷 Make your way over to the Grizzly Peak Recreation Area and experience Soarin' Around the World.* Then get set to get wet on the drenching Grizzly River Run* whitewater raft ride. (Unless they're waterproof, leave valuables in a nearby locker or with a non-riding member of your party.) If you're up for it (and wearing proper footwear), tackle the Redwood Creek Challenge Trail.

(Continued on page 34)

ADVENTURE ACES

If you're short on time, be sure to catch as many of the following four-star attractions at Disney California Adventure as possible:

Toy Story Midway Mania!
Radiator Springs Racers
WEB SLINGERS: A Spider-Man Adventure
Soarin' Around the World
World of Color
Turtle Talk with Crush
Incredicoaster
Mater's Junkyard Jamboree
Guardians of the Galaxy—Mission: BREAKOUT!
Monsters, Inc. Mike & Sulley to the Rescue!
The Little Mermaid—Ariel's Undersea Adventure
Mickey's PhilharMagic

IF YOU HAVE YOUNG CHILDREN

• Head to Hollywood Land for Monsters, Inc. Mike & Sulley to the Rescue! and Mickey's PhilharMagic. Stop in at Disney Animation for Turtle Talk, Sorcerer's Workshop, and to say hello to Anna and Elsa. Then join an interactive shindig at Disney Junior Mickey Mouse Clubhouse Live!

• Zoom into Cars Land for a wild-but-mild ride at Mater's Junkyard Jamboree.

• Amble on over to Pixar Pier. Take a spin on Jessie's Critter Carousel, do Toy Story Midway Mania!, and experience Inside Out Emotional Whirlwind.

• Over at Paradise Gardens, be sure to hit these kid-pleasers: The Little Mermaid—Ariel's Undersea Adventure and Jumpin' Jellyfish.

• Try the kid-friendly obstacle course at the Grizzly Peak area's Redwood Creek Challenge Trail.

• Finally, treat night owls to the dazzling World of Color water show. (The noisy water jets might spook some.) Warn kids that they may get a teeny bit wet.

DISNEY CALIFORNIA ADVENTURE
One-Day Schedule

(Continued from page 33)

🐭 Pick up some wine-pairing tips or sample California's finest at the Golden Vine Winery.

🐭 Explore San Fransokyo Square before proceeding on to Pixar Pier's crowd-pleasing rides, including but not limited to Incredicoaster* and Toy Story Midway Mania!* (don't ride on a full stomach).

🐭 Work your way around Paradise Bay, making sure to stop at The Little Mermaid—Ariel's Undersea Adventure.*

🐭 Be sure to catch the delightful nighttime extravaganza World of Color. Line up for a waterside viewing spot at least 45 minutes before showtime—and know that you might get a little wet if you are up close.

Note: If you're okay with missing World of Color, visit (or revisit) a popular attraction during the show. Wait times may be a bit shorter as park guests watch the wildly popular lagoon-based water show.

LINE BUSTERS

When lines abound at Disney California Adventure, we suggest heading to the following: Jessie's Critter Carousel, Silly Symphony Swings, Redwood Creek Challenge Trail, Disney Animation, and Monsters, Inc. Mike & Sulley to the Rescue!* The line for The Little Mermaid—Ariel's Undersea Adventure* often thins later in the day. If you don't mind splitting up your party, do consider the Single Rider line at Radiator Springs Racers. The wait is usually much shorter than for the standby line.

TOP SHOPS

Shopping at this park can be an adventure in and of itself. These are some of the spots that have earned their place in the spotlight:

Big Top Toys
Elias & Co.
Off the Page
Oswald's
Rushin' River Outfitters
Sarge's Surplus Hut
Trolley Treats

SEE THE CHARACTERS

Guests have many opportunities to catch up with favorite characters at Disney California Adventure. Among the best spots to see them are Buena Vista Street (usually Mickey, Goofy, and Donald Duck), Hollywood Land (Anna, Elsa, Olaf), Avengers Campus (Ant-Man, Black Widow, Captain Marvel, Thor, Black Panther, or others), Redwood Creek Challenge Trail (Chip and Dale), Cars Land (Mater, McQueen, and Red the Fire Engine), and Pixar Pier (Woody, Buzz, and Jessie). All details are subject to change at any time. Check a park Tip Board, the Disneyland app, or *disneyland.com* for appearance schedules.

* Lightning Lane Multi Pass is available for this attraction. Details are subject to change.
** Lightning Lane Single Pass is available for this attraction. Details are subject to change. Fees apply for Multi Pass and Single Pass. To learn about how to use Lightning Lane Passes, see page 22.

A Second Day in
DISNEYLAND PARK

Returning for a second or third day in each of the theme parks means more time to savor the atmosphere, try attractions you missed the first day, and revisit all the old and new favorites. Knowing that there will be a second day to play also makes for a less harried pace on day one.

🔴 Start the morning with grab-and-go breakfast at Jolly Holiday Bakery Cafe or Market House. Or enjoy the morning meal with Disney characters at the Plaza Inn (one can also share breakfast with characters outside the park at Goofy's Kitchen in the Disneyland Hotel or the Grand Californian's Storytellers Cafe). Reservations are necessary for character meals.

🔴 If you missed or would like to revisit Star Wars: Galaxy's Edge, get there early! It is a popular realm.

🔴 Head to Tomorrowland and experience Space Mountain,* Star Tours—The Adventures Continue,* Buzz Lightyear Astro Blasters,* Autopia,* and other futuristic favorites.

🔴 Navigate over to the kid-pleasing area known as Mickey's Toontown. If you haven't done Mickey & Minnie's Runaway Railway* yet, now's the time!

🔴 Visit It's a Small World,* experience the Matterhorn Bobsleds,* and tour Fantasyland.

🔴 Stroll, shop, and break for lunch on (or on your way to) Main Street, U.S.A.

🔴 Ride a Main Street Vehicle up to Town Square and continue on foot toward Adventureland.

🔴 Stop at the Enchanted Tiki Room before heading to New Orleans Square. There, the priorities are Haunted Mansion* and Pirates of the Caribbean. Visit them and navigate to Bayou Country for Tiana's Bayou Adventure and The Many Adventures of Winnie the Pooh.

🔴 Meander through the shops of New Orleans Square, and then stop for a leisurely dinner at a nearby eatery. River Belle Terrace, Tiana's Palace (jambalaya!), and the full-service Blue Bayou and Cafe Orleans are all solid options for a hearty meal.

🔴 Select a viewing location (in Frontierland or New Orleans Square) about 45 minutes before the evening's performance of Fantasmic! (if it is scheduled).

🔴 After the crowds disperse a bit after Fantasmic!, make your way to Big Thunder Mountain Railroad* for one last go 'round before the park closes for the evening.

🔴 Enjoy a final snack on Main Street, U.S.A. and do a bit of people-watching before heading under the train station and saying goodbye to Disneyland for the day.

* Lightning Lane Multi Pass is available for this attraction. Details are subject to change.
** Lightning Lane Single Pass is available for this attraction. Details are subject to change. Fees apply for Multi Pass and Single Pass. To learn about how to use Lightning Lane Passes, see page 22.

A Second Day in
DISNEY CALIFORNIA ADVENTURE

🐭 If you don't have an advance reservation for a table-service meal, stop for a quick-service breakfast at Smokejumpers Grill or Fiddler, Fifer & Practical Cafe (aka Starbucks). Then it's off to see what you missed on day one and revisit favorite attractions.

🐭 Make tracks for the wildly popular Cars Land if you haven't seen it yet, then circle back to Avengers Campus for anything you may have saved for later. The must do's in this super spot: Guardians of the Galaxy—Mission: BREAKOUT!* and WEB SLINGERS: A Spider-Man Adventure.* After exploring the area, pop over to Pixar Pier.

🐭 Thrill-seekers flip for a second go-round on the topsy-turvy Incredicoaster,* and gamers of all ages will swoon over Toy Story Midway Mania!*

🐭 Say hello to Baymax and Hiro at San Fransokyo's Hamada Bot Shop. Then visit the local bakery for a behind-the-scenes tour and discover how sourdough bread is made—and enjoy a free sample. Bonus!

🐭 Take a lunch break at Lamplight Lounge, Flo's V8 Cafe, Award Wieners, or Cocina Cucamonga—or, if the park is open late, head back to your hotel to relax or splash in the pool (be sure to keep track of your park

ticket so that you can return later in the day). Another option is to spend the afternoon in Downtown Disney District—most of its restaurants and shops open by about noon (or earlier).

🐭 Your California adventure picks up again with Soarin' Around the World* (located in Grizzly Peak Airfield), followed by a visit to The Little Mermaid—Ariel's Undersea Adventure,* then on to Grizzly River Run* (if you don't mind the likelihood of getting more than a tad soggy).

🐭 Stop for the parade if one is offered today, then make your way over to Hollywood Land. En route, try to catch a performance by Five and Dime.

🐭 Wander through Hollywood Land, enjoying any impromptu entertainment, take in Turtle Talk with Crush, and see Anna and Elsa inside Disney Animation. Take a tour of Monstropolis at Monsters, Inc. Mike and Sulley to the Rescue!* and don some 3-D glasses at Mickey's PhilharMagic.

🐭 If time permits after the show, revisit some of your favorite attractions or search for last-minute souvenirs at the shops on Buena Vista Street.

🐭 If you haven't seen World of Color yet, check a park Tip Board to see if it's being presented today. If it is, be sure to catch a performance. It's sure to put a smile on your face. (Guests up front may get a little wet.)

*Lightning Lane Multi Pass is available for this attraction. Details are subject to change.
**Lightning Lane Single Pass is available for this attraction. Details are subject to change. Fees apply for Multi Pass and Single Pass. To learn about how to use Lightning Lane Passes, see page 22.*

Fingertip Reference Guide

BARBERS AND SALONS

Disney's Grand Californian Hotel & Spa offers salon services at its Tenaya Stone Spa. One nearby spot at which hair may be cut or coiffed is Pure Escape Beauty Bar at the Hilton Anaheim Hotel (777 Convention Way; 714-740-4628; *pureescapebb.com*).

CAR CARE

The Anaheim office of the Automobile Club of Southern California is located at 420 North Euclid Avenue; *https://travel.calif.aaa.com*; 714-774-2392. To summon emergency roadside service, call 800-400-4222.

DRINKING POLICIES

While Disneyland Park has eased its long-standing no-alcohol policy (currently offering spirited beverages at Oga's Cantina and Blue Bayou), imbibing is an option at many spots at Disney California Adventure and at many venues located within the Downtown Disney District. Alcohol may also be purchased in the lounges and restaurants of the three Disneyland resort hotels. The legal drinking age in the state of California is 21. (Legal proof of age is required.)

GROCERY DELIVERIES

While Disney has no shortage of sublime sustenance, many guests choose to supplement its dining scene by having groceries delivered to their hotel. It's a convenient way to stock up on kids' favorite snack foods, breakfast bars, fresh fruit and veggies, and beverages. Simply order from a local grocery store such as Von's, or from a shopping service: Shipt, Amazon Fresh, Instacart, etc. If you're staying at a Disneyland Resort Hotel, you can meet the driver in the hotel driveway or have the delivery left with Bell Services—where they have a chiller to keep items cold until you pick them up. Delivery fees apply. Note that standard rooms at Disney hotels have mini refrigerators without freezers and do not have microwaves. With the exception of studios, Disney Vacation Club Villas at the Grand Californian and the Disneyland Hotel have full kitchens. Keep that in mind when placing your grocery order. The name of the room reservation holder should be the "deliver to" contact, along with your check-in date. For more info, including the delivery address for each of the Disneyland Resort Hotels, visit *disneyland.com*.

LOCKERS

Lockers of various sizes are available just outside the main entrance of the parks (our preferred location), inside Disneyland on Main Street (behind the Market House), and inside Disney California Adventure (DCA) across from Guest Relations. Prices are $7, $10, $12, or $15 per day, depending on the size and location of the locker. These storage facilities make it convenient to intersperse frolicking on the attractions with shopping; just make your purchases and stash them in a locker. Availability is limited, and during busy periods all the space can be taken well before noon. Disney California Adventure guests may stash items in lockers for free while they ride Grizzly River Run. The lockers are situated on the side of the attraction's entrance.

LOST AND FOUND

Lost and Found is located to the left of the entrance to Disneyland Park. At any given moment, a survey of the shelves might turn up mobile phones, cameras, strollers, handbags, hats, sunglasses, baby shoes, jewelry, and even a few crutches, false teeth, and hubcaps. If you lose something at a hotel, contact the front desk.

MAIL

Postcards are sold in gift shops throughout Anaheim, in a few shops in Downtown Disney District and the Disneyland Resort theme parks, and at the Disneyland Resort hotels. (Bring stamps from home.)

Cards that are deposited in mailboxes in the Disney theme parks are picked up and delivered to the U.S. Post Office once a day, early in the morning. All items

HOT TIP

To avoid the sometimes maddening congestion at the Main Street locker location, consider stowing your stuff at the lockers by the picnic area, just outside Disneyland Park's turnstiles. (You'll find them on the left side of the entrance as you face the park.)

are postmarked Anaheim, not Disneyland. (By the way, don't forget to arrange for your own mail to be held by the post office or picked up by a neighbor while you're on vacation.) Due to the heavy volume, expect delivery to take a whole lot longer than usual—please don't mail anything date-sensitive from the Disneyland Resort.

Post Office: The U.S. Post Office that's closest to the Disneyland Resort is Holiday Station, a half-mile away (1180 W. Ball Rd., Anaheim; 714-533-8182). It's open from 9 A.M. to 5 P.M. weekdays only.

MEDICAL MATTERS

Blisters are the most common complaint received by Disney's First Aid departments, found at the north end of Main Street, next to Lost Children in Disneyland, and at Chamber of Commerce near the main entrance to Disney California Adventure. Be sure to wear comfortable shoes (pack a backup pair)—and carry Band-Aids, just in case. ***In case of emergency, notify an employee and call 911***.

If you have a serious medical problem while on Disney property, call 911 and contact any Disney cast member (aka employee). They will get in touch with First Aid to make further arrangements. First Aid, staffed with registered nurses, will supply breathing machines and crutches for guests if needed. It will not dispense medication to anyone under the age of 18 without the consent of a parent or chaperone.

It's always a good idea to carry an insurance card and any other pertinent medical information. Those with chronic health problems should carry copies of all their prescriptions, along with their doctor's telephone number.

Prescriptions: The pharmacy at CVS, about a mile from the Disneyland Resort, is open 24/7 (480 South Main St.; 714-938-1200). The drive-through pharmacy at Walgreens, about three miles from Disneyland Resort, also operates 24/7 (12001 Euclid Street, Garden Grove; 714-530-1071). At the intersection of Katella Avenue and Harbor Boulevard, there is another CVS with a pharmacy that's open Monday through Friday from 9 A.M. to 6 P.M., Saturdays from 10 A.M. until 6 P.M., and Sundays from 11 A.M. to 5 P.M. (1803 S. Harbor Boulevard, Anaheim; 714-817-9116).

Refrigerator Facilities: In the Disney parks, insulin and antibiotics that must be refrigerated can be stored for the day at First Aid. (It does not store breast milk for nursing mothers.) Outside the theme parks, there are refrigerators in many of the area's hotels and motels. If your room does not come with one, a fridge can usually be supplied for a nominal charge, or the hotel or motel may be able to store insulin in its own refrigerator. Be sure to inquire before you make the reservation.

MONEY

Cash, traveler's checks, Visa, American Express, MasterCard, JCB, Discover Card, Diner's Club, Disney Gift Cards, and Disney Visa Rewards Redemption Cards are all accepted as payment for admission to the theme parks, as well as most merchandise and meals (except at select souvenir and food carts, where it's strictly cash). Personal checks may be used to pay for park admission. Checks must be imprinted with the guest's name and address, drawn on a U.S. bank, and accompanied by proper ID—that is, a valid driver's license or passport. Department store cards are not acceptable identification for check-writing purposes. Disney hotel guests who have left a credit card number at check-in can charge most expenses in the parks to their hotel bill.

Merchandise Mobile Checkout: Guests can use mobile phones to pay for merch at select Disneyland Resort shops. To do so, download the Disneyland app, create a profile, and link a credit card, Disney gift card, Disney Rewards redemption card, and/or Apple Pay (cash purchases must be made at a register). When you're ready to buy an item, open the Disneyland app. Then scan the barcode and tap "check out" to pay with your phone. Show the QR code to a cast member on the way out and you're all set. Note that eligible discounts will be applied for Disney Visa Card members, Disneyland Resort Magic Key holders, and Disney Vacation Club members. (Make sure your pass or membership is linked to your Disney account.)

Disney Gift Cards: Available for purchase at most merchandise locations, these may be redeemed throughout the Disneyland Resort (though there are a few exceptions at Downtown Disney, where select vendors are not equipped to accept gift cards).

Financial Services: There are two Automated Teller Machines (ATMs) within Disneyland park. The first one you'll encounter is near the Disneyana shop at the Bank of Main Street building. The other is in Frontierland, across from Pioneer Mercantile. Disney California Adventure has an ATM near the Embarcadero Gifts shop. The Downtown Disney District has an ATM by Wetzel's Pretzels. Each of the three Disneyland Resort hotels has

at least one ATM. For additional information, inquire at a Guest Relations location.

Personal checks are not accepted in the Disney theme parks. Note that the presence of a bank on Main Street is a tad deceiving: The building does not offer financial services. (Though it does have an impressive selection of Disney keepsakes and souvenirs.)

Foreign Currency Exchange: Foreign currency may be exchanged (at the day's current exchange rate) at City Hall in Disneyland, Chamber of Commerce at Disney California Adventure, and at the front desk at each of the three Disneyland Resort hotels. Paper currency only.

PETS

While there is no longer a Pet Care Kennel inside the Disneyland Resort, it's still possible to travel with Fluffy or Fido—provided they've had all their shots.

Outside the Disneyland Resort: Dogtopia (714-777-3647; www.dogtopia.com/anaheim-hills/), in Anaheim Hills, has both daycare and overnight boarding options. Dog guests spend the day playing and socializing with other pooches in outdoor yards and open play areas. Another option is the Hydrant Pet Hotel in Costa Mesa (949-250-2200; www.hydrantpethotel.com), which accepts dogs (as long as they pass a temperament test) as well as cats for both daycare and overnight boarding. Please note, these companies are not affiliated with or endorsed by The Walt Disney Company.

Some hotels and motels within the Disneyland Resort area, including a number of Disney's Good Neighbor Hotels, accept well-behaved (preferably small) pets, but most do not allow guests to leave animals in a room unattended. For a listing of all pet-friendly area hotels, contact the Anaheim/Orange County Visitor & Convention Bureau (714-765-2800 or search "pets" at www.visitanaheim.org.

PHOTOGRAPHIC NEEDS

Disney's PhotoPass photographers will happily document your park visit. If you bought a PhotoPass package (see page 87) or purchased Lightning Lane Multi Pass for the day (it comes with unlimited PhotoPass downloads) and have questions while at Disneyland Resort, call PhotoPass Guest Support at 407-560-4300. Note that there is no charge when PhotoPass photographers snap your mug using your equipment. Nice!

Try not to use your camera or mobile phone on wet, rough, or bumpy rides. Stash it in a locker or with a non-riding member of your party. Note that selfie sticks are not permitted in any Disney theme parks. If your camera uses memory cards, pack extras from home—they're no longer sold at the Disneyland Resort.

RELIGIOUS SERVICES

Catholic: St. Justin Martyr; 2050 W. Ball Rd., Anaheim, about two miles from Disneyland; www.saintjustin.org; 714-774-2595. Masses are presented in English and Spanish; call or check the website for times.

Episcopal: St. Michael's Episcopal Church; 311 W. South St., Anaheim; http://stmichaelsanaheim.org; 714-535-4654; approximately seven blocks from the Disneyland Resort. Sunday services are at 11:30 A.M. (English) and 9:30 A.M. (Spanish).

Jewish: Temple Beth Emet; 1770 W. Cerritos Ave., Anaheim; 714-772-4720; www.tbe-oc.org; a few blocks from Disneyland. Services are held on Fridays at 6 P.M. and 9 A.M. on Saturdays.

HOT TIP

Disney Genie is a vacation planning tool feature in the Disneyland Resort mobile app. Lightning Lane Multi Pass is a fee-based add-on. It includes booking and redemption of Lightning Lane selections in Disneyland park and Disney California Adventure park (refer to page 22) — plus unlimited downloads of PhotoPass images for the day and Audio Tales that are themed to different areas of the parks. The cost for Multi Pass starts at about $32 per person, per day (and can go much higher). For additional information, visit disneyland.com. Details are subject to change.

Lutheran: Prince of Peace Lutheran Church; 1421 W. Ball Road, Anaheim; *www.princeofpeaceanaheim.com*; 714-774-0993, about one mile from the Disneyland Resort. Sunday services are at 8 A.M. (traditional) and 10:30 A.M. (contemporary divine).

Non-denominational: The Kindred Community Church; 8712 E. Santa Ana Canyon Rd., Anaheim; 714-282-9941. Services are held on Sundays at 8:30 A.M. and 10:30 A.M. The church is approximately 11 miles from the Disneyland Resort; *www.kindredchurch.org*.

United Methodist: Anaheim United Methodist Church; 1000 South State College Blvd., Anaheim; 714-776-5710; *www.anaheimumc.org*; Sunday morning services are held at 10 A.M. (traditional) and 5 P.M. (modern); approximately 3.3 miles from the Disneyland Resort.

SHOPPING FOR NECESSITIES

It's a rare vacationer who doesn't leave some essential at home or run out of it mid-trip. Gift shops in almost all the hotels stock items no traveler should be without, but they usually cost more than in conventional retail shops. One good source is CVS Pharmacy at 1803 S. Harbor Blvd.; 714-817-9116.

Inside the theme parks, aspirin, bandages, suntan lotions, and other sundries are sold; just ask a cast member to direct you to the closest shop. Some items are also available at each park's First Aid location and Baby Care Center.

SMOKING POLICY

Disneyland Resort is a smoke-free zone. Smoking (of any kind) is not permitted anywhere within the boundaries of the Disneyland Resort. This includes Disneyland and Disney California Adventure parks, Downtown Disney District, and all three Disneyland Resort hotels (including guestrooms and balconies). A $250–$500 cleaning fee will be charged for smoking in hotel rooms, on balconies, or on patios. The (enforced) smoking ban includes tobacco, e-cigarettes, and any products creating a vapor or smoke. Smoking of marijuana is prohibited. No exceptions. For more details, visit *disneyland.com*.

TELEPHONES

If you don't have a wireless phone at the ready (or charged), know that local calls from most pay phones in Southern California cost about fifty cents. Most hotels in the area charge an average rate of a dollar or more for all local, toll-free, and credit card calls made from your hotel room.

For long-distance phone calls, policies vary greatly from hotel to hotel, but charges are always higher than they'd be for direct-dial calls made from a pay phone. It makes the most sense to use a calling card whenever dialing long-distance from an in-room telephone.

Phone Cards: Disney offers AT&T prepaid phone cards in values of $10 and $20. They can be purchased at select locations at the Disneyland resort hotels.

Wireless Phones: To ensure a dose of uninterrupted magic for you and those around you, stick to texting while visiting the parks and silence your ringer. You'll be glad you did.

TIPPING

The standard gratuities around Anaheim are about the same as in any other city of its size. Expect to tip bellhops about $1 to $5 per bag. Tip cabdrivers and outstanding shuttle or tour bus drivers 15 to 20 percent. Valets usually get $3 to $5 when you pick up the car. In table-service restaurants, a 15 to 20 percent gratuity is generally the norm. If you are pleased with the condition of your hotel room, it is customary to leave a gratuity of $3 to $6 per day for the housekeeper (please leave a note with the tip to avoid any confusion). Note that room service bills often include an automatic gratuity.

WEATHER

For information such as current weather forecasts, pay a visit to *www.weather.gov, www.weather.com* or *www.wunderground.com*.

DID YOU KNOW?

The real estate on which Disneyland Resort stands was once occupied by groves of orange and walnut trees. Some of the original trees' descendants still call Disneyland home.

ACCOMMODATIONS

The welcome sign is always out at the Hotels of the Disneyland Resort, where themed meals, amenities, and decor are definitely in character and add a layer of fun to a Disney vacation. And the resort's Disneyland Hotel, Pixar Place Hotel, and Grand Californian Hotel & Spa take staying at Disneyland to a lovely level of luxury.

In addition to the three hotels located within the Disneyland Resort, there are dozens of properties in Orange County, known as Disneyland Good Neighbor Hotels, that the Walt Disney Travel Company has hand-picked to round out the Disneyland Resort area lodging options. We have selected a bunch of these recommended hotels, based on services and proximity to the Disneyland Resort, to highlight in this chapter.

If the sole purpose of your trip is to visit Disney, you should plan to stay in the Anaheim area, either on Disneyland property or at one of the surrounding hotels. Once you arrive and check in, you won't need a car again until you leave. Disneyland Resort is easily traversed on foot. Buses, shuttles, and car-sharing companies serve neighboring hotels. And monorails provide nifty transportation from Downtown Disney District to Disneyland Park's Tomorrowland—and back again! If struck with a bit of wanderlust, know that Anaheim is within range of a host of Southern California destinations. Whatever your vacation goals, we've provided a variety of lodging options in the Anaheim area, from old-fashioned to contemporary, simple to sublime.

Disneyland Resort Hotels

Guests planning to stay at a Disneyland Resort Hotel are faced with a rather difficult decision—which of the three thoroughly-themed Disney properties to choose. Some factors to consider:

The whimsical pool area and character meals make the classic Disneyland Hotel appeal to the kids in the family (and the kid in us all).

Meanwhile, Disney's Paradise Pier Hotel has magically morphed into Pixar Place Hotel! It boasts delightful digs, family-friendly dining, and playful touches for all ages.

The design team has really outdone itself with Disney's Grand Californian Hotel & Spa. Located adjacent to Disney California Adventure (it has its own entrance to the park), the hotel's theming and style touch every detail, right down to the floorboards.

Whichever resort hotel you decide on, one thing is certain—a stay on-property is sure to complete the overall Disneyland experience. From resort information on the TV to wake-up calls from Mickey Mouse (or one of his pals), every special touch and detail reminds you that you're in Disney's land.

Exclusive Benefits: Some perks are reserved for guests staying at a Disneyland Resort Hotel. Perhaps the most significant of these is the Early Entry entitlement—a perk that allows entry into a designated Disneyland Resort theme park 30 minutes before it officially opens for the day (at no extra cost, with a valid ticket and park reservation). There are even special entrances to Disney California Adventure park, available only to guests who are registered at Disney's Grand Californian Hotel & Spa or the Pixar Place Hotel (a valid resort key card is required to use these convenient theme park entrances).

One of the most convenient perks is the ability to charge most expenses incurred at a Disney park back to the hotel room with the Disneyland app (if a credit card was provided at check-in). Purchases can be charged to the room from the time of check-in until 11 A.M. on the day of departure.

Hotel guests have preferred access to reservations for select hotel table-service restaurants during their stay. (Reservations are limited and may be booked online after linking a valid Disneyland Resort hotel confirmation number to a *Disneyland.com* account.)

Other on-property perks may include Disney programming in the pool areas, light-up "fireworks" on the headboards (in most rooms at the Disneyland Hotel), hotel-exclusive character interaction (Pixar Place Hotel), special activities, and seasonal events.

Check-in and Checkout: Check-in begins at 3 P.M. (4 P.M. for the Villas at Disney's Grand Californian and the Disneyland Hotel), but guests who arrive early can check in, store their luggage at the Bell Desk, and go have

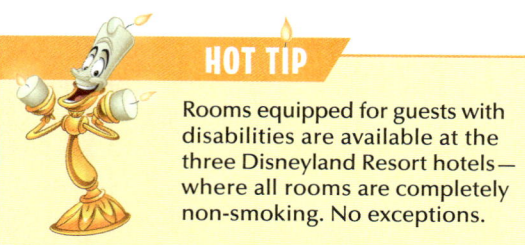

HOT TIP

Rooms equipped for guests with disabilities are available at the three Disneyland Resort hotels—where all rooms are completely non-smoking. No exceptions.

fun. A government-issued photo ID is required at check-in. Guests also have the option of checking in online up to five days before arrival. Those who do so will get a message when their room is ready. Guests using the Digital Key feature in the Disneyland app can go straight to their room once they receive the notification. Checkout is at 11 A.M., and bags can be stored (for free) until guests are ready to depart. Express check-out is available by leaving a credit card number at check-in.

Prices: Starting rates for standard guest rooms range from about $405 to $1,676. Club Level rooms range from about $553 to $1,788. Suites start from about $954 to $2,235. The rates fluctuate based on hotel, view, season, day of the week, etc. Self-parking costs $40 per day for registered guests at a Disneyland Resort hotel ($45 for oversized vehicles); valet parking costs $70 per day. Local calls, fitness center access, and Wi-Fi have no charge.

Deposit Requirements: A deposit equal to one night's lodging (plus tax) is required at time of booking when making a "room only" reservation. Packages require a $200 deposit, due within 38 days of booking. Final payment is due 45 days prior to arrival. Packages booked within 30 days prior to final payment due date (45 days before arrival) don't require a deposit. If you prefer not to use a credit card for the deposit, call 714-520-5050 for direction.

Cancellation Policy: For a room-only booking, the deposit will be refunded if the reservation is canceled at least five days before scheduled arrival. If you need to cancel a package, expect to be charged a $200 fee, plus insurance cost (where applicable), if the package is canceled 29 days or less prior to your scheduled arrival. Details are subject to change. Check *disneyland.com* for updates.

Additional Costs: Portable playpen-like cribs are available upon request (no charge), while cribs may be rented from an outside company such as the Traveling Baby Company (starting at about $20 per day). Self-parking costs $40 per day, while valet parking is available for $70 per day. Note that there is no fee for extra guests (up to room capacity). Bonus!

Discounts: Magic Key passholders may get special discounts throughout the Disneyland Resort. There may be discounts available to California residents, teachers, and members of the military, too—inquire when you make your reservation. Disney Visa® Cardmembers can reap savings on merchandise, guided tours, and dining at the Disneyland Resort. For additional information, visit *DisneyRewards.com*.

Packages: The Walt Disney Travel Company offers packages that feature a stay at one of the Disneyland hotels. Call 714-520-5050.

DISNEYLAND HOTEL: This fanciful resort adjacent to the Downtown Disney District was the first hotel erected at Disneyland Resort—way back in 1955. It has had many looks over the years, and the current one proves the old adage: Everything old is new again! While the motif is a tribute to yesteryear and highlights the original mid-20th-century style of the hotel, there are some delightfully 21st-century touches, such as colorful fiber-optic "fireworks" on many of the guest-room headboards.

The pool area is popular with guests of all ages. With a nod to iconic park signage, "Disneyland" is spelled out in familiar blocks atop a platform supporting two twisting water slides. Reminiscent of the original monorail station at the Disneyland Hotel, a replica monorail train sits at each pool slide's entrance. The larger of the big slides sits 26 feet high and stretches 187 feet. The area also has a two-lane, mini slide for younger guests, as well as bubble jets and a *Steamboat Willie*–themed splash pad. There are three hot tub spas and three poolside cabanas, too (there's a fee for cabana use).

The hotel has more than 1,300 rooms, including 71 suites and 344 villas, spread over several towers. Most tower rooms have two queen beds, and many can sleep up to five people (one of them on a daybed). The 11-story Adventure Tower looks toward the Downtown Disney District on one side and the main pool on the other. The 11-story Fantasy Tower offers rooms with pool views, but only on one side; guests staying on the other side look out over city rooftops, with Disneyland Park to the right, and the best view of the fireworks. The 14-story Frontier Tower's rooms have city and courtyard/pool views.

PHOTO BY JILL SAFRO

A monorail stop is a short walk away in neighboring Downtown Disney District, which allows for extremely easy access to Disneyland Park (it drops guests off in the middle of Tomorrowland)—a nice convenience for folks who relish a break in their park-going with a trip to one of the hotel pools, or to its Fitness Center. The workout room may be used by all registered resort guests (age 14 and above; guests under age 18 must be accompanied by an adult) and is accessed with a valid Disneyland Hotel room key.

Off the lobby of the Fantasy Tower, a large shop called Fantasia sells Disney souvenirs, while Small World Gifts offers sundries and snacks. Goofy's Kitchen, hosted by Chef Goofy and his pals, is a popular eatery open for breakfast and dinner; The Coffee House provides drinks, snacks, and quick meals. Tangaroa Terrace Tropical Bar & Grill, a casual dining spot, serves meals with a South Seas flair, as well as a selection of grab-and-go items. The adjoining bar, Trader Sam's, is a great spot for drinks and appetizers, as are the Broken Spell Lounge and Palm Breeze Bar. (For dining details, see the *Good Meals, Great Times* chapter.)

The convention and meetings area, which is adjacent to Goofy's Kitchen and linked to the lobby via a photo-lined passageway, deserves a look for its Disney-related artwork, including a collage of Disney collectibles and milestones. Created entirely from old toys, souvenirs, name tags, and other memorabilia, it commemorates the colorful and unique history of the Disneyland Resort.

The hotel can provide safe-deposit boxes, currency exchange, and dining reservation assistance. An Automated Teller Machine (ATM) is on the premises. Taxis and car sharing services do pick-ups and drop-offs in the front of the hotel. ChargePoint charging ports are available in the Fantasy self-parking lot. (To use a port, you'll need to scan a ChargePoint card). Charging stations are not available to guests who choose valet parking. Note that Charge-Point is not operated by The Walt Disney Company.

Guest rooms have two queen beds or one king bed, a flat-screen TV, small safe, coffeemaker (with coffee), desk with a telephone, free Wi-Fi, hair dryer, iron with board, and a small (unstocked) fridge/cooling box. Room service may be available.

Room rates start at about $530 to $700, depending on view and season; no charge for roll-aways. Club Level rooms start at about $812. Starting rates for suites range from about $970 to $2,000. (Note that higher rates apply to specialty suites such as the Pirates of the Caribbean Suite and the Mickey Mouse Penthouse Suite.)

Self-parking costs $40 per day ($45 per day for over-size vehicles); valet is $70 a day. Non-resort guests just visiting the hotel pay about $35 for the first four hours and $10 for each extra hour to self-park (with a $75 maximum for 24 hours); $50 for the first hour and $10 for each additional hour of valet parking, with a $120 maximum. Note that all prices were correct at press time but are likely to change.

Disneyland Hotel, 1150 Magic Way, Anaheim, CA 92802; 714-956-6425 (to make reservations) or 714-778-6600 (front desk); *disneyland.com*.

DISNEY'S GRAND CALIFORNIAN HOTEL & SPA: This hotel is in a prime location—right in the middle of the Disneyland Resort. It includes 948 studio rooms, 44 suites, 71 Disney Vacation Club villas, and 3 swimming pools. The hotel has its own entrance to Disney California Adventure park and convenient access to the popular Downtown Disney District.

A border of trees surrounds the six-story hotel, built as a tribute to the American Craftsman tradition of the early 1900s. Cedar and redwood paneling decorates the stupendous lobby, where display cabinets filled with original art and reproductions introduce guests to that rich period of art. The lobby's great hearth fronts a perennially lit fire. Furnishings throughout the hotel feature warm colors and intricate textures.

Each deluxe guestroom and suite features a 55-inch TV, small safe, room service, desk with a phone, Wi-Fi Internet access (no charge), USB chargers, coffeemaker (with coffee and non-dairy creamer), iron with board, and small (unstocked) fridge/cooling box. The bathroom is equipped with a makeup mirror and hair dryer.

THE VILLAS AT DISNEYLAND HOTEL

The most recent addition to the Disney Vacation Club (DVC) family of resort hotels is the 12-story Discovery Tower at the Disneyland Hotel. Having debuted in 2023, the lofty edifice offers about 344 well-appointed villas with a Disney art and animation flair. In addition to the fresh digs, there is a spiffy pool area, outdoor bar, community hall, fitness center, and a nifty play zone for the little ones. Note that The Villas at the Disneyland Hotel are available to everyone when not reserved by Vacation Club members. For information about Disney's vacation ownership program, aka the Disney Vacation Club, call 800-500-3990, or visit *disneyvacationclub.disney.go.com*.

Most of the rooms in the hotel feature two queen beds with a sleeper chair or daybed, or a king bed and sleeper chair. The carved wooden headboards are made of quarter-sawn oak, a hallmark of Craftsman design. They feature a blossoming orange tree mural, complete with two familiar chipmunks frolicking in its branches. California-inspired artwork dots the room walls, including original designs of orange crate labels—paying homage to the history of the Disneyland Resort.

The Disney Vacation Club (DVC) villas reflect the same design as the hotel and are available to all guests when not occupied by DVC members. Each studio has a queen-size bed and queen-size sleeper sofa, plus a kitchenette with microwave, coffeemaker, and mini fridge. Larger (one-, two-, and three-bedroom) villas sleep 5 to 12 and offer dining areas, kitchens, laundry facilities, baths with hot tub spas, and DVD players. They include a king-size bed in the primary bedroom, a living room with queen-size sleeper sofa (and a sleeper chair in the one- and two-bedroom villas), and either two queen-size beds or a queen bed and a double sleeper sofa in extra bedrooms.

Guest services include room service, laundry and dry cleaning (including same-day service), a fitness center, and a business center. The concierge level offers upgraded amenities and services. Guests can relax at the Fountain Pool and Redwood Pool (the two are adjacent) and make a splash at the Mariposa Pool, which includes a hot tub and 6 private cabanas that are available to rent throughout the day. The luxurious Tenaya Stone Spa features an array of body treatments, facials, massage, and salon services. The Disney Imagineer-designed spa has a relaxation room with Craftsman architecture, comfy furnishings, a water feature, and a stained glass window of the rising sun. Acorn's Gifts & Goods, which sells apparel, pins, toys, collectibles, and snacks, is just off the lobby.

Among the dining options are the award-winning Napa Rose, which features fresh California cuisine and wines (plus breakfast with Disney princesses!), and Storytellers Cafe, serving three meals a day in an Old California setting and the backdrop for a breakfast hosted by Disney characters. The GCH Craftsman Grill supplies coffee drinks, made-to-order and grab-and-go selections; GCH Craftsman Bar is a solid choice for a poolside meal, snack, or refreshing beverage. The Hearthstone Lounge (off the lobby) offers tasty bites and a full bar. The Palm Breeze pool bar, at Discovery Tower, offers a lovely lineup of eats and drinks, too.

The hotel can provide safe-deposit boxes and currency exchange. An ATM is on the premises. Guests with electric vehicles may use charging ports based on availability. If you would like to reserve one, let the valet attendant know upon arrival. Valet charges apply. Taxis and car sharing services do pick-ups and drop-offs in the front of the hotel.

Rates for standard guestrooms start at about $683, depending on the view, date, season, etc. Club Level (aka "Concierge") rooms start at about $1,192; suites start at about $1,547. There are no rollaway beds, but portable playpen-like cribs may be requested (no charge). Self-parking costs $40 a day ($45 for oversize vehicles); valet parking is $70 per day. Non-resort guests pay $35 for the first hour of self-parking and $10 for each extra hour (with a $75 max); $65 for the first hour of valet parking, and $10 for each additional hour (with a $120 max). Non-registered guests who dine at Storytellers Cafe receive 3 hours free parking with validation, while Napa Rose and Tenaya Stone Spa patronage (when you spend $125 or more) includes 5 hours free parking with validation.

Disney's Grand Californian Hotel & Spa, 1600 S. Disneyland Drive, Anaheim, CA 92803; 714-956-6425 (for reservations) or 714-635-2300 (front desk); or visit *disneyland.com*.

PIXAR PLACE HOTEL: Previously known as Disney's Paradise Pier Hotel, this playful property has experienced an extremely merry **NEW** makeover. The hotel's theme complements that of its across-the-street neighbor—Pixar Pier at Disney California Adventure Park. Woody, Jessie, Nemo, Dory, and a plethora of Pixar pals are reflected in the resort's cheerful motif. To punctuate the Pixar spirit, the resort even boasts appearances by Bing Bong of *Inside Out* fame and the live piano stylings of *Soul*'s Joe Gardner. The immersive atmosphere takes guests on the creative journey experienced by artists who bring stories to life.

The hotel's two high-rise towers—one 15 stories tall, the other 14 stories—are juxtaposed to create a central atrium, which cradles the lobby and a larger-than-life sculpture of the famous Pixar ball and the beloved Pixar lamp. Each of the 479 guestrooms and suites are peppered with playful Pixar touches, one king-size bed or two queen beds, plus a twin daybed (a nice convenience for larger parties). The Pixar theme extends to the hotel's popular pool deck—including an immersive water play area inspired by the film *Finding Nemo*. The fanciful recreation area features a big pool, 186-foot water slide (complete with Crush the sea

turtle perched at the tippy top), pop-jet splash pad, family play court inspired by Pixar short films, fire pits, fireworks viewing areas, and the Small Bytes snack bar

The hotel's table-service eatery is operated by the team behind SoCal's popular Great Maple. Disneyland's version of the family-friendly restaurant also specializes in elevated comfort classics. Quick-service bites and snacks are offered at The Sketch Pad Café (lobby coffee shop) and the Small Bytes pool bar. Pixar Place Hotel has an exercise room, guest laundry service, concierge lounge, and an ATM (fees may apply). A glass-enclosed elevator provides a lovely bird's-eye view of the resort lobby and the nearby Disney California Adventure theme park.

It may be the smallest of the Disneyland Resort hotels, but it's understandably popular. And now that all of the "Pixar dust" has settled, there's a convenient foot path connecting Pixar Place Hotel with a "back door" to the Disney California Adventure park—making that park a hop, skip, and a jump away. (A valid resort key, park ticket, and park reservation are required to use the special entrance.) For more information, use the Disneyland mobile app or visit *disneyland.com*.

Hotel guests may access the Disneyland Hotel and Downtown Disney by using a handy, landscaped walkway. Guests (with valid admission tickets and a theme park reservation) can access Disneyland park by taking the monorail from the Downtown Disney District station. (The monorail transports guests to the park's Tomorrowland station.) Disneyland park's entrance is within a 10- to 17-minute walk for most pedestrians.

Standard rooms accommodate up to five guests. Rates range from about $405–$550, but vary depending on view, date, season, etc. There's no charge for kids under 18 sharing their parents' hotel room; no charge for rollaways or cribs. For pricing and details about suites (including 2-bedroom signature suites) and Club Level digs, visit *disneyland.com*. Self-parking costs about $40 per day ($45 for oversize vehicles); valet parking is $70 a day.

Pixar Place Hotel, 1717 South Disneyland Drive, Anaheim, CA 92802; 714-956-6425 (reservations) or 714-999-0990 (front desk); *disneyland.com*.

Disneyland Good Neighbor Hotels

With fewer than 2,500 hotel rooms available at the Disneyland Resort and tens of thousands of guests pouring through the parks each day, it's no wonder that a majority of visitors stay off Disney property. To make it easier for guests to narrow down their off-property choices, the folks at Disney have selected local hotels and motels that meet their standards and anointed them Disneyland Good Neighbor Hotels. Before receiving Disney's seal of approval, hotels are reportedly graded on amenities, services, decor, guest satisfaction, price, and location. All Good Neighbor hotels sell tickets to both Disney parks. *(Theme park reservations and tickets should be secured as far in advance as possible).*

Ranging from small operations to big chains, Good Neighbor hotels proliferate along Harbor Boulevard, which flanks Disneyland resort on the east. From Harbor, it's a relatively manageable walk to the Disneyland Resort. (If you're planning to walk to and from Disney's theme parks, be sure to inquire about the distance before you book your hotel.) A few hotels are on Ball Road, the resort's northern boundary. Below Katella Avenue, which borders the resort to the south, side streets lead to the Anaheim Convention Center and major convention hotels. Divided into Superior, Deluxe, Moderate, and Suite categories, there are more than 40 Good Neighbor hotels in all. In these pages, we describe some of our favorites. For a list of Good Neighbor properties not detailed here, flip to page 52.

Prices: Expect to pay approximately $129 to $500 (plus tax), or more, per night for a hotel room for two adults and two kids (youngsters under age 18 usually stay in their parents' room for free), $70 to $250 for a motel room, and $50 to $85 for tent or RV camping. Prices drop a bit in winter; they are usually highest in the summer months and over holidays. The hotel room tax in Anaheim, California, is 15 percent.

Additional Costs: When comparing accommodation costs, do consider hidden zingers, like parking. Hotels usually charge for it (at least $24 a day; more for valet service). Many also charge a fee when more than four people occupy a room. Ask about telephone rates when you check in—hotel surcharges are notoriously huge. Many hotels offer free Wi-Fi. Be sure to ask.

Savings: You may be able to save money by staying in a hotel that offers complimentary breakfast and shuttle service to the Disneyland Resort. Discounts are sometimes offered to folks who are members of automobile or retirement associations.

HOT TIP

For additional information about the Disneyland Resort's Good Neighbor hotels, go to *https://disneyland.disney.go.com/hotels/good-neighbor/*. To learn about any special vacation packages that may be offered during your expected visit, go to *https://disneyland.disney.go.com/vacation-packages/good-neighbor-hotel-package.*

Individual Needs: What is absolutely essential for one vacationer—and well worth an added expense—might seem completely frivolous to another guest: room service, on-site restaurants, live music, a suite, a kitchen, concierge/Club Level service and amenities, large swimming pool, fitness center, or a place that accepts pets.

Packages: The Walt Disney Travel Company offers packages in conjunction with each of the (Disney vetted) Good Neighbor hotels—representing potentially big savings for travelers. For details or to book a Good Neighbor package, contact the Walt Disney Travel Company directly at 714-520-5060, or visit *disneyland.disney.go.com/vacation-packages/good-neighbor-hotel-package.*

Note: The following establishments accept major credit cards and offer accommodations for travelers with disabilities, unless otherwise indicated. Call directly to inquire about deposit requirements and cancellation policies. Rates were correct at press time, but are subject to change and should always be confirmed.

SUITE HOTELS

HYATT HOUSE AT ANAHEIM RESORT: This all-suite hotel around the corner from the convention center prides itself on its larger rooms, ranging from 355 to 790 square feet, which strongly appeal to families and those who will be staying more than a few nights. The 264 rooms and suites are decorated in neutral hues and earth tones, and range from standard to studio suites, one-bedroom or family suites. Breakfast is included, as are Wi-Fi service and a 24-hour workout room.

Suites offer either one king or two queen beds, bunk beds, sofa beds, 42-inch flat-screen TVs, and views of the Disneyland fireworks. Spacious studio and one-bedroom Kitchen Suites have a fully equipped kitchen with a refrigerator, microwave, dishwasher, stove, small appliances, and utensils.

The hotel is home to H Bar and Starbucks. There's an outdoor pool, hot tub, barbecue pit, patio, and meeting room. Rates range from about $333 to $763 per night. Parking runs about $26 a day.

Hyatt House at Anaheim Resort, 1800 South Harbor Boulevard, Anaheim, CA 92802; 714-971-1800; *www.hyatt.com.*

CLEMENTINE HOTEL & SUITES ANAHEIM: Nestled in a garden-like setting, this residential-style hotel, formerly the Residence Inn by Marriott, is about a half-mile from Disneyland Resort. The 200 spacious suites, set inside sunny orange and yellow buildings, are offered in different room configurations, including a studio suite (one king bed and a sofa bed, which sleeps four), a one-bedroom suite (two queen beds and sofa bed, which sleeps six), and a bi-level loft suite (two queen beds, sofa bed, king bed, and two bathrooms, which sleeps eight). All rooms have a flat-screen TV, full kitchen with stove, microwave, dishwasher, a full-size refrigerator, and cooking utensils. Rates range from $252 to $499. Cribs and baby gates are available; rollaway beds are not.

Facilities include a swimming pool, kiddie pool, whirlpool, and a single adaptive sport court that can be used for tennis, basketball, or volleyball (equipment is available to borrow). Court hours are usually 9 A.M. to 9 P.M. There is a 24/7 guest laundry, mini market, fire pit and barbecue patio, and an on-site playground.

Amenities include a business center with free Internet and printing services, and Wi-Fi in all suites. The $30 daily resort fee includes a (daily) hot breakfast buffet (including eggs, waffles, fruit, pastries, oatmeal, and more) and self-parking (studios and one-bedroom suites have a one car limit, while larger suites can park two cars; additional vehicles incur a daily fee of $15, plus tax). Furry pets are accepted for a flat fee of $250 per stay. Anaheim Resort Transit provides bus transportation for a fee.

Clementine Hotel & Suites Anaheim, 1700 S. Clementine Street., Anaheim, CA 92802; *www.clementinehotel.com* or 714-533-3555.

HOT TIP

If you stay in the 1300 to 1500 block of Harbor Boulevard, you can cross the street and walk to both theme parks. Of course, once you reach Disneyland property, it's another 5- to 15-minute walk to get to the theme park turnstiles.

SUPERIOR HOTELS

ANAHEIM MARRIOTT: Conveniently located next door to the Anaheim Convention Center, the Marriott is a perennial favorite among visitors. Guest rooms offer a modern feel and a SoCal vibe. Room amenities include a 55-inch flat-screen TV, hardwood style floors, private balconies, and a choice of one king-size, two double, or two queen-size beds. Wireless Internet is available for a fee.

The main restaurant/lounge—nFuse—offers California cuisine with a global twist, a full-service bar, and a pleasant area with sofas, a shuffleboard court, and a pool table. For a more casual bite, Slice Pizzeria offers custom-made pizza with house-made dough. The Market Café offers a variety of food and drink options, including Starbucks drinks, grab-and-go selections, juices, sodas, and more.

The Anaheim Marriott has a fitness center, outdoor pool, and whirlpool. The hotel is a couple of (long) blocks from the Disneyland Resort—for some folks, it's within walking distance. Shuttle service to the Disney theme parks is provided by Anaheim Resort Transit for a fee; transportation to area airports may also be arranged.

Room rates for two start at $189 (there is no charge for children under age 18 sharing their parents' room); suites start at about $399. Rollaway beds are $20 per stay, and cribs are free. Self-parking costs $42 per day; valet parking is $44 per day. The hotel is not pet-friendly.

Anaheim Marriott, 700 W. Convention Way, Anaheim, CA 92802; call 714-750-8000 or 800-228-9290, or visit *www.anaheimmarriott.com.*

HILTON ANAHEIM: The 14-story glass exterior of this property reflects the Anaheim convention center, a relatively short walk away, while the bustling lobby area invites the outdoors (and legions of conventioneers) inside. Hilton Anaheim, the largest hotel in the Anaheim

resort area, boasts 1,572 rooms, including 93 suites, decorated in contrasting dark wood tones, with crisp white linens and warm wall coverings. Highlights include a chic lobby lounge, fifth- and 14th-floor Presidential Suites, and a Starbucks coffee shop.

The hotel's outdoor recreation area, located on the fifth floor, features a heated swimming pool, two whirlpools, and a kids' splash zone. Dining options include the Mix Restaurant & Lounge and the Pool Bar & Grill for outdoor dining (the latter operates on a seasonal basis). There is also a small food court known as Corner Eatery. Room service is offered, too.

Add to that a business center, FedEx store, gift shop, and Pure Escape Beauty Bar. The 25,000-square-foot Fitness Center has all manner of exercise equipment.

Rates for a room with two queen beds typically range from $179–$379 (there is no charge for kids under 18 when sharing their parents' room with existing bedding); suites start at about $299. Each room has a coffeemaker (with coffee and non-dairy creamer), a safe, small TV, and Wi-Fi (about $13 per day; free for Hilton Honors members. There is no extra charge for cribs, but rollaway beds cost about $35 per night. There is an Enterprise rental car location in the lobby. Self-parking costs $24 per day; valet parking, $39. Pets are not permitted.

Hilton Anaheim, 777 Convention Way, Anaheim, CA 92802; *www.hiltonanaheimhotel.com*; 714-750-4321 or 800-445-8667.

HYATT REGENCY ORANGE COUNTY: The hotel, in Garden Grove, is one mile south of Disneyland Resort. Its dramatic, 17-story atrium encloses palm trees and greenery and houses Starbucks, a gift shop, and an arcade. The hotel has 655 guestrooms (242 of which are suites). Rooms feature either a king-size bed or two queen beds, and modern design.

Amenities include coffeemaker, hair dryer, iron, mini fridge, 65-inch TV, and free Wi-Fi. The one- and two-bedroom suites also have a living room, mini fridge, and microwave. Suites can accommodate up to 8 guests.

Kids' Suites include a room for the little ones, complete with bunk beds and a TV. The parents' room has a king bed, TV, mini fridge, and microwave.

The hotel's recreational facilities, located on the South Tower's third-story roof, include a heated pool, a fitness center, basketball court, table tennis, a pickleball court, and a fire pit. Another pool and whirlpool are on the ground floor of the North Tower. Transportation to and from the Disneyland Resort is provided for a fee.

Room rates start at about $199 (there is no extra charge for kids under age 18 occupying their parents' room), plus $25 for each additional adult; $238 and higher for suites. Cribs are free (subject to availability). Self-parking is $30 per day; valet parking is $36 per day.

Hyatt Regency Orange County, 11999 Harbor Boulevard, Garden Grove, CA 92840; 714-750-1234; *orangecounty.regency.hyatt.com*.

ANAHEIM MAJESTIC GARDEN HOTEL: With its turrets and Tudor design, this 13-acre hotel looks like a castle, surrounded by grounds that incorporate three courtyards, a rose garden, and koi pond. The lobby has a colorful fish tank, fireplace lounge for evening story time, and two knights standing guard. There's even a resident princess who visits during breakfast (and is available to schedule a special tuck-in or wake up for young guests.)

The hotel has 463 rooms and 26 suites. The rooms—all large (490 square feet on average)—have two queen- or one king-size bed, cable TV, in-room movies, a safe, voice mail, iron, mini fridge, hair dryer, and coffeemaker (with coffee). Rooms are designed to capture the hotel's castle theme with backdrops evoking an enchanted forest. Each suite features a sitting area with a sofa bed. Some family suites offer castle bunk beds. Most rooms can be connected to accommodate larger parties.

There's the Hanagi Japanese Restaurant, the Garden Court Bistro and Patio, a deli/gift shop, and a lounge with small plates and nightly happy hour. Also available: an arcade, heated pool, whirlpool, fitness center, and guest laundry. Rates range from about $129 to $275. Self-parking is $30 per day. This property is pet-friendly. The hotel offers complimentary (first-come, first-served) shuttle service to and from the Disneyland Resort on its "Dream Machine."

Anaheim Majestic Garden Hotel, 900 S. Disneyland Dr., Anaheim, CA 92802; *www.majesticgardenhotel.com*; 714-778-1700, or 844-227-8535.

SHERATON PARK HOTEL AT THE ANAHEIM RESORT:
This 14-story tower is easy to spot, and the 490 rooms and ten suites have balconies (some large, some small) that have a view of the pool or the Disneyland Resort (and its fireworks). Rooms offer either one king or two queen beds, 55-inch TV, mini fridge, coffeemaker, and hair dryer.

The hotel features a lobby bar, Morton's Steakhouse, The World Market, Savor Stone Hearth Pizza & Wine (breakfast, lunch, and dinner), Splash pool bar, and a coffee shop. There's a 24-hour fitness center and a large, heated pool.

Shuttle service to Disneyland is provided by Anaheim Resort Transportation (for a fee). Room rates start at about $205 and vary depending on occupancy and season; Club Level rooms are higher. Rollaways cost about $15 extra; cribs are available free of charge. Parking rates start at about $35 per day. Small pets may stay for $100 per stay.

Sheraton Park Hotel at the Anaheim Resort, 1855 S. Harbor Blvd., Anaheim, CA 92802; call 714-750-1811 or 866-837-4197; or visit *www.marriott.com/SNAPS*.

CAMELOT INN & SUITES:
Directly across the street—and a relatively short walk away—from the Disneyland Resort, this family-friendly hotel, with its shingled roof, clock tower, turrets, and window boxes, looks like something out of a Bavarian village. Each of the 121 rooms and suites has a 49-inch TV, microwave, mini fridge, coffeemaker, safe, free Wi-Fi, hair dryer, and an iron with board. It also has a mobility scooter and stroller rental shop, and a guest laundry facility (fees apply). There is a pool (with a view of the Matterhorn Bobsleds attraction in Disneyland park), whirlpool, and terrace sundeck. Complimentary

luggage storage is available in the lobby. While there's no on-site eatery, there are many places to eat within reasonable walking distance.

Deluxe standard rooms, most with two queen-size beds, range from $199 to $329 year-round; family suites range from about $309 to $499 and accommodate up to six guests, but they have only one bath. All rooms have a sleeper chair. Cribs are available for free. The front desk is staffed 24/7. Adjoining guestrooms are usually available upon request. There's no shuttle service, but it is possible to walk to the Disneyland Resort entrance via Harbor Boulevard. Anaheim Resort Transit provides transportation to Disneyland Resort (for a fee). There is a daily fee for valet parking.

Anaheim Camelot Inn & Suites, 1520 S. Harbor Blvd., Anaheim, CA 92802; call 714-635-7275 or 800-828-4898, or visit *www.camelotinn-anaheim.com*.

MODERATE HOTELS

FAIRFIELD BY MARRIOTT ANAHEIM RESORT:
Fronted by palms and pines, this inviting 467-room hotel is about a 7- to 10-minute walk to the Disneyland Resort theme park entrances. Its rooms, some accented with Disney artwork, are in two towers (one tower is nine stories high; the other, eight). Each room has a king-size bed or two queen beds, child-size sleeper sofa, smart TV, free high-speed Internet, an iron and board, a hair dryer, refrigerator, and coffeemaker (with coffee).

Other facilities include a fitness center, heated pool, whirlpool, 24/7 mini market, gift shop, arcade, and free Wi-Fi in the lobby and other public areas. Guestrooms may be occupied by up to five people, and rates range from about $245 to $375; cribs are available. Parking costs $27 a day.

Anaheim Fairfield Inn by Marriott, 1460 S. Harbor Blvd., Anaheim, CA 92802; call 714-772-6777 or 800-228-2800, or go to *www.marriott.com*.

COURTYARD BY MARRIOTT ANAHEIM THEME PARK ENTRANCE:
Located across the street from Disneyland Resort is the first entirely "family-geared" Courtyard. All rooms sleep up to six and feature bunk beds, two separate showers in the bathroom, and a 47-inch TV with Netflix. Guestrooms at this property start at a roomy 532 square feet. Suites are available, too. This is the only four-star hotel within true walking distance of the two Disneyland theme park entrances (about a 10-minute walk, give or take). Dining options include The Bistro and Starbucks. There is a fitness center, two laundromats, and a gift shop. Rates for a double room start at about $322. Parking is valet only ($35 per day).

The 20,000-square-foot Surfside Waterpark has super slides, tot-friendly slides, a 400-gallon "drench bucket"; lap pool; and hot tub. (Access is included, but reservations are required. Make them up to 30 days prior to arrival.) The pool deck offers views of the Disneyland fireworks.

Courtyard Marriott Anaheim Theme Park Entrance, 1420 S. Harbor Boulevard, Anaheim, CA 92802; visit *www.marriott.com/snadt*, or call 714-254-1442.

BEST WESTERN PLUS STOVALL'S INN: This inn is known for its fanciful topiary garden. The property features 288 guestrooms, complimentary continental breakfast, fitness center, business center, and a pair of pools (one is heated), two whirlpools, a wading pool, and a gift shop. Room configurations include two queen, one king, or two double beds, and a bathroom with a separate sink and lots of counter space.

Accommodations come with a mini refrigerator, microwave, coffee/tea maker, hair dryer, iron (with board), and TV. Room rates for up to five guests run $175 to $309. Rollaways are $15; cribs are free. Parking costs $20 a night (one car per room).

Best Western Plus Stovall's Inn, 1110 W. Katella Ave., Anaheim, CA 92802. Visit *www.stovallsinn.com*, or call 714-778-1880 or 800-854-8177, ext. 3.

CANDY CANE INN: There's a lot to like about this sweet, two-story hotel—fountain out front, relaxed ambience, wrought-iron touches, and lots of fresh flowers. Located down the street from the entrance to Disneyland Resort (a manageable walk for many adults and non-toddlers), the Candy Cane Inn is family run and well maintained.

Each of the 171 rooms, most of which face a court-yard, has a fridge, safe, free Wi-Fi, coffeemaker, iron, hair dryer, and two queen beds with custom bedding. Add to that a laundry (fees apply), pool, gazebo-covered whirlpool, and fitness center. Free continental breakfast is served daily. Premium rooms have robes (to borrow), microwaves, in-room breakfast, turndown service, and 2 P.M. checkout. Sightseeing services are available, as is free shuttle service to and from the Disneyland Resort. Transportation to airports can be arranged. Parking is free.

Rates for a double room with two queen-size beds start at about $279, depending upon the time of year. Rollaways, available in deluxe and premium rooms, are $20; cribs are free. The inn is located across the street from a shopping area with fast-food eateries.

Candy Cane Inn, 1747 S. Harbor Boulevard, Anaheim, CA 92802. Visit *www.candycaneinn.net*, or call 714-774-5284 or 800-345-7057.

HOWARD JOHNSON BY WYNDHAM ANAHEIM HOTEL & WATER PLAYGROUND: This property's lush landscaping is a big reason to stay here. Flowers and trees proliferate; a central fountain anchors the four, two-story units. The hotel is close to Disneyland and local eateries. Anaheim Resort Transit (ART) offers Disneyland Resort shuttle service (for a small fee).

The 296 non-smoking rooms are spread among several buildings on seven acres. Most have two queen beds, and all have a small fridge, microwave, safe, and free Wi-Fi. The rooms are relatively spacious. Most rooms have a full balcony. Family suites are available.

There is a heated swimming pool with a hot tub, plus Castaway Cove—a splashy pirate playground featuring water slides, water cannons, toddler pool, and fountains. There are 2 guest laundries and a gift shop. Room rates range from $214 to $639, depending on the time of year. Parking is $25 per day, plus tax (there's a limit of one vehicle per room, no RVs or oversized vehicles). Rollaways cost $15 per day; cribs are free.

Howard Johnson by Wyndham Anaheim Hotel & Water Playground, 1380 S. Harbor Blvd., Anaheim, CA 92802; Visit *www.hojoanaheim.com*, or call 714-776-6120 or 800-422-4228.

TROPICANA INN & SUITES: This contemporary hotel is conveniently situated across from a pedestrian cross-walk that connects to the Disneyland Resort (it is about a 10-minute walk, but the time varies depending on the pace). Each of its 197 rooms has a 43-inch flat-screen TV, coffeemaker (with coffee), mini fridge, small safe, microwave, hair dryer, iron, and free Wi-Fi. Standard rooms have two queen beds and a single sleeper chair. Guests may use a computer in the lobby free of charge. Some rooms have a view of the Disneyland Resort's fireworks presentations.

The inn is home to a cafe/shop known as The Cove on Harbor Market and Coffee House. It sells food, drinks, souvenirs, and sundries. There are many eateries in the area (some within easy walking distance). Anaheim Resort Transportation provides shuttle service for a fee. Parking costs about $22 per day. (An additional vehicle may be parked for about $29 per day, pending availability.)

The inn also has a heated Junior Olympic pool, whirl-pool spa, and a guest laundry (fees apply). Guest room rates are about $199 to $329. Suites sleep up to 8 guests and range from $309 to $499. Some suites have kitchens.

Tropicana Inn & Suites, 1540 S. Harbor Boulevard, Anaheim, CA 92802; *www.tropicanainn-anaheim.com*; 714-635-4082 or 800-828-4898.

The Rest of the Best

Here's a roundup of the remaining Good Neighbor hotels. They have amenities and rates similar to those described in this chapter. However, some are a bit far from the Disneyland Resort.

Note: The various properties that boast Good Neighbor status are subject to change during the year; visit *disneyland.com* for updates.

SUPERIOR HOTELS

- **Delta Hotels by Marriott Anaheim Garden Grove**, 12021 Harbor Blvd., Garden Grove; 714-867-5555
- **JW Marriott Anaheim Resort**, 1775 S. Clementine St., Anaheim; 714-294-7800
- **Sheraton Garden Grove — Anaheim South Hotel**, 12221 Harbor Blvd., Garden Grove; 714-703-8400
- **The Viv, Anaheim, a Tribute Portfolio Hotel**, 1601 S. Anaheim Blvd., Anaheim; 657-276-0145
- **The Westin Anaheim Resort**, 1030 W. Katella Ave., Anaheim; 657-279-9786

DELUXE HOTELS

- **Cambria Hotel and Suites Anaheim Resort**, 101 E. Katella Ave., Anaheim; 714-520-3200
- **Courtyard by Marriott Anaheim Resort**, 2045 S. Harbor Blvd., Anaheim; 714-740-2645
- **Desert Palms Hotel & Suites Anaheim Resort Convention Center**, 631 West Katella Ave., Anaheim; 714-535-1133
- **Hampton Inn & Suites by Hilton Anaheim/Garden Grove**, 11747 Harbor Blvd., Garden Grove; 714-703-8800
- **Hampton Inn & Suites by Hilton Anaheim Resort Convention Center**, 100 W. Katella Ave., Anaheim; 714-533-1500
- **Hilton Garden Inn Anaheim Resort**, 1441 S. Manchester Ave., Anaheim; 714-844-2808
- **Hilton Garden Inn Anaheim/Garden Grove**, 11777 Harbor Blvd., Garden Grove; 714-703-9100
- **Holiday Inn Hotel & Suites**, 1240 S. Walnut St., Anaheim; 714-535-0300
- **Hotel Lulu Anaheim**, 1850 S. Harbor Blvd., Anaheim; 714-750-2801
- **Hyatt Place at Anaheim Resort Convention Center**, 2035 S. Harbor Blvd., Anaheim; 714-750-4000
- **Sonesta Anaheim Resort Area**, 1915 S. Manchester Ave., Anaheim; 714-748-7777
- **SunCoast Park Hotel Anaheim**, 1640 S. Clementine St., Anaheim; 714-598-0600

MODERATE HOTELS

- **The Anaheim Hotel**, 1700 Harbor Blvd., Anaheim; 714-772-5900
- **Anaheim Portofino Inn & Suites**, 1831 S. Harbor Blvd., Anaheim; 714-782-7600
- **Best Western Plus Anaheim Inn**, 1630 S. Harbor Blvd., Anaheim; 714-774-1050
- **Best Western Plus Park Place Inn & Mini Suites**, 1544 S. Harbor Blvd., Anaheim; 714-776-4800

- **Best Western Plus Pavilions**, 1176 W. Katella Ave., Anaheim; 714-776-0140
- **Best Western Plus Raffles Inn & Suites**, 2040 S. Harbor Blvd., Anaheim; 714-750-6100
- **Castle Inn & Suites**, 1734 S. Harbor Blvd., Anaheim; 714-774-8111
- **Clarion Hotel Anaheim Resort**, 616 W. Convention Way, Anaheim; 714-750-3131
- **Cortona Inn & Suites**, 2029 S. Harbor Blvd., Anaheim; 714-971-5000
- **Four Points by Sheraton Anaheim**, 1221 S. Harbor Blvd., Anaheim; 714-758-0900
- **Grand Legacy at the Park**, 1650 S. Harbor Blvd., Anaheim; 714-772-0440
- **Motel 6 Anaheim Maingate**, 100 W. Disney Way, Anaheim; 714-520-9696

SUITE HOTELS

- **Anaheim Marriott Suites**, 12015 Harbor Blvd., Garden Grove; 714-750-1000
- **Candlewood Suites Anaheim Resort Area**, 1773 S. Anaheim Blvd., Anaheim; 714-635-5555
- **Doubletree Suites by Hilton Anaheim Resort Area**, 2085 S. Harbor Blvd., Anaheim; 714-750-3000
- **Element by Westin Anaheim Resort Convention Center**, 1600 S. Clementine St., Anaheim; 714-326-7800
- **Embassy Suites by Hilton Anaheim-North**, 3100 E. Frontera St., Anaheim; 714-632-1221
- **Embassy Suites by Hilton Anaheim-South**, 11767 Harbor Blvd., Garden Grove; 714-539-3300
- **Holiday Inn Express & Suites Anaheim Resort Area**, 1411 S. Manchester Ave., Anaheim; 714-844-2801
- **Home2 Suites by Hilton Anaheim Resort**, 1441 S. Manchester Ave., Anaheim; 714-844-2811
- **Homewood Suites by Hilton Anaheim–Main Gate Area**, 12005 Harbor Blvd., Garden Grove; 714-740-1800
- **Homewood Suites by Hilton Anaheim Resort Convention Center**, 2010 S. Harbor Blvd., Anaheim; 714-750-2010
- **Residence Inn by Marriott Anaheim/Resort Area**, 11931 Harbor Blvd., Garden Grove; 714-591-4000
- **Residence Inn by Marriott Anaheim Resort/Convention Center**, 640 W. Katella Ave., Anaheim; 714-782-7500
- **Sonesta ES Suites Anaheim**, 1855 S. Manchester Ave., Anaheim; 714-748-7700
- **SpringHill Suites by Marriott Anaheim Maingate**, 1160 W. Ball Road, Anaheim; 714-215-4000
- **SpringHill Suites by Marriott Anaheim Resort Convention Center**, 1801 S. Harbor Blvd., Anaheim; 714-533-2101

DISNEYLAND PARK

When you wish upon a star, your dreams come true. That's how the song goes, and it's always possible in Disneyland—Walt Disney's own dream come true. He envisioned "a place of warmth and nostalgia, of illusion and color and delight." The result: a place where imagination is given free reign, grins and giggles are encouraged, and everyone can see the world through a child's eyes.

The undisguised pleasure on the faces of park-goers reveals that they have fallen under the spell of a turreted pink castle; the oompah of a band marching down Main Street, U.S.A.; the pleasant clip-clop of a horse-drawn trolley; a cheerful greeting from Mickey and Minnie and a fireworks spectacle more fantastic than an elaborate, pyrotechnic dream.

Those who first entered Disneyland as wee ones now return with their own kids—and grandkids—to find the park of their memories unchanged in spirit and heart. Shows and attractions have come and gone since it opened back in 1955 and whole new "lands" have been added, while many beloved classics endure. The newest neighborhood, Star Wars: Galaxy's Edge, promises high-flying intergalactic adventures for generations to come. Of course, the overall enchantment that guests experience when they walk through the portals of "The Happiest Place on Earth" remains constant. That may well be Disneyland park's most enduring accomplishment. Enjoy!

"TO ALL WHO COME TO THIS HAPPY PLACE: WELCOME."

—WALT DISNEY

DISNEYLAND PARK

Getting Oriented

Disneyland Park's layout—a basic hub-and-spokes configuration—is simple, but it was quite innovative when the park opened in 1955. The design makes getting around easy, though it's not altogether effortless, since the numerous nooks, crannies, and alleyways can be a bit confusing at first.

The hub of the park's wheel is Central Plaza, which fronts Sleeping Beauty Castle. From it extend five spokes leading to nine "lands": Main Street, U.S.A.; Adventureland; Frontierland; New Orleans Square; Bayou Country; Fantasyland; a vibrantly re-imagined Mickey's Toontown; Tomorrowland; and Star Wars: Galaxy's Edge. As you face Sleeping Beauty Castle, the first bridge to your left takes you to Adventureland; the next one, to Frontierland and New Orleans Square. To your right, the first walkway goes to Tomorrowland, and the next one—known as Matterhorn Way—leads to Fantasyland and Toontown. If you cross the Castle's moat and walk through the archway, you will reach Fantasyland. Bayou Country occupies its own cul-de-sac, extending north from New Orleans Square. Star Wars: Galaxy's Edge is just beyond Bayou Country (and may be accessed from there, as well as from Fantasyland and Frontierland).

Study the map at left to familiarize yourself with the park layout. When you arrive, check a park Tip Board, which includes details about times and locations of the day's entertainment, as well as how to see favorite Disney characters. Entertainment information is offered via the Disneyland app, too.

PARKING

Guests are directed to park vehicles in the Mickey & Friends and Pixar Pals parking structures or the Toy Story lot on Harbor Boulevard. If one parking area is full, a cast member will direct you to one that has space. Courtesy tram service transports guests from the parking decks, while buses service the Toy Story lot.

Parking areas open an hour before the park does—but getting a space can take a while if there are a lot of folks also hoping to get a head start on the day. Guests using wheelchairs will be directed to a special parking area and have access to ramps in the tram-loading area.

Parking Fees: Guests arriving in regular passenger vehicles or motorcycles pay about $35 to park for the day. (The fee for oversized vehicles, motor homes, or tractors without trailers is $40 [Toy Story parking area only]. The fee for buses or tractors with extended trailers is $45 at the Toy Story parking area only.) Preferred parking starts at $55. You may leave the lot and return later the same day at no additional charge. (Keep the parking stub as proof of payment.) Prices are subject to change.

Lost Cars: Even if you take careful note of where you park your car, you might have trouble remembering or recognizing the exact spot when you return hours later. (Hundreds more vehicles will likely be parked around yours!) To keep track of your vehicle, use the Car Locator feature in the Disneyland app. The free service uses Location Services to find and save your parking details.

GETTING AROUND

The Disneyland Railroad's five narrow-gauge trains make a loop around the park, stopping at Main Street, U.S.A., New Orleans Square, Mickey's Toontown, and Tomorrowland. It takes approximately 20 minutes to come full-circle on the train. Horse-drawn streetcars, horseless carriages, and an old-time motorized fire engine make trips up and down Main Street, U.S.A.

To travel outside Disneyland Park, consider taking the monorail, which glides between Tomorrowland and Downtown Disney. From the Downtown Disney District, you can walk to any of the three on-property hotels: Pixar Place Hotel, the Disneyland Hotel, and Disney's Grand Californian Hotel & Spa.

The Grand Californian Hotel & Spa is a short walk to the Disneyland entrance and has its own entrance to Disney California Adventure. (The gate is reserved exclusively for Grand Californian Hotel guests—you will have to flash a valid Grand Californian room key to use it.) Note that the theme parks require separate admission, unless you have a Park Hopper ticket; see page 57 for ticket pricing and structures.

Park Primer

BABY FACILITIES

The Baby Care Center, on Main Street, U.S.A., by First Aid, provides changing tables, high chairs, toddlers' toilets, and a nursing area. Bottles can be warmed here, and diapers, formula, and food are sold. There are no napping facilities or babysitting services.

FIRST AID

First Aid is at the north end of Main Street, next to the Baby Care Center. A nurse is on duty during park operating hours. *In case of emergency, notify an employee and call 911.* The center can store medications that require refrigeration and provide containers for hypodermic needle disposal.

GUIDED TOURS

Disneyland's backstage tours originate from the Guided Tour Gardens, just left of City Hall on Main Street. They include (but are not limited to) the *Walt's Main Street Story Tour* and *Holiday Time at the Disneyland Resort* (offered seasonally). Park admission is required for both tours. Details are subject to change at any time. For more information, flip to page 21 and visit *disneyland.com.*

HOURS

Disneyland park is usually open daily, year round. Monday through Thursday hours are usually from about 8 A.M. to 8 P.M., Friday and Sunday from about 8 A.M. to 11 P.M., Saturday from 8 A.M. to 12 A.M., with extended hours during the summer and holiday periods. Park-hopping is allowed after 11 A.M. Details are subject to change. For updates, visit *disneyland.com,* or call 714-781-4565.

During the inevitably busy spring break, summer, and Christmas holiday seasons, it's especially wise to arrive early so that you can visit the most popular attractions before the lines get long. If you arrive at Disneyland too late, the parking structure and surrounding lots could be more crowded than usual; this is almost always the case in the summer and the last week of December.

INFORMATION

Cast members at City Hall on Main Street, Guest Relations kiosks (Fantasyland, Tomorrowland, Frontierland, and New Orleans Square), and the Central Plaza Information Board can answer questions. Be sure to get a park guidemap as you enter. They're free.

Information Board: A valuable resource, the Central Plaza Information Board (aka the Tip Board) is on Main Street, U.S.A. It lets you know how long the waits are for most shows and attractions, what is not operating that day, and where and when park entertainment will take place—as do the Disneyland app and *disneyland.com.* Cast members can answer questions and provide information. They can help locate favorite Disney characters, too.

LOCKERS

Storage lockers are outside the main entrance (on the left) and on Center Street (about halfway up Main Street). Inside-the-park lockers cost about $7 or $10 per day, depending on size. Items may be stored during park hours only. You'll also find a kiosk from which to rent smartphone power packs. The cost is $30 per day and includes unlimited pack-swapping, plus power cords for iPhones and Android devices. The lockers outside the park cost $7, $10, $12, and $15 per day (depending on size).

LOST & FOUND

Disneyland's Lost & Found is located on the left side of the Disneyland park entrance. If you realize that you've lost something after you have gotten home visit *https:// disneyland.disney.go.com/guest-services/lost-and-found/.*

LOST CHILDREN

Report lost children to the closest cast member (park employee) so security personnel can assist you. Kids who become separated from parents or guardians while in the park will be escorted to the nearest Baby Care Center by a cast member. To expedite reunions, supply youngsters with a copy of your mobile number before you visit the park.

MONEY MATTERS

Cash is accepted throughout the Disneyland Resort. Debit cards, American Express, Visa, MasterCard, Discover, JCB Card, Disney Visa Rewards redemption cards, and Apple Pay may be used too. Payment features in the Disneyland mobile app may be used at many shops and eateries.

Main Street's City Hall can assist with some foreign currency exchange. Disneyland Resort hotel guests may charge most in-park purchases to their hotel bill if they gave a credit card number at check-in.

Disney gift cards are accepted at the three Disneyland Resort hotels, Disney California Adventure, Downtown Disney, and Disneyland park.

There are two Automated Teller Machines (ATMs) within Disneyland park. The first one you'll encounter is near the Disneyana shop at the Bank of Main Street building. (Though one might expect the Bank to be, well, a bank, it is not. It's a shop.) The other ATM is in Frontierland, across from Pioneer Mercantile.

PARK RESERVATIONS

To enter a Disneyland Resort theme park, guests must have valid park admission *and* a park reservation for the day. Park reservations can (and should) be made in advance via the Disneyland app or *disneyland.com*. We recommend checking for reservation availability before purchasing tickets, as reservations have been known to sell out. Details may change in 2026.

SAME-DAY RE-ENTRY

All Disneyland park guests have their picture taken upon initial entry to the park. (The photo links with their ticket.) This makes for speedy and convenient re-entry, with the presentation of said park ticket. If you'd like to visit two parks on one day, you'll need to purchase the "hopper" option prior to entering the first park. (Disneyland and Disney California Adventure are with n walking distance of each other, which allows for hassle-free hopping between the parks.)

SMOKING RULES

Disneyland Resort is a smoke-free zone. Smoking (of any kind) is not permitted anywhere within Disneyland Resort boundaries—this includes all of Disneyland Park, Disney California Adventure, Downtown Disney, the Disneyland hotels, and the esplanade between the parks. The ban includes tobacco, e-cigarettes, and any products creating a vapor or smoke. Smoking of marijuana or illegal substances is prohibited. No exceptions.

STROLLERS & WHEELCHAIRS

Strollers ($18 for singles; doubles $36) and wheelchairs ($15 with a $20 refundable deposit and a credit card) may be rented outside the park entrance. Electric Conveyance Vehicles (ECVs) cost $60 for the day, with a $20 deposit and major credit card. Wheelchair and ECV supplies are limited. Misplaced strollers may be replaced at the park entrance and The Star Trader shop in Tomorrowland.

SECURITY CHECK

All guests are subject to a thorough security check before entering the Disneyland Resort. Bags are screened and guests must pass through a metal detector. For a complete rundown of the current Park Rules, visit *disneyland.com/parkrules*.

Expect car trunks to be searched when entering Disney parking facilities.

Guests checking into a Disneyland Resort hotel must present a valid government-issued photo ID.

TICKET PRICES

Although prices[†] will likely increase, the following should give an idea of what you will pay for tickets in 2025/2026. Note that 1-Day tickets purchased in 2026 must be used by 12/30/26. The first day of use of multi-day tickets must be on or before 12/30/26. Multi-day tickets must be used within 13 days of first use or by January 12, 2027, whichever occurs first. For updates, use the Disneyland app or visit *disneyland.com*. Details are subject to change.

	ADULTS	CHILDREN*
1-Day Ticket (1 park)	$104/206	$98/196
1-Day Ticket (hopper) **	$169/281	$163/271
2-Day Ticket	$330	$310
2-Day Ticket (hopper) **	$415	$395
3-Day Ticket	$415	$390
3-Day Ticket (hopper) **	$505	$480
4-Day Ticket	$474	$444
4-Day Ticket (hopper) **	$569	$539
5-Day Ticket	$511	$476
5-Day Ticket (hopper) **	$616	$581
Enchant Key pass		$974
Believe Key pass		$1,374
Inspire Key pass		$1,749

† One-day prices represent the range in which you can expect to pay. Prices vary based on date. For dates, visit *disneyland.com*.
* 3 through 9 years of age; children under 3 free
** Guests with Park Hopper tickets and valid park reservations must enter the park as designated in their park reservation, and may hop between parks on the same day starting at 11 A.M. (subject to availability). After 11 A.M., guests with Park Hopper tickets who have a reservation for Disneyland park or Disney California Adventure, but have not yet entered that park, may enter either theme park (subject to availability).

There is a single price (for adults and kids) for Enchant Key, Believe Key, and Inspire Key passes. Said passes are part of the "Magic Key" pass program that replaced traditional annual passes. There is a limited number of Magic Key passes available and sales may be suspended at any time. For more information on Magic Key passes, use the Disneyland mobile app or visit *disneyland.com*.

Main Street, U.S.A.

This pretty thoroughfare represents Main Street America in the early 1900s, complete with the gentle clip-clop of horses' hooves on pavement, melodic ringing of street-car bells, and strains of nostalgic tunes such as "Bicycle Built for Two" and "Coney Island Baby."

The sounds of brass bands, a barbershop quartet, and ragtime piano fill the street. An old-fashioned steam train huffs into a handsome brick depot. Rows of picturesque buildings line the street. Authentic gaslights, which once lit up Baltimore and St. Louis, flicker at sundown in ornate lampposts lining the walkways, and the storefronts—painted in a palette of pastels—could not be more inviting. Walt Disney was a master of detail: throughout Main Street, even the doorknobs are historically correct.

To make the buildings appear taller, a set designer's technique called forced perspective was employed. The first floor is seven-eighths scale (this allows guests to enter comfortably); the second story is five-eighths scale; and the third, only half size. The dimensions of the whole are small enough for the place to seem intimate and comforting, yet the proportions appear correct. (Forced perspective was also used to make the Matterhorn and Sleeping Beauty Castle seem taller than they are.)

The following attractions are listed in the order in which you'll encounter them while walking from the entrance up Main Street, U.S.A., toward Sleeping Beauty Castle.

CITY HALL: Before strolling up Main Street, U.S.A., stop briefly at the Guest Relations and Information Center at City Hall, on the west side of Town Square, for assistance with dining reservations, ticket questions/upgrades, or to help you plan your Disneyland day.

FIRE DEPARTMENT: Next door to City Hall, this was Walt Disney's home away from home during the construction of Disneyland. His private apartment, on the top floor, looks just the same as when Walt called it home. It's decorated with antiques and items he and his wife Lillian picked up during their travels around the world. A light shines in the window in Walt's memory. The apartment is not open to the general public, but all guests are welcome to visit the firehouse. Kids love—and are welcome—to climb on the fire wagon parked inside the firehouse. It's a realistic copy of a truck from the early 1900s and provides a great photo opportunity.

Note: Guests who wish to visit Walt's Disney's apartment may do so via Walt's Main Street Story guided tour. Fees apply. See page 21 for details.

DISNEYLAND RAILROAD: Walt Disney loved trains so much he actually built a one-eighth-scale model of one, the Carolwood Pacific, in the backyard of his home. So it was only natural that his first theme park include a

BIRNBAUM'S ★BEST★

Stamps like this one indicate the shows and attractions that we find superlative in one (and usually more) of the following ways: state-of-the-art technology, theming, beauty, novelty, thrills and spills (make that splashes), and overall whimsy. Each "Birnbaum's Best" promises to deliver a dynamite Disneyland experience. Enjoy!

railroad—five narrow-gauge steam trains have circled Disneyland Park since it opened in 1955. Two of the locomotives were constructed at the Walt Disney Studios, while three had other lives before finding a permanent home at Disneyland.

Guests who ride the train between Tomorrowland and Main Street, U.S.A., are in for a few surprises. In 1958 Walt Disney added a diorama of the Grand Canyon, depicted from its south rim on a seamless, handwoven canvas that is 306 feet long and 34 feet high, and is covered with 300 gallons of paint. The accompanying music is the "On the Trail" section of American composer Ferde Grofé's Grand Canyon Suite.

PHOTO BY JILL SAFRO

The train travels across an elevated trestle, affording panoramic views of five waterfalls gracing the Rivers of America. Disneyland veterans may also take note of some old Frontierland friends during the journey.

NEW **MAIN STREET OPERA HOUSE PRESENTING WALT DISNEY—A MAGICAL LIFE:** The Main Street Opera House makes the perfect backdrop for a tribute to "The Happiest Place on Earth," and the man who created it, one Walter Elias Disney. A unique collection of art, models, and mementos—as well as a film—marks more than 70 years of Disneyland magic. In celebration of Disneyland's 70th Anniversary, a new show debuted here on July 17, 2025. Walt Disney—A Magical Life tells the story of Walt's journey from Kansas City paperboy to Hollywood moviemaker. Guests visit Walt's office and see the first ever Audio-Animatronics figure of Walt himself. Once the 70th Anniversary celebration is complete, Walt Disney—A Magical Life will play in rotation with longtime Opera House show Great Moments with Mr. Lincoln.

PHOTO BY JILL SAFRO

MAIN STREET VEHICLES: Main Street's motorized fire wagon, horseless carriages, and horse-drawn streetcars lend the thoroughfare a real touch of nostalgia, while at the same time giving guests a lift from one end of the street to the other. The fire truck is modeled after those that might have been discovered on an American Main Street in the early 1900s, except that it has seats where the hose was meant to be carried.

The horse-drawn streetcars, inspired by those in 19th-century photographs, carry up to 30 passengers each. Most of the horses that pull the cars are Belgians (characterized by white manes and tails and lightly feathered legs) and Percheron draft horses.

PRESS A PENNY!

The art of pressing pennies—believed to have started in Austria in 1818—took the U.S. by storm when it was introduced at the 1892–1893 World's Columbian Exposition in Chicago. About a century later, Disneyland introduced guests to the joy of smushing a penny into a shiny souvenir! The first two machines proved so popular, Disney has been adding new ones ever since. Now it's possible to press pennies (plus dimes and quarters) into more than 150 different Disney-themed souvenirs. (In case you're wondering, the first Disneyland penny press machine yielded (appropriately) an image of Mickey Mouse, while the second featured the beloved bruin and Disneyland darling, Big Al.) Most of the pressed-coin machines feature images from the area in which they are located—it's fun to discover them while wandering in the park.

How does it work? For starters, Disney provides the penny. You simply place your credit card or four quarters into the machine, hit the button, and *presto*: The coin is squeezed between rollers, flattened into an oval, and engraved with a Disney design of your choosing. (If you prefer to press a dime or quarter, the fee is higher.) In true old-timey fashion, some of the classic machines may not accept credit cards. Coins only, please.

While some guests get rather crafty with their coins (turning them into key chains, jewelry, belts, wind chimes, and more), others preserve them in a scrapbook or Disney-branded souvenir book (available for purchase at many shops throughout the Disneyland Resort).

Note: Coin-press machines are available at Disney California Adventure, Downtown Disney District, and the Disneyland Resort hotels, too. They're easily located by using the Disneyland app, visiting *disneyland.com*, or asking a cast member.

MAIN STREET CINEMA: This small, standing-room-only movie theater features classic, early Mickey Mouse cartoons. The six animated shorts, which play continuously throughout the day, were originally aired before feature films. The addition of several benches has made this cinema an even-more-pleasant place to soak up some Disney nostalgia.

PENNY ARCADE: This place is more of a candy shop than an arcade, but the air of nostalgia remains. Those who have frequented it in the past will be happy to find Esmeralda front and center, ready as always to tell your fortune. The arcade still has Mutoscopes, machines that feature hand-cranked moving pictures and require a penny to operate.

PHOTO BY JILL SAFRO

Save some change for the arcade's penny presses. You insert a credit card (or a few coins) to pay for the service, and the penny will be flattened and imprinted with the image of Sleeping Beauty Castle or the face of one of the Disney characters.

CENTRAL PLAZA: Main Street, U.S.A., ends at Central Plaza, the hub of the park, and four of the park's lands are directly accessible from here. At its center stands the Walt and Mickey Partners statue. It's one of the park's most popular picture spots.

One of Disneyland's Information Centers is located here, near the Plaza Inn restaurant. Besides the information desk, there is a handy Information Board, (aka Tip Board) updated frequently, that posts wait times for many attractions, which attractions offer Lightning Lane service, what (if anything) is not operating that day, and where and when park entertainment will take place.

Adventureland

PHOTO BY MIKE CARROLL

For someone who grew up in Marceline, Missouri, around the turn of the 20th century, as Walt Disney did, the far-flung regions of the world must have seemed most exciting. So it's not surprising that when he was planning his new park, he designated one area, called Adventureland, to represent all the (then) remote and mysterious corners of the world.

The original South Seas–island ambience all but disappeared with the opening of the Indiana Jones Adventure in 1995, and Adventureland became a 1930s jungle outpost. Today, the entrance to the Jungle Cruise is a walk-through headquarters, with old photographs and radios playing big band music interrupted by news flashes about Professor Jones's latest exploits and discoveries. Shops here sell wares that are meant to appeal to modern-day adventurers.

WALT DISNEY'S ENCHANTED TIKI ROOM: Introduced in 1953, this was the first of the park's Audio-Animatronics attractions and the precursor of more elaborate variations, such as "Great Moments with Mr. Lincoln" and the above-mentioned Dr. Jones. Housed in a vaguely Polynesian complex situated at the entrance to Adventureland, the 15-minute show was given a spiffy face-lift not too long ago.

The stars are four feathered emcees (José, Michael, Pierre, and Fritz), backed up by a company of pastel-plumed parrots and an eclectic chorus of orchids, carved wooden tiki poles, drummers, singing masks, bird-of-paradise flowers, macaws, Amazon parrots, toucans, fork-tailed birds, cockatoos, and several other species.

The 225 performers all sing and drum up a tropical storm with so much animation that it's hard to resist a smile. Their repertoire includes "The Tiki, Tiki, Tiki Room" and "Let's All Sing Like the Birdies Sing."

JUNGLE CRUISE: The spiel delivered by the skipper on this 10-minute river adventure has its share of corny jokes, but your navigator may turn out to be a natural comic with a funny delivery. Just remember that the cornball humor is part of the fun.

As jungle cruises go, this one is as much like the real thing as Main Street, U.S.A., is like life in an actual small town—long on loveliness and short on the visual distractions and minor annoyances that constitute the bulk of human experience. There are no venomous vipers and no Montezuma's revenge. And the Bengal tiger and king cobras at the ancient Cambodian shrine, and the great apes, gorillas, crocodiles, alligators, hippos, elephants, and lions in the water and along the shores represent no threat to passersby—though according to maintenance crews, mechanical critters are almost as much trouble as real ones.

Movie buffs should note that Bob Mattey, who helped develop these jungle creatures, also worked on the giant squid for the Disney film *20,000 Leagues Under the Sea*, the man-eating plants in many Tarzan movies, and the menacing mechanical shark in *Jaws*.

The large-leafed upright tree in the Cambodian ruins section of the attraction is a Sacred Fig (Ficus religiosa), the same species of tree under which Buddha received enlightenment in India many centuries ago.

This classic attraction was refreshed a few years back. Expect an increased wildlife presence, surprise scenarios, and, of course, a ton of tomfoolery.

ADVENTURELAND TREEHOUSE—INSPIRED BY WALT DISNEY'S SWISS FAMILY ROBINSON: The 80-foot-tall, 150-ton *Disney-odendron semperflorens grandis*, or "large, ever-blooming Disney tree," cradled the original Swiss Family Treehouse from 1962 to 1999, and until 2021 embraced another lofty dwelling: Tarzan's Treehouse. And now, we are very happy to report, the famous shipwrecked family is back! They've spruced up their moss-and-vine-covered "high-rise apartment"— and you're invited to an open house (open treehouse?). The aerial abode, which overlooks the Jungle Cruise and the Temple of the Forbidden Eye (the setting for the nearby Indiana Jones Adventure attraction), is accessed near a giant waterwheel.

Throughout the climb up (and down) the numerous stairs, you can drink in the sights and sounds of Adventureland while peeking into the refurbished rooms. The digs include a music room, nature room, and astronomer's loft. Ground-level spaces include a well-appointed kitchen and dining room, plus an art studio—all easily traversed by folks who wish to skip the vertical trip through the tree.

F.Y.I. The *Disney-odendron semperflorens grandis* is entirely human-made, with concrete roots and steel limbs. And its 300,000 leaves were all attached by hand.

BIRNBAUM'S ★BEST★ **INDIANA JONES™ ADVENTURE:** **MP** Hidden deep within the dense jungles of India, the Temple of the Forbidden Eye was built long ago to honor the powerful deity Mara. According to legend, Mara could "look into your very soul" and grant the "pure of heart" one of three gifts:

unlimited wealth, eternal youth, or future knowledge. But legend also issues a rather stern warning: "A terrible fate awaits those who gaze upon the eyes of Mara!" Dr. Jones would only comment, "Records indicate that many have come, but few have returned."

Now you can take an expedition through the ancient temple ruins in this high-octane attraction based on the George Lucas/Steven Spielberg films. The experience, including the pre-show and queue area, can take more than an hour (without a Lightning Lane Multi Pass; see page 22), though the ride itself lasts about 3½ minutes. You follow the jungle path through Dr. Jones's cluttered encampment, then enter the temple via the path marked by his original team. The queue area gives adventurers a hint of what's to come. What it does not reveal is that Indy has entered the temple and disappeared.

Following in his footsteps, you will see warning signs that indicate there still may be booby traps that have not yet been disarmed. (The fun is in ignoring the warnings and letting the spikes fall where they may.) Inside the temple, guests board 12-passenger vehicles reminiscent of 1930s troop transports. One person sits by the wheel and serves as the expedition driver, but not until all are securely fastened in their seats for the twists and turns ahead. Hold on to your hat!

The search for Indiana Jones is on, and an encounter with the fearsome Mara is unavoidable. The trip reveals a world of mummies, glowing fires, falling lava, worrisome snakes, and poisonous darts.

Surprises lurk around every bend, and escape is only temporary (just as in the movies), as you suffer an avalanche of creepy crawlies, traverse a quaking suspension bridge, and find yourself on a collision course with a giant rolling boulder that threatens to flatten everything in its path. At the end of the ride, Indy himself is waiting for you, with a flippant parting remark, such as "That wasn't so bad" or "Next time you're on your own" or "Tourists. Why'd it have to be tourists?"

Thanks to the creative wizardry of Disney Imagineers, no two rides are exactly the same, so each time you enter the Temple of the Forbidden Eye, the overall experience may be slightly different. Hang on!

Note: Pregnant women and guests who suffer from heart conditions, motion sickness, sore necks or backs, and have other physical concerns should avoid this wild and exceptionally bumpy attraction. Guests must be at least 46 inches tall to board; children under age 7 must be accompanied by a person who is at least 14 years old. Spooked by snakes? There are more than a few in here. They may not be real, but they're still rather creepy.

New Orleans Square

Though New Orleans Square did not figure in the Disneyland layout until 1966, it's certainly among the park's most evocative areas. This would be true even if it were home to just the superb Haunted Mansion and Pirates of the Caribbean. But there's also its picturesque site near the shores of the Rivers of America, and its architecture, a pastiche of wrought iron, pastel stucco, French doors, and beckoning verandas.

Not to be missed are the pleasant open-air dining spots; the charming Blue Bayou restaurant overlooking the moonlit lagoon inside Pirates of the Caribbean; the unique assortment of boutiques; and the music—lively jazz and Dixieland, performed in traditional New Orleans style.

As you relax on a warm evening, snacking on freshly made beignets and mint juleps, notions of Disneyland-as-amusement-park may start to evaporate. Just as Main Street, U.S.A., makes the theme park a delightful place to shop, New Orleans Square makes it a fine spot to spend a few relaxing hours. Those perpetual click-click sounds emanating from the railroad station are the Morse code version of the actual dedication speech given by Walt Disney on the opening day of Disneyland back in 1955. It begins: "To all who come to this happy place: welcome."

The attractions that are described on the following pages are listed in the order in which you'd encounter them while strolling from east to west in Disneyland's New Orleans Square.

BIRNBAUM'S ★BEST★ **PIRATES OF THE CARIBBEAN:** The most swashbuckly adventure you'll find at Disneyland, this 16-minute boat ride takes guests through a series of sets portraying a rowdy

pirate raid on a Caribbean village. Bursting with cannon fire, stolen loot, a gluttonous feast, and a raucous band of unruly mercenaries, Pirates of the Caribbean has been a fan favorite for more than half of a century. It was the last attraction built under Walt Disney's direct creative supervision.

The experience begins with a peaceful voyage through a bayou, where will-o'-the-wisps glow just above the grasses. Fireflies twinkle nearby, while stars spangle the twilight-blue sky overhead. The attention to detail nearly boggles the mind. The Audio-Animatronics cast includes plastered pigs whose legs actually twitch in their soporific contentment, singing marauders, and wily wenches. The observant may notice a couple of familiar rapscallion residents. Yep, that beloved scally-wag Captain Jack Sparrow has dropped anchor here, as has his nefarious nemesis, Captain Barbossa. And there's a new pirate in town—the famous redhead resident of this attraction has teamed up with the local marauders! Redd hopes to help the townspeople "unload" their valuables at the Mercado Auction.

While it's by no means the most politically correct attraction, the theme song, "Yo-Ho, Yo-Ho (A Pirate's Life for Me)," manages to transform some rather blatant buccaneering into a rousing time for all. A must—again and again.

BIRNBAUM'S ★BEST★ **HAUNTED MANSION:** **MP** In a British radio interview, Walt Disney once explained how sorry he felt for those homeless ghosts whose haunt-able mansions had fallen

to the wrecker's ball. Feeling that these lost souls sorely needed a place of their own, he offered this Haunted Mansion, unquestionably one of Disneyland's top attractions. From its stately portico to the exit corridor, the special effects are piled on to create an eerie, but never terrifying, mood. Just frightfully amusing.

Judicious applications of paint and expert lighting effects heighten the shadows that play ghoulishly on the walls outside. The jumble of trunks, chairs, dress forms, and other assorted knickknacks in the attic are left appropriately dirty, and extra cobwebs, which come in convenient liquid form, are strung with abandon. The eerie music and the slightly spooky tones of the Ghost Host often set small children to whimpering, and soon their Mickey Mouse ears have been pulled tightly over their eyes. Still, the spirits that inhabit this house on the hill—999 in all—are a tame lot for the most part, though they are always looking for occupant number 1,000. Any volunteers?

What makes the seven-minute attraction so special is the attention to, and abundance of, details—so many that it's next to impossible to take them all in during the first, or even the second or third, time around. In the Portrait Chamber—a room full of fearsome-looking gargoyles that adjoins the chandeliered and lace-curtain-adorned foyer—it's fun to speculate on whether the ceiling moves up or the room moves down. (It's one way here and the opposite way at the Haunted Mansion's counterpart at Walt Disney World's Magic Kingdom park.)

Once seated in your Doom Buggy, look for the bats' eyes on the wallpaper, the tomb-sweet-tomb plaque, and the rattling suit of armor in the Corridor of Doors. Can you spot a Hidden Mickey in the haunted dining room? And keep your eyes peeled for the infamous "Hatbox Ghost" in the attic scene. Absent from the manse for decades, he's made a creepy comeback!

Then there are the dead plants, withered flowers, and broken glass in the Conservatory, where a hand reaches out of a half-open casket; the terrified cemetery watchman and his mangy mutt in the Graveyard; the ghostly teapot that pours spectral tea; the ectoplasmic king and queen on the teeter-totter; the bicycle-riding spirits; the transparent musicians; and the headless knight and his supernatural Brunhilde. Nice stuff all.

Construction of the mansion was completed in 1963, inspired by the Shipley-Lydecker House in Baltimore, Maryland; the attraction opened in 1969. The signature song "Grim Grinning Ghosts" was composed especially for the Haunted Mansion attraction.

Frontierland

PHOTO BY JILL SAFRO

This is the America experienced by the pioneers as they pushed westward: rough wilderness outposts and dense forests, and rugged mountains delineating the skyline.

The sights in Frontierland are just about as pleasant as they come in Disneyland park, and the atmosphere just as inviting.

FRONTIERLAND SHOOTIN' EXPOSITION: This rustic shooting gallery, set in an 1850s town in the Southwest Territory, is completely electronic. Eighteen rifles are trained on Boothill, a mining town complete with a bank, jail, hotel, and stables. They fire invisible infrared beams that trigger silly results whenever they strike the little red targets. The most challenging target is the moving shovel, which, when struck, causes a skeleton to pop out of a grave. There are nearly 100 targets on which to test your marksmanship.

Note: Park admission does not include use of the Frontierland Shootin' Exposition. Pay a buck for about 25 shots—then fire away. Pricing and other details are subject to change.

BIRNBAUM'S
★BEST★ **BIG THUNDER MOUNTAIN RAILROAD:** **MP** Hold on to your hats and glasses, because this here's the wildest ride in the wilderness! Inspired by peaks in Utah's Bryce Canyon and Arizona's Sedona, Big Thunder Mountain is entirely a Disney creation. The name comes from an old legend about a sacred mountain in Wyoming that thundered whenever anyone tried to excavate its gold. The now classic attraction took five years of planning and two years of construction, and it cost about as much to build as the rest of the original Disneyland attractions put together.

As roller coasters go, this one is relatively tame. It's short on steep climbs and precipitous drops that put hearts in throats and make stomachs protest, but long on tight curves that provoke giggles of glee. Adding to the appeal of this thrill ride is the scenery that the runaway mine train passes along the way: a pitch-black bat cave, giant stalactites and stalagmites, a waterfall, a natural-arch bridge that affords fine views over the Big Thunder landscape, and mine walls ready to cave in.

The queue area sets the scene of the quaint mining town, with two hotels, a newspaper office, dance hall, saloon, and general store. If you listen closely, you may hear a local barmaid flirting with a miner to the tune of "Red River Valley" or "Listen to the Mockingbird."

As you approach the ride's loading area, notice the brownish stone walls on each side of you. They were made from a hundred tons of real gold ore from the former mining town of Rosamond, California, which also yielded the 10-foot-tall stamp mill designated "Big Thunder Mine 1880."

Note: Pregnant women and guests who have heart conditions, weak backs, are prone to motion sickness, or other limitations should not ride. Guests must be at least 40 inches tall to experience Big Thunder Mountain Railroad. Kids under age 7 must be accompanied by a guest age 14 or older.

MP = Lightning Lane Multi Pass attraction (see page 22) **65**

PHOTO BY JILL SAFRO

MARK TWAIN RIVERBOAT: One of the original Disneyland attractions, this five-eighths-scale vessel circumnavigates Tom Sawyer Island. Along the way, it passes the River Belle Terrace, the Royal Street Veranda, piney Bayou Country, a waterfall, abandoned railroad tracks, and lovely dense woods filled with alders, cottonwoods, maples, and willows that might have been found along the Missouri frontier more than a century ago. Moose, elk, and (real) ducks complete the scene. The 14-minute ride offers a pleasant respite from the crowds. And if you manage to get one of the few chairs in the bow, the *Mark Twain* also provides a rare opportunity to rest your weary feet.

GOLDEN HORSESHOE SALOON: Western flair is the key ingredient at this entertaining dining venue, where frontier-style vittles are served for lunch and dinner. The hall itself is resplendent with chandeliers, polished floors and banisters, and a long brass railing. One of several O.G. Disneyland buildings (it opened with the park in 1955), the longhorns that line its walls were selected by Walt Disney himself. Walt kept a private box here, just to the left of the stage, on the upper level. (It's open to the public now.)

The Golden Horseshoe Saloon is a worthy stop during a Disneyland day—especially if your stomach's growlin' for some tasty grub. Yee-ha!

PHOTO BY JILL SAFRO

SAILING SHIP COLUMBIA: A full-scale replica of the 10-gun, 3-masted "Gem of the Ocean," the *Columbia* operates seasonally and on busy days at Disneyland. The original ship, built in Plymouth, Massachusetts, in 1787 and christened the *Columbia Redivivia* ("freedom reborn"), was the first American craft to circumnavigate the globe. (Back then, that took about three years to do!)

Disney's *Columbia*, dedicated in 1958 and renovated in 1984, was the first ship of its kind to be built in more than a century. It circumnavigates the Rivers of America in 15 minutes. It has a steel hull and a deck planked with Douglas fir, and measures 110 feet from stem to stern, with an 84-foot mainmast. Usually moored at Fowler's Harbor, opposite the Haunted Mansion, the sailing ship towers majestically above the treetops of Frontierland.

Below Decks: The *Columbia's* maritime museum, found below the main deck, celebrates the dedication and sacrifice of the brave explorers who filled in the final details of the world's map. It has historical displays and re-creates the living conditions of 18th-century sailors, based on reports in the ship's log and in letters between the captain and the owners.

PIRATE'S LAIR ON TOM SAWYER ISLAND: Yes, you read that right—there has been a pirate invasion in Frontierland. Tom Sawyer Island has been transformed into a pirate-y paradise, complete with hidden treasure, creepy caves, and shipwrecks.

The only way to reach the island is by pirate-piloted raft. Once there, guests have many areas to investigate. Among them is Smuggler's Cove, which incorporates the island's beloved bridges and invites guests to man the bilge pumps in an effort to raise sunken treasure. Then there's the Castle Rock lookout point, with its spyglasses and peepholes (perfect for spying on scallywags or fellow park guests); Will Turner's Blacksmith Shop offers a glimpse at some of his works in progress; Dead Man's Grotto is a dark and labyrinthine set of caves sporting some spooky yet snazzy special effects. Purists are pleased by the preservation of Tom and Huck's Tree House. (Tom Sawyer Island is the only attraction designed by Walt Disney himself.)

Small signs point to places of interest on the island. Time spent here is worthwhile and could unexpectedly encompass some of your happiest moments in Disneyland.

Note: Tom Sawyer Island closes early to allow for Fantasmic! preparation. Check at the dock for excursion times, particularly the last raft departure of the day.

Bayou Country

Lush, shady forests of pines, locusts, white birches, coastal redwoods and evergreen elms surround Bayou Country, one of the most pleasant corners of Disneyland. In 1972, this land debuted as Bear Country, the backwoods home of the since-departed Country Bear Playhouse. From 1956 through 1971, the area was called the Indian Village and was considered part of Frontierland.

Disney Imagineers dubbed this zone Critter Country in 1989. (That's the year an attraction known as Splash Mountain made its Disneyland debut). Now called Bayou Country, the area is home to bunnies, beavers, raccoons, opossums, and many of the other cuddly critters that make up the Audio-Animatronics cast of Tiana's Bayou Adventure.

BIRNBAUM'S
★BEST★
NEW

TIANA'S BAYOU ADVENTURE: **MP**
Originally known as Splash Mountain, this re-imagined crowd-pleaser celebrates Mardi Gras in jubilant fashion—thanks to a splashy new *Princess and the Frog*–inspired storyline and jazzy original songs. The theme of the attraction is new, but the giddy thrills of the classic experience endure.

In this 9-minute ride, guests board hollowed-out logs and drift on a waterborne journey through bayous (where glowing fireflies light up the night sky), down waterfalls, and over the top of a super-steep spillway into an H_2O-filled splash zone five stories below. Along the way, they join Princess Tiana and jazz-loving alligator Louis as they prepare a special celebration for the people of New Orleans. Throughout the journey, the sounds of jazz, rara, and zydeco music fill the air, courtesy of a band of cuddly critters—including an otter, raccoon, beaver, and a turtle playing cleverly hand-crafted (or paw-crafted) instruments. (FYI: Zydeco is a blend of rhythm and blues that was born in Louisiana, and rara is a form of festival music that originated in Haiti.)

It may be a challenge for a first-time rider to take in all the details, since the tension of waiting for the big drop is all-consuming. It's more than a tad terrifying at the top, but once back on the ground, it seems most riders just can't wait for another trip—even though they may get drenched. (Water-wary guests have be seen wearing rain ponchos on this attraction. On the other hand, if you would like to get soaked, try to sit up front; seats in the back may receive a slightly smaller splash.)

By the second or third time around, it's possible to relax a bit, enjoy the interior scenes, and take in the spectacular bird's-eye views of the park from the top of the attraction. At this point, you may even manage

PHOTO COURTESY DISNEYLAND RESORT PUBLIC RELATIONS / DisneylandNews.com

HOT TIP

If you want to get totally soaked on Tiana's Bayou Adventure, sit in the front of the log; the spray has less of a dampening effect in the back. Though nobody stays dry! We recommend stashing electronics and other non–waterproof items in a nice dry locker or with a non-riding member of your party.

to keep your eyes open for the duration of the final fall—or at least part of it.

This splashy attraction boasts one of the planet's tallest and sharpest flume drops—52½ nail-biting feet at a 47-degree angle! That drop makes for one of the fastest rides ever operated at Disneyland Park.

Note: Guests must be at least 40 inches tall to ride Tiana's Bayou Adventure. Children under age 7 must be accompanied by a guest age 14 or older. Most seats are arranged single file. If you'd like to ride side by side with a timid tyke, request seating in the back of the log. Details are subject to change. For updates, use the Disneyland app or visit *disneyland.com*.

DAVY CROCKETT'S EXPLORER CANOES: Part attraction, part workout, Davy Crockett's Explorer Canoes require teamwork and elbow grease to make the trip around the Rivers of America. The 35-foot-long canoes hold about 20 passengers at a time and they are definitely not on a track. Modeled after boats used by early Native Americans and European explorers, the canoes are powered entirely by handheld paddles. Though a helmsman and sternman guide the rowing, guests' contributions are vital when it

comes to completing the 2,400-foot voyage. Small kids must wear (provided) life jackets while in a canoe.

Note: Davy Crockett's Explorer Canoes operate on select days, and the attraction closes at dusk. It may not operate during certain times of day or during inclement weather. Check at the landing for excursion times.

THE MANY ADVENTURES OF WINNIE THE POOH: There's a cuddly critter in town, and he goes by the name of Winnie the Pooh. In this whimsical attraction, everyone's favorite honey-lovin' cub treats Disneyland park guests to a wild and whimsical 3½-minute tour of his home turf.

The attraction features a most unlikely form of transportation: beehives. They whisk (and bounce) guests through the Hundred Acre Wood, where the weather's most blustery. The wind is really ruffling the feathers of one of the locals. It seems Owl's tree house has been shaken loose and just may topple to the ground—and onto the beehives below.

Similar sight gags abound, from a bubble-blowing Heffalump (hey, this is Disneyland) to a treacherous flood that threatens to sweep Tigger, Piglet, and the rest of the gang away. When the Pooh bear saves the day, it's time to celebrate—and everyone is invited to the party.

Note that, like many of the attractions in Fantasyland, this Bayou Country ride has a few scenes that take place in near darkness. Some timid youngsters may find these moments a bit unsettling. (If your kids can handle the likes of Mr. Toad's Wild Ride and Pinocchio's Daring Journey, they should be within their comfort level while in the Hundred Acre Wood.)

Fantasyland

Walt Disney called Fantasyland a timeless land of enchantment. We couldn't agree more. The skyline, dominated by the peak of the Matterhorn, bristles with chimneys and weather vanes, turrets and towers. At the center of it all, as if deposited here by an itinerant carnival, is the regal King Arthur Carrousel.

Note: Parents of young children should be aware that many of Fantasyland's attractions—while tame—have moments that take place in the dark. (In fact, they are often referred to as "dark rides.") These include Peter Pan's Flight, Mr. Toad's Wild Ride, Alice in Wonderland, Snow White's Enchanted Wish, Pinocchio's Daring Journey, and Storybook Land Canal Boats.

SLEEPING BEAUTY CASTLE: Rising above the treetops at the end of Main Street, U.S.A., it could be a figment of your imagination or a mirage created by Tinker Bell's pixie dust. Closer inspection proves this architectural confection is as real as the ducks gliding across the moat that surrounds it. A composite of medieval European castles, primarily in the French and Bavarian styles, Sleeping Beauty Castle, the gateway to Fantasyland, is constructed of concrete, with towers that rise 77 feet above the moat. Trimmed in 22-karat gold leaf, it appears shiny even on gray days. The structure seems larger than it really is due to its designers' use of forced perspective, down to the bricks.

From the Central Plaza, you're actually looking at what was originally intended to be the back of the castle; Walt Disney decided it was prettier that way and had the builders turn it around. The drawbridge, lowered when the park first opened in 1955, is like a real one—though it has been raised (and lowered again) only once since that day. The historic event took place in 1983, at the re-dedication ceremony for Fantasyland.

One of the two graceful trees to the right of the drawbridge bears hundreds of tiny yellow flowers in spring, and the other is covered with lavender flowers for several weeks in early summer.

SLEEPING BEAUTY CASTLE WALK-THROUGH: This classic Disneyland experience features extra scenes and enhanced special effects. The show, which features a series of dioramas, tells the story of *Sleeping Beauty*—including the magic of fairies Flora, Fauna, and Merryweather and the sinister spells of the evil Maleficent.

Guests enter the walk-through from the right, on the Fantasyland side of the castle. Note that it is rather dark

PHOTO BY JILL SAFRO

inside (which may spook tots) and there are some stairs to climb. Guests who are unable to do stairs or navigate the narrow passageways of the castle may experience the walk-through "virtually" in a special room on the ground floor.

FANTASY FAIRE: Once upon a time . . . in a storybook village nestled beside Sleeping Beauty Castle, folks of all ages were invited to mix and mingle with Disney characters and enjoy a live (and lively!) stage show. That time is now, and the guest list includes you. The Royal Hall and The Royal Theatre are the highlights of Fantasyland's newest neighborhood.

ROYAL HALL: Behind the richly detailed facade of this regal residence, you'll find a gorgeous gothic interior fit for a princess. A rotating group of royals is always on hand to greet guests. Expect favorites such as Belle, Cinderella, Snow White, and more.

ROYAL THEATRE: Take your funny bone to this theatre—the antics onstage are meant to make you chuckle. The show features a madcap and original retelling of a classic and beloved Disney tale. The action recently regaled tales from the films *Beauty and the Beast* and *Tangled*. The theatrical yarns are presented by Mr. Smythe and

Mr. Jones, Renaissance bards with vastly vaudevillian vigor, and a multitasking cast. It's fun for the whole family. Tales change periodically. Shows typically last about 22 minutes. The Royal Swing Big Band Ball may be offered on select evenings.

PIXIE HOLLOW: Where do Disney fairies live? In Pixie Hollow! Disneyland guests may enter the world of Tinker Bell and her friends. As guests walk along the garden path, they feel as though they are shrinking down to fairy size as the landscape gets larger and larger. This miniature realm is extra sparkly on summer nights, when it glows with the "magic" of pixie dust. You will find it between Sleeping Beauty Castle and the entrance to Tomorrowland.

SNOW WHITE WISHING WELL & GROTTO: Tucked off Matterhorn Way, at the eastern end of the moat around

Sleeping Beauty Castle, this is one of those quiet corners of the park easily overlooked by some guests. (Though not everyone, as it is a popular spot to "pop the question.") If you stand by the wishing well, you might hear Adriana Caselotti, the original voice of Snow White, singing the lovely melody "I'm Wishing," written for Walt Disney's Oscar-winning 1937 film.

F.Y.I.: All coins tossed into the well go to children's charities—so your wish will help fulfill other wishes.

BIRNBAUM'S ★BEST★ PETER PAN'S FLIGHT: "Come on, everybody, here we go! Off to Never Land!" This attraction is one of the park's loveliest— and consistently one of the most popular. Based on the story by Sir James M. Barrie about a boy with an immunity to maturity and an affinity for flying—by way of Disney's 1953 animated feature—the ride's effects soar to celestial heights. Pirate ships embark from the Darling kids' nursery and carry travelers through the clouds and into a starry sky.

Water ripples and gleams softly in the moonlight; the lava on the sides of a volcano glows with an intensity that mimics the real thing. After an ephemeral few minutes, the ships drift back into reality, an unloading area that is all the more jarring after the magic of the trip through Never Land.

Of the approximately 350 miles of fiber optics throughout Fantasyland, the majority is used in this attraction. The twinkling London scene is actually an enlarged model of an authentic map of the city.

Peter Pan's Flight is atop the popularity list with guests of all ages and usually has a line consistent with its status. Head here first thing in the morning, or late in the day (after little ones have gone to bed).

BIRNBAUM'S ★BEST★ MR. TOAD'S WILD RIDE: Based on the 1949 Disney animated film *The Adventures of Ichabod and Mr. Toad*—which was inspired by Kenneth Grahame's novel *The Wind in the Willows*—this simple, zany attraction is housed in an English manor bristling with ornate chimneys that really smoke. The wild, low-tech ride is experienced from the perspective of the eccentric but lovable Mr. Toad.

Of course, he is as inept a driver as you'd expect a toad to be. During the excursion, you crash through the fireplace in his library, burst through a wall full of windows, careen through the countryside, charge headlong into a warehouse full of TNT, lurch through the streets of London, then ram into a pub and veer out again. During the 2-minute journey, you'll also be berated by

DID YOU KNOW?

There is a shadow of Sherlock Holmes (complete with pipe and cap) in the second-story window of the Constabulatory building inside the Mr. Toad's Wild Ride attraction.

a judge in court, nearly collide head-on with a railroad train, and be banished to a fiery inferno. (Yes, you read that right.) Some effects may be too intense for tots.

ALICE IN WONDERLAND: This Fantasyland staple (which made its debut in 1958) features a delightful Alice figure, animated flowers, and a rolling hedgehog. It is Alice in *Wonderland*, after all.

Traveling in oversize caterpillars, visitors fall down the rabbit hole and embark upon a bizarre adventure in that strange world known as Wonderland. They come face-to-face with Tweedledee and Tweedledum, a garden filled with singing roses, the Cheshire Cat, the Queen of Hearts and her playing-card soldiers, the White Rabbit, and other characters from Lewis Carroll's beloved story *Alice's Adventures in Wonderland*.

At the conclusion of the nearly four-minute journey, a giant un-birthday cake explodes (thanks to a dynamite "candle"), providing a suitable finish to this sweet and surreal interlude. It's understandably popular with the under-age-7 demographic.

MAD TEA PARTY: The sequence in Walt Disney's 1951 release *Alice in Wonderland* in which the Mad Hatter hosts a tea party for his "un-birthday" is the theme for this ride—a group of colorful oversize teacups whirling wildly on a spinning tea table. Festive, colorful lanterns hang overhead. One of the park's original attractions, this dizzying ride lasts only 1½ minutes—but it may feel a bit longer!

Note: The teacups may look mild, but it's a good idea to let a reasonable interval pass after eating before you take one for a spin.

BIRNBAUM'S
★BEST★ **MATTERHORN BOBSLEDS:** **MP** Though it's 100 times smaller than the actual peak, Disney's version of the Matterhorn is still a credible reproduction. The use of forced perspective makes the snowy summit look

much loftier than the approximately 147 feet it does reach. Even the trees and shrubbery contribute to the illusion. Those at the timberline are far smaller than the ones at the bottom.

The ride itself, like the Space Mountain and Big Thunder Mountain Railroad attractions, has to be counted among the most thrilling at Disneyland. At the time the Matterhorn Bobsleds were dedicated, in 1959, they were considered an engineering novelty because their dispatch system allowed more than one car to be in action at once. The ride was also the world's first tubular steel roller coaster. This classic is also considered Disney's first thrill ride. The old favorite has enhanced snowcaps, lighting, and visual effects.

The somewhat jolting adventure begins with a climb into the frosty innards of the mountain, then makes a speeding, twisting, turning descent through a cloud of fog and past giant icicles and ice crystals. The wind howls as you hurtle toward a brief encounter with the Abominable Snowman (take note of the effects!). The speed of the downhill flight away from the creature seems greater than it really is because much of the journey takes place inside tunnels. Splash down is in an alpine lake.

Note: Pregnant women and guests who suffer from weak backs (the seats are hard and the ride is bumpy), heart conditions, motion sickness, or other physical limitations should not take the ride. Guests must be at least 42 inches tall. Children under age seven must be accompanied by an adult.

PHOTO BY JILL SAFRO

STORYBOOK LAND CANAL BOATS: This 7-minute cruise through Monstro the Whale and past miniature scenes from Disney's animated films is not one of Disneyland's major attractions, yet few who take the trip would deny that the journey is one of the park's sweetest. No detail was spared, from the homes of the Three Little Pigs, to the Old English village of *Alice in Wonderland* (where the White Rabbit boasts his very own mailbox), to the London park that Peter Pan and Tinker Bell flew over with Wendy, John, and Michael Darling on their journey to Never Land.

Other storybook locales include the marketplace where Aladdin met Princess Jasmine, the Seven Dwarfs' home and jewel mine, and Cinderella's castle. At the end of the cruise, the boat drifts past Geppetto's village, Prince Eric and Ariel's castle, King Triton's castle—and *Frozen's* Kingdom of Arendelle.

IT'S A SMALL WORLD: **MP** The background music for this attraction is cheerful and singsong, sometimes maddeningly so. It does grab your attention, starting with the cheery facade, embellished with stylized representations of the Eiffel Tower, the Leaning Tower of Pisa, Big Ben, the Taj Mahal, and other landmarks. The 30-foot-tall clock with the loud ticktock and the syncopated swing is frosting on the architectural cake. The whirring of gears that marks every quarter hour alone warrants a trip to the attraction's plaza.

Boats carry guests into a land filled with close to 300 Audio-Animatronics dolls representing children (and popular Disney characters) from 100 regions of the world. It's a pageant for the eyes, even if the ears grow weary. (If you find yourself humming "It's a Small World" for the next several hours, you can blame Richard M. and Robert B. Sherman, the Academy Award–winning composers of the music for *Mary Poppins,* among many other renowned Disney scores.)

Topiary (sculpted shrub) figures in the shapes of a giraffe, elephant, rhinoceros, lion, horse, and other friendly beasts bid guests farewell at ride's end.

Note that It's a Small World is transformed inside and out between Thanksgiving and New Year's to become as close to a winter wonderland as you're likely to find in Southern California. The dolls even sing "Jingle Bells" along with "It's a Small World."

PHOTO BY MIKE CARROLL

CASEY JR. CIRCUS TRAIN: One of the key sequences in the film *Dumbo*, in which an engine named Casey Jr. pulls a circus train up a steep hill, became the inspiration for this 3½-minute train ride that circles Storybook Land. The Storybook Land Canal Boats are better for viewing the landscaping and miniature details there, but it's worth a ride inside one of the wild-animal cage cars. Each train has two of them—plus a real caboose. Listen as the engine chugs, "I think I can" and then, "I thought I could" as it negotiates the hill.

DUMBO THE FLYING ELEPHANT: As cherished a symbol of Fantasyland as Sleeping Beauty Castle, this attraction reminds all who see it of the baby elephant immortalized in Disney's 1941 feature film. In it, Dumbo discovers that his large ears actually enable him to fly. A mechanical marvel, Dumbo the Flying Elephant is full of filigreed metalwork, with a system of cogs, gears, and pulleys. Brass pipes spew water from the base, and music is supplied by a vintage band organ housed in a small, ornate structure nearby. That tiny figure atop the ride is Dumbo's trusty sidekick, Timothy Q. Mouse.

PHOTO BY JILL SAFRO

SNOW WHITE'S ENCHANTED WISH: As guests enter this classic attraction, they gaze upon the pages of a storybook. It sets the stage for what's to come: "Once upon a time, a lovely princess named Snow White had a wish"—and it warns that the cruel Queen aims to thwart Snow's wish for happiness. It's a rather ominous start to a primarily pleasant adventure.

The two-minute journey begins with a visit to the Seven Dwarfs' unkempt cottage, where they're enjoying a dance party with Snow White (that's Grumpy playing the pipe organ!). From there, the story takes a very brief dark tone, as the ride vehicle whisks through the inky Enchanted Forest and past the dreaded Queen—who is clearly up to no good. The mood quickly lightens as Dopey, Doc, and their diminutive comrades head off to work. Heigh-ho, heigh-ho, it's off to the diamond mine everyone goes.

After passing through that short-but-happy scene, ride vehicles visit a darkened chamber where the evil Queen engages with her magic mirror and morphs into a wicked witch before your very eyes. She's next seen laboring over a bubbling cauldron, perfecting the poison apple into which Snow White promptly bites. A mirror shatters! A storm hits the Forest! And then, *poof*—it all ends in true storybook fashion: Snow White awakens, and with her Prince and their seven sidekicks, is set to live happily ever after. Her wish has come true.

Note: While dark moments in this attraction can be too intense for some children, recent enhancements make the adventure a little less scary.

PINOCCHIO'S DARING JOURNEY: Based on Disney's 1940 animated feature, this is a 3-minute morality play of sorts, with Jiminy Cricket serving as host and guide. Pinocchio, who is the creation of the toy maker Geppetto, pays a somewhat scary visit to Pleasure Island and soon discovers the right way to live.

As the ride vehicles whisk guests from the cheerful land of popcorn and Ferris wheels to the seamy world of Tobacco Road, Pleasure Island hues are replaced with dreary shades of brown and gray. Here, little boys are turned into donkeys and sold to work in the salt mines.

PHOTO BY MIKE CARROLL

Pinocchio escapes that fate, nearly becomes supper for Monstro the Whale, and winds up back home in the care of his dad, Geppetto—another happily-ever-after ending. The final scene, in which the Blue Fairy turns into a cloud of sparkles and then disappears, leaving a smattering of sparkly pixie dust on the floor, is partially accomplished via fiber optics.

KING ARTHUR CARROUSEL: Guests come upon this graceful park landmark as they stroll toward the Sleeping Beauty Castle passageway into Fantasyland. One of the few attractions in the park that is an original rather than a Disney adaptation, the carrousel contains 68 horses—all movable, as Walt Disney wished. Crafted over a century ago, no two are alike, and they are as pampered as the live Belgian horses on Main Street, U.S.A. The ornamentation on them is gold, silver, and copper leaf. The nine hand-painted panels on top of the carrousel's main face tell the story of Princess Aurora, aka Sleeping Beauty.

PHOTO BY JILL SAFRO

LIGHTNING LANE ATTRACTIONS

Long lines got you down? Not to worry—many major Disneyland attractions offer Lightning Lane Access (fees apply). The Disneyland park attractions listed here may change and Lightning Lane service may not be offered at all times during the year.

Lightning Lanes may be accessed two ways: Lightning Lane Multi Pass and Lightning Lane Single Pass. You may purchase one, both, or neither (standby lines are always available!)

The following attractions fall into the Multi Pass category (one daily fee covers them all, except for Star Wars: Rise of the Resistance). At press time, it was designated a Lightning Lane Single Pass attraction and comes with a separate fee. (Lightning Lane Single Pass attractions are not included with Multi Pass). For additional info about the Lightning Lane attraction access system, see page 22 and visit *disneyland.com*. All details are subject to change.

ADVENTURELAND
• Indiana Jones Adventure

BAYOU COUNTRY
• Tiana's Bayou Adventure

FANTASYLAND
• Matterhorn Bobsleds • It's a Small World

FRONTIERLAND
• Big Thunder Mountain Railroad

MICKEY'S TOONTOWN
• Roger Rabbit's Car Toon Spin
• Mickey & Minnie's Runaway Railway

NEW ORLEANS SQUARE
• Haunted Mansion

TOMORROWLAND
• Space Mountain • Autopia
• Star Tours—The Adventures Continue
• Buzz Lightyear Astro Blasters

STAR WARS: GALAXY'S EDGE
• *Millennium Falcon*: Smugglers Run
• Star Wars: Rise of the Resistance
(available for Lightning Lane Single Pass)

Mickey's Toontown

Disneyland lore tells us that when Mickey Mouse burst onto the movie scene in 1928 in *Steamboat Willie*, the first synchronized-sound cartoon, his success was so great that his busy schedule demanded he practically live at the Walt Disney Studios. Thirty cartoons later, in the early 1930s, he was one tired mouse, so he moved into a quiet residence in a "toon only" community south of Hollywood. Over the years, many toon stars gravitated to Mickey's Toontown, as it quickly became known. Mickey, Minnie, and Goofy have long maintained homes here, and Donald Duck docks his boat, the *Miss Daisy*, on his neighbor's pond. Other toons known to frequent this land: Daisy, Pluto, Clarabelle, and Pete.

One afternoon, while Mickey Mouse and his close friend Walt Disney were relaxing on Mickey's front porch, Walt revealed his idea for a theme park that would appeal to "youngsters of all ages." Mickey suggested that he build it next to the secret entrance to Toontown, and the rest is history. Disneyland opened to the public in 1955, but little did anyone realize as they were drifting through It's a Small World that they were actually right next door to Mickey's Toontown.

In the 1990s, Mickey and his friends decided to open up their neighborhood to non-toons, and, in preparation, all of Toontown received a new coat of ink and paint.

Legend aside, the development of Toontown was a real challenge: to create a three-dimensional cartoon environment without a single straight line. Yet, as topsy-turvy as it is, Mickey's Toontown is a complete community, with a downtown area, including a commercial zone, a suburban neighborhood (home to everyone's favorite mice), and CenTOONial Park. The best part is that everything is meant to be touched, climbed, and jumped on. Children do just that, while adults relish the attention to detail and the assortment of sight gags. All guests are welcome to relax under a majestic tree in the park, which is just one of the enhancements to enjoy now that this cheery place has been re-imagined. (After a thorough refreshment, the grand reopening of this land took place on March 19, 2023.)

This booming toontropolis is home to a cluster of youngster-friendly attractions—including Mickey & Minnie's Runaway Railway, Goofy's How-to-Play Yard, and Donald's Duck Pond (a splash zone where Donald anchors his boat), plus opportunities to dine and play.

Guests enter this colorful zone by walking under the Toontown train depot. You never know just what to expect once inside—but it's all bound to be goofy! Note that Toontown tends to keep shorter hours than the rest of the park.

PHOTO BY JILL SAFRO

CENTOONIAL PARK: As guests cross the border from Fantasyland to Mickey's Toontown, they enter a sprawling nature-inspired zone dubbed CenTOONial Park. This grassy space is a great place for families to play, relax, and unplug. In the heart of the park stands an interactive fountain that pays tribute to Toontown's most famous residents: Mickey and Minnie. The fountain does double duty as the land's central icon and a focal point for fun. In addition to the usual fountain-y features, this spot sports several interactive water tables. Guests of all ages are encouraged to splish and splash till their hearts' content. At night, this special spray spot comes to life in a "unique spectacle" of color and light.

Another landmark of note is the majestic "Dreaming Tree." It was inspired by the tree that Walt Disney used to dream under when he was a kid. Toontown's leafy homage to Walt's original tree supplies shade, inspiration, plus a plethora of places for kids to crawl, climb, explore, and—of course—dream.

ROGER RABBIT'S CAR TOON SPIN: MP This chaotic, rollicking ride combines the technology of the Mad Tea Party teacups and the tracks of Fantasyland attractions such as Mr. Toad's Wild Ride. In it, Lenny the cab (Benny's "twin" cousin), Jessica Rabbit, and Roger Rabbit embark on a dizzying chase, which takes guests through the back

alleys of the toon underworld made famous in the classic feature film *Who Framed Roger Rabbit.*

It seems Jessica Rabbit, who is now a private eye, is on a mission to thwart the evil weasels (while avoiding the dreaded DIP!) and she takes you along for the ride. During the 3-minute adventure, expect to crash into Bullina's China Shop, slide through the Power House, and spin wildly into the Gag Warehouse storage area, where the Weasels are waiting to take aim at your cab.

This "hare-raising" attraction is fun for all ages, but it does have some dark moments that may spook timid tots. Note that the ride vehicles can spin a full 360 degrees as they travel along the track. If the whirling teacups over in Fantasyland make your head spin (or worse), you should probably sit this one out. And please don't eat just before climbing aboard Lenny.

MINNIE'S HOUSE: It's hard to miss Minnie Mouse's humble abode. This lavender-and-pink creation has a sweetheart theme for the sweetheart inside. Here, guests can peek at Minnie's living room with its chintz sofa and sophisticated magazines (*Cosmousepolitan* and *Mademouselle*) on the coffee table.

There are messages from Goofy and Mickey on the answering machine in the hallway. Guests are invited to create new fashions for Minnie on the computer in her dressing room.

In Minnie's kitchen, a cake in the oven rises when a knob is turned, pots and pans clank out a melody when the stove is switched on, and the dishwasher churns after a button is pushed. Her fancy Cheesemore refrigerator is stocked with an assortment of dairy products, including

Golly Cheeze Whiz, and the shopping list left on the outside of the fridge hints at this mouse's cheeses of choice. Be sure to check out the cookies on Minnie's kitchen table (and be prepared for a sweet practical joke, courtesy of Ms. Mouse).

As you leave Minnie's House, you'll pass the wishing well in her yard. Don't think you're imagining things: It's been known to share a few parting thoughts.

MICKEY'S HOUSE: A short path leads from Minnie's backyard to the front door of Mickey's House. The welcoming yellow dwelling with a tile roof, huge green door, and green shutters is home to the toon who started it all. Not only is Mickey's face on the mailbox out front, but his welcome mat is in the instantly recognizable shape of three circles—his head and ears.

In the living room stands a player piano and a curio cabinet filled with all manner of memorabilia, including Mickey's baby shoes and a picture of him with his friend Walt Disney, as well as some of Pluto's favorite

PHOTO BY JILL SAFRO

treasures—a bone and a half-eaten shoe. In the laundry room, the washing machine chugs merrily away, and laundry supplies, such as Comics Cleanser and Mouse 'n' Glo, are at the ready.

From here, make your way through the greenhouse and into Mickey's backyard, where you may catch a glimpse of Pluto's doghouse and a vegetable garden with mysteriously disappearing carrots. If you'd like to meet Mickey Mouse, be sure to visit the movie barn out back. He's there to greet guest throughout the day.

CHIP 'N' DALE'S GADGETCOASTER: Gadget Hackwrench is a brilliant inventor. (You may recognize her from *Chip 'n' Dale Rescue Rangers*). Her latest creation is a one-of-a-kind mini-thriller crafted for the denizens of Toontown and its venturesome visitors.

Gadget, the ultimate recycler, created this coaster from an assortment of gizmos that once served other purposes. Gigantic toy blocks are now support beams for the tracks; hollowed-out acorns have become the cars of the train; and bridges have been created from giant combs, Popsicle sticks, golf tees, pencils, paper clips, and such. The thick steel tracks give the impression of a tame ride, but there are a few thrills, right up to the final turn into the station.

Note: Guests must be at least 35 inches tall to experience Chip 'n' Dale's GADGETcoaster. Those under age 7 must be accompanied by someone age 14 or older. It may be a small coaster, but the 51-second ride is wilder than one might expect. Pregnant folks should skip the trip.

GOOFY'S HOW-TO-PLAY YARD: Our good friend Goofy has one honey of hobby: candy-making! In fact, he's such an enthusiast that his house was built around a giant candy-creating contraption. Sound like something you would like to get your hands on? Well, go right ahead. Goofy is a very hospitable fellow and his interactive Toontown abode is always open to Disneyland visitors. Sweet!

Youngsters (ages 2 to 12) are invited to explore the Goof's How-to-Play Yard, too. Dedicated to all things play related, the yard features an elevated clubhouse, plus a sound garden—where visitors can discover whimsical ways to produce wacky noises. Another aspect of note at Goofy's homestead? A pond large enough to fit his pal Donald's boat.

DONALD'S DUCK POND: Everyone's favorite seafaring fowl has docked his boat (aka the *Miss Daisy*) in Donald's Duck Pond (which is technically on Goofy's property, but that's for them to sort out). The vessel sports larger-than-life spinning water lilies, balance beams,

ROOTS OF THE DREAMING TREE

Toontown's newest landmark, The Dreaming Tree, was inspired by a majestic Cottonwood that once stood in Marceline, Missouri. When Walt Disney was a young kid, he would often lie under the tree and daydream beneath its dappled, heart-shaped leaves. He named it The Dreaming Tree and considered it the birthplace of his imagination.

Walt had many imaginative adventures in the shadow of The Dreaming Tree. He and his little sister, Ruth, liked to study birds, bugs, and nature while under the tree—and enjoyed splashing about in a nearby spring.

As a grown-up, Walt often visited his childhood home of Marceline. While there, he'd always make time to sit beneath his old friend, The Dreaming Tree. Today, thanks to saplings from the tree, a new Cottonwood grows near where the original once stood. This "Son of The Dreaming Tree" has two siblings: one is in the Lakota Village in Disneyland park (it's behind a large teepee and can be seen from the *Mark Twain* riverboat, the Sailing Ship *Columbia*, and Davy Crockett Explorer Canoes), and the other is kept safe in a top-secret location (at the ready to spawn more saplings to sustain the family tree).

And now a fourth version of The Dreaming Tree has been added to Mickey's Toontown. Meant as a tribute to Walt and the roots of his imagination, it's here to inspire the dreamer in all of us.

and rocking toys that should garner giggles from your littles. Guests may peer into the boat via portholes, enjoy "bubbles of fun" inside, and frolic beside familiar ducklings Huey, Louie, Dewey, and Webby.

BIRNBAUM'S ★BEST★ MICKEY & MINNIE'S RUNAWAY RAILWAY: MP Prepare to enter a wild and wacky cartoon realm via Mickey & Minnie's Runaway Railway—a fanciful, family-friendly attraction that chugged its way into Mickey's Toontown in January of 2023. Housed inside a spiffy theater, the "2.5-D" (no glasses required) adventure begins with the premiere of a new cartoon that guests watch in the pre-show area. In it, Mickey and Minnie are preparing for a picnic. When a train driven by Goofy pulls up beside them, it's all aboard for everyone! Thanks to a bit of movie magic, guests are invited to step into the action and enter the zany, unpredictable world of a Mickey Mouse Cartoon Short. The train zigs and zags through multiple scenes, while a happy tune underscores the jolly journey. ("Nothing

Can Stop Us Now" is a gift that keeps on giving—you will be humming the optimistic earworm long after the ride comes to an end).

In addition to dozens (possibly hundreds?) of Hidden Mickeys, this delightful experience features a bounty of Easter eggs for eagle-eyed Disney fans—including the number 1928 (the year our friends Mickey and Minnie entered the world).

There is no height requirement to enjoy Mickey & Minnie's Runaway Railway. The attraction is suitable—and enjoyable—for guests of all ages. The experience can be a tad herky-jerky (especially while the ride vehicle weathers a cyclone). Folks with back or neck issues may want to avoid this adventure. At press time, this attraction offered a standby queue, and Lightning Lane service (via Multi Pass). Details are subject to change. For updates, use the Disneyland app, or visit *disneyland.com*.

Tomorrowland

When Walt Disney was alive, the future seemed simple: We would all dress in Mylar and travel in flying saucers. The Tomorrowland he created in the '50s was set in the distant year of 1987, part Buck Rogers and part World's Fair. The current incarnation of Tomorrowland retains that spirit and is based on a classic vision of the future, one that looks at it from the perspective of the past. The result is an innocent and hopeful place—imagine, for instance, a planet that renews itself. Visit Tomorrowland today, and you enter a realm more in keeping with the rest of Disneyland than with the sterile, less positive future world often depicted on television and in the movies.

Cross the bridge into this sleek land and enter a visually engaging terrain, where the palette of colors is not otherworldly, but still forward-thinking. Futuristic boulders and dreamlike architecture coexist with apple, orange, lemon, and pomegranate trees that line pathways created from gray, mauve, and burgundy bricks. This landscape aims to fire up the intellect as well as the imagination.

Galileo Galilei, Leonardo da Vinci, Jules Verne, H.G. Wells, and Walt Disney would have felt right at home here. Aldous Huxley probably wouldn't have. Several of Tomorrowland's attractions are also located at Walt Disney World in Florida: Space Mountain, Star Tours—The Adventures Continue, Astro Orbitor, and Buzz Lightyear Astro Blasters (known in Walt Disney World as Buzz Lightyear's Space Ranger Spin). Other classic Tomorrowland attractions include the Finding Nemo Submarine Voyage, the Disneyland Monorail, and Autopia.

A replica of the Moonliner, a Tomorrowland icon from 1955 to 1966, sits on the site of its predecessor. Monorail trains glide to and from the Downtown Disney District, while traditional Disneyland Railroad trains chug their way into the Tomorrowland station, a vibrant reminder that the past is indeed prologue. (The Disneyland Railroad has stations at Main Street, U.S.A., New Orleans Square, and Mickey's Toontown, too).

Attractions described on the following pages were operating at press time, but specifics are subject to change. Check *disneyland.com* for updates.

PHOTO BY JILL SAFRO

ASTRO ORBITOR: Towering high above the entrance to Tomorrowland, this big whirligig with spinning orbs and speeding starships is a fitting symbol for Tomorrowland. Astro Orbitor, modeled on a drawing made by Leonardo da Vinci almost six centuries ago, is the successor to the Rocket Jets, which gave Disneyland guests a lift for 30 years. Each ride vehicle accommodates two passengers (or two adults and one small child), who can maneuver it up and down while spinning clockwise for 1½ minutes, reveling in sweeping views of Tomorrowland, (Main Street's) Central Plaza, the Matterhorn, and Sleeping Beauty Castle.

Note: The minimum age to ride Astro Orbitor is one year. Children under the age of 7 are required to be in the company of an adult.

BIRNBAUM'S ★BEST★ **BUZZ LIGHTYEAR ASTRO BLASTERS:** **MP** The evil Emperor Zurg is up to no good—and it's up to that Space Ranger extraordinaire Buzz Lightyear and his Junior Space Rangers (that means you) to save the day.

So goes the story line of Tomorrowland's video game–inspired spin through the toy universe. The adventure is experienced from a toy's point of view. Guests begin their 4½-minute tour of duty as Space Rangers at Star Command Action Center. This is where Buzz gives his team a briefing on the mission that lies ahead. Then it's off to the Launch Bay to board the ride vehicles. The ships feature dual laser cannons, glowing lights, and a piloting joystick.

In addition to Buzz and the evil Emperor, you may recognize some other toy faces swirling about—the little

HOT TIP

To maximize your scoring potential at Buzz Lightyear Astro Blasters, aim for targets that are lit up, moving, or far away. They tend to reward you with the most points.

green, multi-eyed alien toys, best known for their awe of "the claw." The Little Green Men have been enlisted to help in the fight against Zurg.

Once Junior Space Rangers blast off, they find themselves surrounded by Zurg's robots, who are mercilessly ripping batteries from toys. As Rangers fire at targets, beams of light fill the air. For every target hit, you will be rewarded with sight gags, sound effects, and points. The points, which are tallied automatically, are accumulated throughout the journey. Although the vehicles follow a rigid "flight" path (they're on a track), the joystick allows riders to maneuver the ships, arcing from side to side or spinning in circles while taking aim at their surroundings.

PHOTO BY JILL SAFRO

When the star cruiser arrives at Zurg's spaceship, it's showdown time. Will good ultimately prevail over evil? Or has time run out for the toy universe? And will you score enough points to be a Galactic Hero? (Most folks improve their scores with a little practice.)

BIRNBAUM'S ★BEST★ **STAR TOURS—THE ADVENTURES CONTINUE:** **MP** Inspired by George Lucas's beloved blockbuster series of Star Wars films, this is one of the most enjoyable attractions in Tomorrowland. It offers guests the opportunity to ride on droid-piloted StarSpeeders—the exact same type of flight simulator used by military and commercial airlines to train pilots—and explore the galaxy in a bumpy 3-D adventure. The action here takes place throughout the time period covered by the major Star Wars movies and TV shows. The best part? There are dozens of different adventures to experience and new scenes may be added at any time. (Characters from *Ahsoka, Andor,* and *The Mandalorian* were the most recent additions.) Multiple visits will undoubtedly yield multiple surprises.

This is a rather turbulent trip—seat belts are definitely required. Passengers must be free of back problems, heart conditions, motion sickness, and other physical limitations to ride. Guests under 40 inches tall may not ride. Pregnant women must skip this one. Make sure young children understand the significance of wearing 3-D glasses (and keeping them on) before you board the attraction—it's a concept lost on most tots. Battle scenes and sudden appearances by Star Wars villains have been known to spook little ones.

STAR WARS LAUNCH BAY: Star Wars Launch Bay offers an immersive atmosphere in which to experience both the Light and Dark sides. Housed in the space formerly occupied by Innoventions, Launch Bay features props, videos, and movie memorabilia celebrating Star Wars and the recently reawakened Force. In addition to Light and Dark galleries, guests may meet characters such as everyone's favorite Wookiee, Chewbacca and that menacing Sith Lord, Darth Vader. Star Wars Launch Bay may not be open in all of 2026. Use the Disneyland app, or check *disneyland.com* for updates.

BIRNBAUM'S ★BEST★ **SPACE MOUNTAIN:** MP When Space Mountain first opened in 1977, it quickly rocketed to the top of just about everyone's list of favorite attractions—where it remains to this day. While the classic facade and essence of the thrilling attraction remain intact, the experience is decidedly 21st century. Brave voyagers blast off from a realistic

launch port. Once they've shot through a disorienting tunnel, riders may have a close encounter with a meteorite. After that, it's all about screeching through the inky darkness, past spinning stars and whirling galaxies. Add to that an edgy soundtrack (which is impressively synchronized to each ride vehicle), and you have got one out-of-this-world attraction.

If your courage fails you, just ask an attendant to direct you to the nearest escape route (aka "the chicken exit"). Space Mountain is an astronomically popular attraction—get there early and take advantage of Disney's Lightning Lane service if budget allows.

Note: Pregnant women and guests who have weak backs or necks, heart conditions, motion sickness, or any other physical limitations must sit this one out. Kids under age 7 must be accompanied by an adult. Guests must be at least 40 inches tall to experience Space Mountain.

F.Y.I.: *Mercury 9* and *Gemini 5* astronaut Gordon Cooper worked with Disney Imagineers to create Space Mountain. He wanted to give guests a realistic feeling of actual space flight. Mission accomplished!

AUTOPIA: MP The only attraction remaining from the original Tomorrowland, Autopia was dubbed "The Freeway of the Future" back in 1955. Kids have always loved guiding the small sports cars around the twisting roadways (for them, a top speed of seven miles per hour is thrilling). The Tomorrowland and Fantasyland roadways now comprise a single attraction (yes, there were two Autopias; the one in Fantasyland opened in 1959 to accommodate spillover crowds). Guests travel in restyled race cars through 21st-century terrain, experiencing a series of happy roadside surprises along the way. Featuring a real working gas pedal and steering wheel, each car can seat 2 adults or 3 children and navigates curves and inclines just like the real thing. Don't let the lack of a brake pedal scare you—to slow down or stop the car, simply ease off the accelerator. This attraction is quite popular with those who've not yet reached Driver's Ed age.

Note: Guests must be at least 54 inches tall to drive solo. Park-goers who are at least 32 inches tall are also permitted to drive, as long as they are accompanied by someone who is at least 54 inches tall. Kids under age 7 must be accompanied by someone at least 14 years of age. Pregnant women; guests with heart, back, or neck problems; and those sensitive to motion should not ride. Intentionally bumping the vehicle in front of you is not allowed.

PHOTO BY MIKE CARROLL

DISNEYLAND MONORAIL: Who doesn't love the monorail? The first daily operating monorail in the Western Hemisphere was a novelty when it was introduced at Disneyland in 1959. Today, it's still a thrill to watch them glide through the park. The sleek, Mark VII trains were designed to evoke images of their 1959 predecessors. Straddling a concrete beamway, the monorail has rubber tires—which enable it to glide quietly—as well as braking wheels atop the concrete beam and guiding and stabilizing wheels on either side.

The 2½-mile-long "highway in the sky" is a distinctive and integral part of Tomorrowland. The electrically powered ride takes guests around the periphery of Tomorrowland, over to Downtown Disney and its diverting activities, and then back to Tomorrowland.

For a special experience, inform the cast member on the boarding ramp that you'd like to sit up front in the pilot's cabin. It can usually accommodate up to five passengers. If all the seats are taken, you can always wait for the next monorail and try your luck again.

By boarding the monorail in Tomorrowland, you are actually leaving Disneyland Park. If you get off at the Downtown Disney station, be sure to retain your valid park ticket. You will need to show it (and photo ID) to reboard the monorail or pass through Disneyland Park's turnstiles. Know that walking back to the park is an option—as Disneyland is about a 5-minute stroll from the Downtown Disney monorail station.

FINDING NEMO SUBMARINE VOYAGE: Uh-oh. It seems that curious little clownfish has wandered off again. And this time he's done so in Tomorrowland's submarine lagoon. The good news is the subs that used to take guests to the North Pole now provide the perfect means for monitoring the fin-challenged fish and his high-spirited underwater hijinks.

The submarine adventure begins as a quiet expedition to observe an undersea volcano. But faster than you can say, "All drains lead to the ocean," our frisky friends from *Finding Nemo* start floating and fluttering in front of a personal porthole. The whole gang's here, including Nemo's overprotective dad, Marlin; the faithful-if-forgetful royal blue tang, Dory; that totally awesome turtle dude, Crush; and more. They're on a quest to catch up with their buddy Nemo, and you're invited along for the slightly frenetic, completely kinetic undersea search. Oh, and remember that volcano you were going to observe? It erupts.

Will you survive the sub-shaking volcanic quaking and find Nemo? Yep. They don't call this "The Happiest Place on Earth" for nothing.

The relatively gentle, underwater experience is appropriate for guests of all ages, provided they're claustrophobia-free. A few moments may be too intense for some tots.

HOT TIP

A trip on the monorail yields lovely views of Disney California Adventure park and its neighbor, the Grand Californian Hotel & Spa. However, it does not stop at either place. It's strictly a Tomorrowland Express!

Star Wars: Galaxy's Edge

There's an out-of-this-world adventure zone waiting to be explored in Disneyland Park—Star Wars: Galaxy's Edge! The land is set on the planet Batuu, a remote outpost on the far reaches of the galaxy. As the story goes, Batuu was once a busy crossroads along the old sub-light-speed trade routes. Now, thanks to the rise of hyperspace travel, Batuu has pretty much fallen off the radar. It's far from deserted, however. In fact, the largest settlement on the planet, Black Spire Outpost, has become quite the haven for folks who prefer to fly under the radar: smugglers, rogue traders, and space-traveling adventurers. It's also an excellent destination for anyone trying to avoid the First Order.

The land is accessed via pathways connected with Fantasyland, Bayou Country, and Frontierland. There are two major attractions here—*Millennium Falcon*: Smugglers Run and Star Wars: Rise of the Resistance. Each invites guests to live out their own Star Wars adventures.

BIRNBAUM'S ★BEST★ **MILLENNIUM FALCON: SMUGGLERS RUN:** **MP** Are you eager to jump into hyperspace on the "fastest hunk of junk in the galaxy"? Here's your chance to fly in Han Solo's beloved bucket of bolts, the *Millennium Falcon!*

It seems Hondo (from the animated shows *Star Wars: The Clone Wars* and *Star Wars Rebels*) is now running a "legitimate business" out of a spaceport and he needs extra flight crews to make some runs for him—provided they don't ask too many questions, of course. That's where you come in.

Before entering the cockpit of the legendary starship, you and five fellow crew members are assigned a role. There are three roles (pilot, gunner, and engineer) and one goal: complete the mission without banging up the ship. At the end of the thrilling (and bumpy) flight, your crew will receive a point total—and a few choice words from Hondo himself.

Guests must be at least 38 inches tall to ride this attraction and should be free of motion sickness and any other health issues. Expectant mothers are advised to skip *Millennium Falcon*: Smugglers Run.

BIRNBAUM'S ★BEST★ **STAR WARS: RISE OF THE RESISTANCE:** What happens when Star Wars heroes and villains end up on the same planet? A *massive* battle breaks out!

In one of the most ambitious adventures ever produced by Walt Disney Imagineering, this immersive attraction places you in the middle of an epic battle between the First Order and the Resistance—including a face-off with the infamous Kylo Ren.

The journey takes guests aboard a full-size transport shuttle and a Star Destroyer. It's a thrilling and harrowing adventure—and not for the faint of heart. To ride, guests should be free of health issues (including, but not limited to, pregnancy and motion sickness), and at least 40 inches tall.

Note: At press time, Rise of the Resistance was a Lightning Lane Single Pass attraction. As such, it has a traditional standby line to ride (included with the price of admission) and offers an expedited wait time for a fee (purchased through the Disneyland mobile app). For details, use the app or visit *disneyland.com,* and refer to page 22.

Shopping

Until you get to know Disneyland park, you might not expect that anyone would visit just to go shopping. But among Southern Californians, it's definitely a top draw for the Disney-themed merchandise and gift items. Mickey Mouse paraphernalia, such as key chains, mugs, T-shirts, ear hats, and other souvenirs, is found here in abundance, of course, but there may be surprises along the lines of character-inspired costumes for youngsters, mobile phone accessories and items for the office, plus assorted upscale items (art collectibles, jewelry, products for the home, and custom-made lightsabers, etc.).

MAIN STREET, U.S.A.

CANDY PALACE: An old-fashioned pageant in pink and white, this candy kitchen is enticing at any time of day, but never more than when the candymakers are at work in the glass-walled display kitchen confecting candy canes, caramel apples, toffee, fudge, and many other sweet temptations for anyone with a sweet tooth. Many of the products made on the premises are available for purchase, along with a veritable bounty of chocolates, licorice, taffy, and other tasty treats.

CHINA CLOSET: If you're in the market for kitchenware, mugs, figurines, picture frames, snow globes, or Christmas ornaments, this is the place to go.

CRYSTAL ARTS: Glasses and pitchers, frames, trays, and other sparkly mementos can be engraved (for an added fee) and monogrammed while you wait, or you can get them without personalization. The shop also sells tiaras, glass miniatures, bells, and paperweights.

DISNEY CLOTHIERS, LTD.: Disney character merchandise has always been popular, but if you want something a little more stylish, this is where to find it. The spot caters to fashion-conscious shoppers with a love for Disney-themed gear. Almost every item in the selection of men's, women's, and children's clothing and accessories sold here incorporates Mickey and Minnie in some way.

DISNEY SHOWCASE: Specializing in the latest seasonal merchandise (Disney style), this shop also offers hats, shirts, home decor items, park logo merchandise, and assorted souvenirs. Personalization is offered (for a fee).

DISNEYANA: Serious collectors and the simply curious alike will discover rare and unusual Disney merchandise here, such as limited-edition art and hand-painted cels inspired by Disney animated classics. Popular pieces have included sculptures from the Walt Disney Classics Collection. This amusing shop is in what was once the Bank of Main Street building, next to the Opera House.

   Note: Disney artists often drop by the shop to sign reproduction artwork, sculptures, recently published books, and other items.

EMPORIUM: Much like an old-time variety store, this large and bustling shop offers an incredible assortment of wares, and it is home to Disneyland logo selections. Decorative figurines, mugs, home decor, clothing, plush toys, character hats, jewelry, and a variety of souvenirs make up the bulk of the stock.

PHOTO BY JILL SAFRO

PHOTO BY JILL SAFRO

FORTUOSITY SHOP: Merchandise in all shapes and sizes, including trendy fashions and accessories like Mickey Mouse watches and character-laden novelty clocks, beckons from this unique emporium.

MAD HATTER: This hat shop stocks Mickey Mouse ear hats in black and various colors and designs. You can even get your name stitched on the back.

MAIN STREET MAGIC SHOP: Small but well stocked with gags and tricks—and books about how to pull them off—this shop has the wherewithal to inspire budding illusionists. In the market for an invisible pooch? A magic wand? An ice cube with a bug in it? This corner store just may have it.

MARKET HOUSE: This Disneyland version of an old-fashioned general store is actually a cleverly themed Starbucks coffee shop. Stop here for fresh-brewed coffee and specialty drinks, plus cookies, cake pops, sandwiches, salads, savory snacks, and much more.

NEW CENTURY JEWELRY: Among the delicate offerings here are 14-karat-gold charms of Tinker Bell, Donald Duck, Minnie Mouse, and/or other subjects. The marcasite character jewelry is subtle and somewhat sophisticated.

NEWSSTAND: While no actual news is offered here (no news is good news, right?), this modest stand stocks a

small selection of Disney-themed souvenir items.

PENNY ARCADE: Adjacent to the Gibson Girl Ice Cream Parlor is a virtual Coney Island of food and fun. Freshly made treats fill ornate shelves, and scrumptious salt-water taffy is available in an array of flavors. To add to the classic carnival atmosphere, old-fashioned arcade games that still cost just a penny to play and a Welte Orchestrion line the walls. And for 25 cents, you can have beloved fortune teller Esmeralda predict your future.

PLAZA POINT HOLIDAY SHOPPE: A Victorian-era emporium, Plaza Point is holiday central all year long. Festooned with garlands and festive decor, the space celebrates a host of holidays, including (but certainly not limited to): Hanukkah, Lunar New Year, Easter, Halloween, and Christmas. Stop here to discover ornaments, housewares, linens, and accessories—all with a holiday theme.

SILHOUETTE STUDIO: Working at the rate of about 90 seconds per portrait, Disneyland's silhouette artists truly are a wonder to behold. Individual and group portraits are available.

20TH CENTURY MUSIC COMPANY: This little place carries a selection of collector pins and pin lanyards, plus books and classic Disney music.

NEW ORLEANS SQUARE

CRISTAL D'ORLEANS: Glasses and chandeliers, tiaras, decanters, glass slippers, pitchers, and paperweights are typical treasures here. Engraving (and some mono-gramming) is available for a fee.

EUDORA'S CHIC BOUTIQUE: Tiana has teamed up with her mom, Eudora, to create this special shop—and share some gourmet secrets. Within their epicurean emporium you'll find cookbooks, beignet mixes, chowder bowls, fancy oyster knives, and other handy household items. You're likely to discover *Princess and the Frog*–inspired clothing and accessories, too.

LA MASCARADE D'ORLEANS: A compact and brightly lit showcase for Pandora products, this shop has a variety of its signature items: necklaces, earrings, rings, and charm bracelets—many with a Disney theme. In fact, some items are part of the Disney Parks Collection.

GET YOUR EARS DONE HERE

Since Disneyland first opened in 1955, there has been no more coveted souvenir than a pair of Mickey Mouse ears personalized with the lucky owner's name. And never have there been more styles from which to choose. Most hats can be embroidered (for a nominal fee) at both locations of the Mad Hatter (in Fantasyland and on Main Street, U.S.A.), and other select locations. Shops will not embroider company names on hats. (Note that it's possible to get ear hats at World of Disney in the Downtown Disney District and at a shop in Disney California Adventure park, too.)

NEW MADAME LEOTA'S SOMEWHERE BEYOND: Welcome, foolish mortals, to this delightfully mystical shop. Located just outside the Haunted Mansion attraction, Leota offers goods themed to said spooky attraction. There is also a selection of merchandise inspired by *Tim Burton's Nightmare Before Christmas*.

MLLE. ANTOINETTE'S PARFUMERIE: This pleasantly fragrant boutique carries classic and chic fragrances for men and women. The parfumerie "blends the essence of French-style elegance with American-style spontaneity." It's in the heart of New Orleans Square.

PIECES OF EIGHT: Wares with a pirate theme are purveyed at this shop beside the Pirates of the Caribbean exit. You will also discover T-shirts, key chains, glasses, and other souvenir items imprinted with the Pirates of the Caribbean logo.

PORT ROYAL CURIOS AND CURIOSITIES: Ready to give your treasured Mickey Mouse T-shirt a day off? Stop at this boutique to augment your Disney-oriented closet. Expect to find shirts, hats, scarves, jewelry, and more.

PORTRAIT ARTISTS: Sit for a portrait—done in pastel or watercolor—amidst the quaint charm of a New Orleans *rue* (street). Individual and group portraits are offered.

FRONTIERLAND

BONANZA OUTFITTERS: Oozing rustic ambience, this cozy yet quaint shop offers traditional frontier-wear with a trendy twist. Look for cowboy hats and coonskin caps. They sell a variety of collector pins and Disney-themed merchandise, too.

PIONEER MERCANTILE: Inspired by the paraphernalia of the pioneer period in American history, this shop is home to a vast array of Disneyland merchandise. Expect to find plush toys, shirts, books, bags, towels, and more. There's a large selection of headwear, too. Have a quarter handy? Drop it in the shop's classic Ho-Down machine and watch Woody dance! Details are subject to change.

WESTWARD HO TRADING COMPANY: This rustic store stocks something for the whole pin-trading frontier family, including pins, lanyards, and other pin-collecting accoutrements. We dig the antler light fixtures— Gaston would likely approve.

MICKEY'S TOONTOWN

ENGINEAR SOUVENIRS: Conveniently stationed at the exit of Mickey & Minnie's Runaway Railway, this shop stocks items themed to the attraction, plus some nifty souvenirs (or souven-ears!).

BAYOU COUNTRY

NEW LOUIS' CRITTER CLUB: Stop at this spot for apparel, accessories, toys, and home goods featuring favorite cuddly critters and Princess Tiana. The Critter Club inhabits the left side of Pooh Corner, near the exit of Tiana's Bayou Adventure.

POOH CORNER: This *hunny* of a store is home to a candy kitchen filled with sweet treats. Lining its many shelves are other Disneyland logo merchandise and items with a Winnie the Pooh theme. Pooh's pals from the Hundred Acre Wood are also represented. Look for plush toys, children's clothing, items for infants, sleep shirts, slippers, etc. There is also a sumptuous selection of freshly baked cookies and chocolates.

NEW RAY'S BERETS: The famous firefly from *The Princess and the Frog* operates a hat shop in a cozy Bayou Country cabin. In addition to headwear, Ray offers plush toys, accessories, and other keepsakes.

STAR WARS: GALAXY'S EDGE

BLACK SPIRE OUTFITTERS: Guests who'd like to blend in on Batuu can suit up at this boutique. Costumes that represent the light and dark sides of the Force are available for guests of all ages.

CREATURE STALL: Stop here to adopt an otherworldly pet. Creatures from which to choose include tentacle-beast rathtars, cooing baby tauntauns, tongue-lashing worrt frogs, and growling puffer pigs.

DOK-ONDAR'S DEN OF ANTIQUITIES: The mysterious Dok-Ondar has stuffed this shop with everything from jewelry and ancient tools to rare kyber crystals, statues, and high-end lightsabers.

DROID DEPOT: If you have ever dreamed of owning your own droid, dream no more: Mubo has miniature droids waiting for you to customize. There are three basic models: an R (like R2-D2 or R5-D4), a BB unit (the ball-droid style similar to BB-8 and the evil BB-9E), or a C

unit (like C1-10P). Once you choose all your droid pieces, you can piece them together in the assembly area. Then head to the chip station to select a personality circuit. Last but not least, bring your droid to life at the activation center. It is highly recommended that you make a reservation (up to 60 days in advance via *disneyland.com*) for this experience, as walk-ups are not always available.

SAVI'S WORKSHOP—HANDBUILT LIGHTSABERS: The First Order would not allow the manufacture of lightsabers—so Savi took that task underground. Head here to build your own high-end lightsaber. Colors include Sith red, Jedi blue and green, and Mace Windu purple. Choose wisely. Reservations are recommended.

TOYDARIAN TOYMAKER: Visit this street market to peruse a variety of hand-crafted toys and other playthings crafted by local artisans.

ADVENTURELAND

ADVENTURELAND BAZAAR: The plush and hand-carved jungle animals corralled here include lions, tigers, and hippos. You may also find rain sticks, drums, collector pins, Indiana Jones™ items, and California-themed apparel.

FANTASYLAND

BIBBIDI BOBBIDI BOUTIQUE: Nestled inside Sleeping Beauty Castle, this boutique offers young guests (ages 3 through 12) the chance to be transformed into "elegant princesses" and princely "shining knights." For more information and to make reservations, use the Disneyland Resort app, visit *disneyland.com*, or call 714-781-7895.

Among the wares available for purchase are sparkly crowns, swords, and regal costumes that dazzle the eyes of many a young royal.

DISNEY'S PHOTOPASS

As you wander the parks, Disney cast members are happy to snap your picture (with your camera and/or theirs). The photographer will scan a code in the Disneyland app (on your phone), or give you a PhotoPass card. That'll link your photos for viewing online. You can ogle the low-res images for free (with watermarks) or purchase favorites for up to 45 days after they are taken. Disney's Lightning Lane Multi Pass includes unlimited downloads of photos taken on any one day (see page 22 and go to *disneyland.com* for details). Another option is a PhotoPass+ One Day Package. It includes the whole day's worth of Disney photographer-snapped shots, plus select attraction and dining photos. High-quality prints, plus mugs, shirts, and other items are for sale. To purchase or just peruse, use the Disneyland Resort mobile app, or visit *disneyland.com*. It's a splurge, but we think PhotoPass is a great way to get images of your whole party.

Note that PhotoPass is included with the purchase of Lightning Lane Multi Pass. For more information, visit *disneyland.com*, use the (free) Disneyland mobile app, and turn to page 22.

FAIRY TALE TREASURES: Conveniently situated next to the Royal Theatre, this spot is all princesses all the time: Elena of Avalor, Elsa of Arendelle, and more.

IT'S A SMALL WORLD TOY SHOP: A small, whimsical open-air structure near It's a Small World is stocked with Disney-themed toys, dolls, pins, and plush items featuring Disney characters and the It's a Small World attraction (of course!).

LE PETIT CHALET GIFTS: Designed to look like a little bit of Switzerland and as cozy as a warm cup of cocoa on a winter evening, this spot is the repository of traditional Disneyland gifts and souvenirs. Included in the wares are coloring books, autograph books, headbands, and a variety of hats—many of which can be personalized on the spot (for a fee). The small Swiss shop is situated near the base of the Matterhorn, along the park's parade route. Handy!

MAD HATTER: Always a great place for hats and plush character caps—and Mouse ears, of course (they will embroider them for you for a small fee). The selection of novelty headgear always includes a few surprises.

PIN TRADING, DISNEY STYLE

It's one of the biggest—and most enduring—collectible crazes to sweep through Disney's land—pin trading! These small enamel pins can be purchased throughout Disneyland Resort property, but buying them is only half the fun. The real joy comes when you encounter another pin trader with a worthy swap. To get a head start, bring some Disney pins from home (*disneystore.com* carries pins, too). Once on-property, keep an eye out for cast members sporting a good selection of pins—they tend to be agreeable to almost any trade. And when negotiating a trade with a cast member, always remember the rules: (1) Only Disney pins may be traded, and (2) Every trade must be an even pin-for-pin exchange.

MERLIN'S MARVELOUS MISCELLANY: A stone's throw from Disneyland's Sword in the Stone (near the King Arthur Carrousel), this whimsically appointed shop has shelves lined with Disney-themed merch: shirts, bags, notebooks, cups, and collectibles, among other things.

STROMBOLI'S WAGON: Located near Red Rose Taverne, this stand offers a wagonful of wares—everything from plush toys to sunglasses. Some of the items available include key chains, pens, buttons, popcorn, and candy. The shop is named after one of the villains from Disney's 1940 classic, *Pinocchio*.

TOMORROWLAND

AUTOPIA WINNER'S CIRCLE: Racing enthusiasts will enjoy the Autopia-inspired souvenirs and toys offered at this small shop. Soft drinks are sold, too.

LITTLE GREEN MEN STORE COMMAND: Sharp traders know they can find an assortment of toys and collectibles at this spot. Disneyland's commanding pin destination, the store offers clothing, accessories, souvenirs, and items featuring Disney/Pixar characters.

THE SPIRIT OF REFRESHMENT: There's a red-and-white rocket perched on a 12-foot pedestal near Alien Pizza Planet! Head there to score a fizzy soft drink and admire the two-third's scale, 53-foot high replica of Disneyland's original Moonliner rocket. The Moonliner was part of a futuristic exhibit that opened with Disneyland Park in 1955. A fine mist cools guests in the warm weeks of summer.

THE STAR TRADER: The Star Trader is the repository of everything from T-shirts and jewelry to novelty headwear, mugs, key chains, candy, and more—many emblazoned with the likenesses of Disney pals and characters from the Star Wars universe.

Entertainment

PHOTO BY JILL SAFRO

Disneyland is famous for festive, live entertainment. What follows is typical of the variety that is traditionally available. However, details are subject to change and some offerings may be modified, or replaced. For updates, check a park Tip Board, the Disneyland Resort mobile app, or *disneyland.com*.

PERFORMANCES & LIVE SHOWS

Performers stroll, march, croon, and pluck their way through Disneyland every day—so frequently that all you usually have to do to find them is follow your ears.

MAIN STREET, U.S.A.

ATMOSPHERE BANDS: Look and listen for the musical groups that perform near the Fire House and Sleeping Beauty Castle on select days.

DAPPER DANS OF DISNEYLAND: The official greeters of Main Street, U.S.A., this classic barbershop quartet performs standards in perfect four-part harmony. The colorfully clad performers may be found strolling on the sidewalk, planted by a storefront, or whizzing by on a trolley or a bicycle built for four.

DISNEYLAND BAND: A presence in the park since opening day in 1955, Disneyland's signature musical group specializes in turn-of-the-century band music and Disney tunes, but it can play just about anything. The band performs inside the main entrance when the

park opens, in Town Square (at the South end of Main Street), and at other locations.

The Disneyland Band's first performance of the day often takes place in front of the train station, just inside the turnstiles. It's an interactive and magical way to start the day. Kids of all ages simply love it.

FLAG RETREAT: The flag at Town Square is lowered just before sunset each day (times vary). The ceremony is often highlighted by a performance by the Disneyland Band or the Dapper Dans. The band has been known to perform several rousing marches per show. On the band's day off, the Dapper Dans perform a capella renditions of American classics. "The Star-Spangled Banner" makes for a stirring finale. (We always get choked up during this touching ceremony.) It's a rewarding experience that captures the essence of what Walt Disney hoped guests would feel as they experienced Main Street, U.S.A. It's usually presented daily.

MAIN STREET PIANO PLAYER: Piano players are often on hand to tickle the ivories on the snow-white upright piano at the Corner Cafe. Presented daily.

THE STRAW HATTERS: This small jazz band, named for their classic headwear, fill the Main Street air with rousing ditties throughout the day.

NEW ORLEANS SQUARE

THE BOOTSTRAPPERS: Yo, ho! Yo, ho! A pirate band for you! These musical buccaneers wander about New Orleans Square and perform on Tom Sawyer Island. They're known for sea shanties, Disney classics, and the occasional ode to Captain Jack Sparrow. *Arrrr!*

JAMBALAYA JAZZ: This group plays down-home New Orleans jazz with plenty of soul. Fetch yourself a mint julep (sans alcohol) or a bowl of gumbo, and let the music wash over you like the mighty Mississippi.

FANTASYLAND

"IT'S A SMALL WORLD" ENCANTO PROJECTION:
On select nights, the facade of this attraction is awash in an enchanting tribute to fan-favorite film, *Encanto*. Note that Disneyland Park's projection shows change from time to time. This show may not be offered during your visit to the park. Check *disneyland.com* for updates.

FRONTIERLAND

GOLDEN HORSESHOE PIANO PLAYER: Yee-ha! A piano player bangs out familiar ditties of the Old West and even takes requests from the audience. Shows take place throughout the day. Note that this classic dance/dining hall opened with Disneyland in 1955.

PARADES

No Main Street is complete without a peppy parade, and Disneyland's Main Street is no exception. The usual route runs between Town Square and the promenade in front of It's a Small World—or vice versa. The direction and route can vary, so it's wise to ask at the Information Center at City Hall or the Central Plaza Tip Board. The park traditionally offers an afternoon and an evening parade. For parade updates, visit *disneyland.com*.

BIRNBAUM'S ★BEST **MAGIC HAPPENS PARADE:** Relatively new to Disneyland, this peppy parade celebrates Disney's long-standing tradition of magic-making—the awe-inspiring moments at the heart of its storytelling. The afternoon spectacular features stunning floats, elaborate costumes, and, of course, a bevy of beloved Disney characters. Look for favorites such as Anna and Elsa, Moana, Miguel and Dante, folks from *Peter Pan*, *The Princess and the Frog*, *Cinderella*, *Aladdin*, *Pinocchio*, and many others. The inspirational processional usually wends its way from Fantasyland through Main Street in the afternoon. For showtimes, check a park Tip Board or the Disneyland Resort mobile app.

Where to Watch the Parade: Some of the best points from which to watch a parade are the platform of the Disneyland Railroad's Main Street depot, Town Square near the flagpole, and the curb on either side of Main Street, U.S.A. If you'd like to avoid crowds, any viewing location other than Main Street may be better for you.

Two other options are the terrace outside the Plaza Inn (but be aware that seating is limited) and the tables in the courtyard of the Carnation Café, where the view may be partially obstructed.

You can also stand on either side of the promenade area in front of It's a Small World whose facade provides a whimsical, only-at-Disneyland backdrop. Wherever you decide to station yourself for the parade, plan to arrive about 30 to 45 minutes early to claim your piece of parade-viewing real estate.

BIRNBAUM'S ★BEST **CHARACTER CAVALCADES:** Often a happy surprise (though some have been known to run on a schedule), character cavalcades are often described as "mini parades." One recent favorite, the Mickey and Friends Band-Tastic Cavalcade featured Mickey and assorted pals (Minnie, Pluto, Donald, Genie, Terk, Tigger, Sadness, Captain Jack, and many more) as they promenaded down Main Street, U.S.A., with the world-famous Disneyland Band. Holiday-themed cavalcades have been presented, too. What will be offered during your Disneyland day? Check an in-park Tip Board or the Disneyland Resort app to find out!

FIREWORKS

FIREWORKS SPECTACULAR: Disneyland park is famous for impressive, nostalgic fireworks extravaganzas. With typical run-times of about 14-minutes, each spectacle dazzles guests with a thrilling combination of pyrotechnics, lights, a stirring soundtrack, and clever special effects projected onto and high above Disneyland park icons.

First presented to mark The Walt Disney Company's 100th anniversary, Wondrous Journeys—intended to ignite the wonder in all of us—treats park guests to an extraordinary celebration of Disney magic, imagination, and animation. The explosive presentation is offered on select nights throughout the year. It features nods to nearly every Walt Disney Animation Studios feature to date and appearances by favorite Disney characters thanks to some nifty projection technology. (Projections may be seen on Sleeping Beauty Castle, Main Street, U.S.A., and the facade of "It's a Small World.") The show's stellar soundtrack features an original tune dubbed "It's Wondrous." Check a park Tip Board or the Disneyland app for the schedule. The show—which debuted in 2023 for a limited engagement—may be replaced at any time. Will it be offered during your visit? Use the Disneyland app or visit *disneyland.com* to find out.

A longtime Disneyland tradition, specially themed fireworks presentations take place throughout the year. Patriotic pyrotechnics fill the sky on the Fourth of July, while a special, spooky spectacular is presented during the Halloween season, and the December holidays feature Believe . . . in Holiday Magic.

Where to Watch: The best area is about midway down Main Street, U.S.A., near Refreshment Corner up to the Castle hub area, but the area near It's a Small World and waterfront in New Orleans Square afford excellent views, too. Note that Main Street tends to be rather congested during the show.

Note: The fireworks spectacular is usually presented on select holidays and weekends. The show may be modified or canceled due to inclement weather, including high winds. All details are subject to change at any time.

Glow with the Show: "Made with Magic" accessories such as MagicBand+ wristbands let guests be part of Disneyland Resort's nighttime spectaculars. Other light-up accessories have included glowing mouse ear hats, Mickey Mouse gloves, and magic wands.

SPECIAL OCCASIONS

Along with plenty of special events in the parks and hotels year-round (some of which require special admission tickets), Disneyland park celebrates three major seasons each year: summer (including the Fourth of July holiday), Halloween (late August through October), and the winter holidays (mid-November through early January).

SUMMER: While plenty of folks are on vacation, Disney offers a satisfying slate of atmosphere entertainment and spectaculars from Memorial Day to Labor Day. Expect longer wait times at attractions, and consider using Lightning Lane access if budget allows. (For details about Disney's fee-based, expedited wait time system, see page 22, and use the Disneyland app.) Past summers have seen a patriotic, pyrotechnic tribute to the U.S.A. on Independence Day in a rousing (and wildly popular) celebration known as Disney's Celebrate America! A Fourth of July Concert in the Sky.

HALLOWEEN: Halloween Time at the Disneyland Resort brings a palette of fall colors, festively carved pumpkins, Disney characters dressed in Halloween

costumes, and trick-or-treat touches, along with an extra-spooky Haunted Mansion transformation inspired by *Tim Burton's The Nightmare Before Christmas* and a spirited fireworks display dubbed Halloween Screams.

WINTER HOLIDAYS: This jolly period generally stretches from November through the first week of January, when the entire park glows with holiday themes. (We've witnessed Yuletide holiday decorations in place as early as October.) Expect the park to be festooned with holiday decor and perhaps even the occasional snow flurry (which is known to make Olaf very happy). The Disneyland Resort officially begins to celebrate the holidays in November, when the merriest attraction on Earth—It's a Small World Holiday—returns for the season.

It's a Small World Holiday celebrates Yuletide customs around the world. The singing Small World dolls add "Jingle Bells" to their repertoire in numerous languages, and the big clock on the attraction's whimsical facade dons a Santa Claus hat.

Main Street, U.S.A., is decked out in traditional red and green, including hundreds of poinsettias and a huge Christmas tree that's surrounded by oversize holiday packages. Highlights include the chance to meet the man in the red suit, Santa himself. Sleeping Beauty Castle gets in on the fun: Each evening during the holiday season, guests watch the castle transform into a shining, icicle-adorned spectacle. As the snow falls and music fills the air, Sleeping Beauty's Winter Castle glimmers with thousands of twinkling lights, illuminated in stages. On a very limited number of December nights, a candlelight processional ending at Town Square takes place. Music is provided by a large choir, and a holiday story is read by a well-known entertainer. **A Christmas Fantasy Parade**, a fan-favorite, takes place throughout the holiday season. The merry, 40-minute processional traditionally includes favorite Disney pals, dancing gingerbread cookies, toy soldiers, colorful floats, and Santa Claus. (Note that all parades at Disneyland Park are dependent on weather conditions and are subject to change or cancellation.) **Believe . . . In Holiday Magic** is Disneyland's festive fireworks show. Set to seasonal music, the 15-minute pyrotechnic spectacular takes place above and around Sleeping Beauty Castle, with excellent vantage points on Main Street, U.S.A., and throughout the park.

Live entertainment and a truly dazzling fireworks show on **New Year's Eve** (no special ticket required) provide a grand finale for this happy holiday season.

For details about seasonal happenings in the park, use the Disneyland Resort app or visit *disneyland.com*.

WHERE TO FIND THE CHARACTERS

Look for Disney characters in Town Square on Main Street, U.S.A., throughout the day. Tinker Bell and her friends may appear at Pixie Hollow. Princesses hold court at Fantasy Faire in Fantasyland, just off Main Street. Winnie the Pooh and his pals are known to converge in Bayou Country. Mickey, Minnie, Donald, Daisy, Goofy, Clarabelle, and Pete (Mickey's arch-nemesis) may be seen in Mickey's Toontown. Tiana makes appearances in New Orleans Square. Aladdin and Jasmine have been known to mingle near Snow White's Wishing Well (near the castle) and the Fantasy Faire courtyard. Friends and foes interact with travelers on Batuu (aka Star Wars: Galaxy's Edge).

Cast members at park Tip Boards can help you locate characters, as can *disneyland.com*. This book's *Good Meals, Great Times* chapter explains where to dine with character friends. Another excellent source for character appearance updates and schedules? The Disneyland Resort app. Details are subject to change.

BIRNBAUM'S ★BEST★

A beloved Disneyland nighttime spectacular, Fantasmic! lights up the Rivers of America in dramatic, high-tech fashion. The newly refreshed production features cutting-edge projection and pyrotechnic technology, a re-imagined battle scene between Sorcerer Mickey and Maleficent, plus the return of a classic *Peter Pan* scene in which The Lost Boys join Peter and Wendy as they take on Captain Hook!

An amalgam of music, magic, special effects, and live performances, Fantasmic! is a fan favorite. The show, which lasts about 25 minutes, lights up the Rivers of America on weekends, holidays, and throughout the summer. More than 100 cast and crew members put on an unforgettable show in a dazzling display of pyrotechnics, giant props, video, and light.

Fantasmic! is a good vs. evil tale, and it is up to Mickey Mouse to overcome an array of villains. Draped in his red sorcerer's robe, Mickey first appears at the tip of Tom Sawyer Island and uses his imagination to make comets shoot across the sky while the river waters dance about. He materializes in a cone of light, and a shower of sparks dramatically shoots from his fingertips.

Top-notch technology makes Fantasmic! all the more impressive. Mickey works his magic and a film sequence appears in midair, above the Rivers of America. The effect is achieved by projecting digital images onto giant screens of seemingly magical mist.

The illusions build toward a confrontation of good and evil in which Disney villains—conjured up by the Evil Queen and her trusty magic mirror—disrupt Mickey's wondrous fantasy.

In fact, said villains have the audacity to transform Mickey's dreams into nightmares, and he must overcome the bad guys with his own powers of imagination—with a little help from his friends. The Sailing Ship *Columbia* glides through the show with members of the aforementioned cast of *Peter Pan* on board, and the *Mark Twain* riverboat brings along a host of familiar Disney friends.

Where to Watch: The best spots are in front of the Pirates of the Caribbean (be sure you can see the water and have a view of Tom Sawyer Island). Get there early. (Late arrivals can sometimes find a place to watch near the Haunted Mansion, in New Orleans Square.)

If you decide to splurge—and it's offered during your planned visit to the park—consider a Fantasmic! Dining Package. It includes lunch or dinner at a Disneyland eatery and space in a reserved viewing area for Fantasmic! The cost starts at about $35 to $89 per adult, $25 to $45 per child (ages 3 to 9). Tax and gratuity are extra. For additional information and to make reservations, visit *disneyland.com* or use the Disneyland resort app. We recommend booking exactly 60 days before your desired date. Park admission is required, but not included with a Fantasmic! dining package. For updates, use the Disneyland app or visit *disneyland.disney .go.com/dining/disneyland/fantasmic-dinner-packages*.

Note: Fantasmic! may be performed twice nightly during the summer. If so, the later presentation is usually a bit less crowded. The special effects are quite realistic, and may be a bit too intense for some tots. For updates and showtimes, visit *disneyland.com*. Details are subject to change.

HOT TIPS

🐭 Tuesday, Wednesday, and Thursday tend to be the least crowded days to visit year-round. If you must come on a weekend, choose Sunday over Saturday.

🐭 Measure your kids before your Disneyland visit so you will know in advance which attractions they may be too short to ride. This can help avoid disappointment later on.

🐭 Wear comfortable shoes. Blisters are the most common malady reported to First Aid.

🐭 Main Street, U.S.A., may open a bit before the rest of the park. Take advantage of this to grab a quick snack, shop, or say hello to some Disney character friends.

🐭 Avoid attractions such as Star Tours, *Millennium Falcon: Smugglers Run*, Star Wars: Rise of the Resistance, Tiana's Bayou Adventure, the Matterhorn Bobsleds, and the Mad Tea Party immediately after meals (for obvious reasons).

🐭 Check the daily entertainment offerings at one of the park's Tip Boards or by using the Disneyland mobile app and plan your day accordingly.

🐭 Wait times are posted at Disneyland attractions themselves, and on the Information Board at the north end of Main Street, U.S.A. (on the Adventureland side of the street), and on the Disneyland app. The times are updated frequently.

🐭 An attraction may reach its Lightning Lane limit before the end of the day, especially if the park is packed. Be sure to book any must-do early if you don't want to wait in the standby line. Note that fees apply for Disney's Lightning Lane Service. For details, see page 22 and visit *disneyland.com*.

🐭 During busy afternoon hours, go to lower-key attractions, where the waits may be shorter. The afternoon is also prime time for shopping, enjoying an outdoor performance, enjoying a parade, taking in a show at the Royal Theatre, or watching the daily Flag Retreat on Main Street, U.S.A.

🐭 Try to enjoy lunch before 11:30 A.M. or after 2 P.M., and dinner before 5 P.M. or after 8 P.M. to avoid long register lines (which may be shorter toward the left of fast-food counters). Keep in mind that many quick-service eateries offer Mobile Order service. (See page 127 for details.)

🐭 Try to visit the major attractions—*Millennium Falcon: Smugglers Run*, Star Wars: Rise of the Resistance, Space Mountain, Star Tours, the Indiana Jones Adventure, Big Thunder Mountain Railroad, Finding Nemo Submarine Voyage, Haunted Mansion, the Matterhorn Bobsleds, and Tiana's Bayou Adventure—early or during parades. The lines are often shorter during those periods.

🐭 If you're traveling alone or willing to split up your party, be aware that Space Mountain, Matterhorn Bobsleds, and *Millennium Falcon:* Smugglers Run usually offer Single Rider lines—potentially much shorter than the standby lines. Just know that parties will be split up. They don't call it Single Rider for nothing!

🐭 For a change of pace food-wise, head over to Downtown Disney District or to one of the hotels on property. They have something for almost every budget and taste—from simple to sublime, ravioli to rack of lamb—as well as buffet meals with popular Disney characters (at the Disneyland resorts only).

🐭 The monorail transports guests from Tomorrowland to the Disneyland Hotel end of Downtown Disney. Guests may be asked to disembark, but it's okay to reboard if you'd like to complete the round-trip journey. Keep your park ticket handy— you'll need it to get back on to Disney's "highway in the sky."

🐭 Main Street shops are a good place to escape the midday heat, but try to steer clear of them at the end of the park's operating hours, when they tend to be the most crowded.

🐭 For most attractions, if you're in line up to one minute before the park's closing time, you'll be allowed on. It's a good tactic for popular attractions such as Space Mountain, Peter Pan's Flight, and the Indiana Jones Adventure.

🐭 Avoid the crowds by returning your stroller (and getting your deposit back) before the evening's fireworks presentation comes to an end.

🐭 Break up your time in the park (unless you have only one day). Arrive early, see major attractions until things get busy, return to your hotel for a swim or a nap, then go back to the park. Remember, you must present your valid ticket to re-enter Disneyland Park later in the day.

DISNEY CALIFORNIA ADVENTURE

Fame, fortune, and fun in the sun have lured adventurous spirits to California for centuries. But now visitors have an alternative way to enjoy the glories of the Golden State: through Disney's eyes. In February 2001, The Walt Disney Company officially unveiled its new California Adventure theme park—and it was a work in progress for quite some time. To that end, an ambitious growth-spurt is complete. Fresh themes and attractions joined the landscape, while some veteran rides and lands have been cleverly "re-imagined," with new shows, attractions, and eateries forever on the horizon. The result? A theme park adventure to impress even the most devoted Disneyland Park devotees.

Disney California Adventure sits snugly in the heart of the Disneyland Resort, sharing an entrance esplanade with Disneyland, neighboring Downtown Disney District, and the Disney hotels. But once you set foot inside the park, you're in a world all its own. Regions blend into each other, and no matter where you stand, you are sure to see (or hear whoops and hollers coming from) one of the park's eye-catching icons—Guardians of the Galaxy—Mission: BREAKOUT!, WEB SLINGERS: A Spider-Man Adventure, the majestic Sierra-inspired Grizzly Peak mountain, Pixar Pier's Incredicoaster, and the wildly popular Radiator Springs Racers.

With a small vineyard, several upscale restaurants, scream- and smile-inducing thrill rides, and attractions tailored for every member of the family, the 66-acre theme park has something for everyone to enjoy. California, here we come!

DISNEY CALIFORNIA ADVENTURE

PIXAR PIER

PARADISE GARDENS PARK

SAN FRANSOKYO SQUARE

GRIZZLY PEAK

CARS LAND

AVENGERS CAMPUS

HOLLYWOOD LAND

BUENA VISTA STREET

N

HOLLYWOOD LAND
1. Disney Animation
2. Hyperion Theatre
3. Monsters, Inc. Mike and Sulley to the Rescue!
4. Disney Junior Mickey Mouse Clubhouse Live!
5. Mickey's PhilharMagic

GRIZZLY PEAK
6. Soarin' Around the World
7. Grizzly River Run
8. Redwood Creek Challenge Trail

PARADISE GARDENS PARK
9. The Little Mermaid—Ariel's Undersea Adventure
10. Golden Zephyr
11. Jumpin' Jellyfish
12. Goofy's Sky School
13. Silly Symphony Swings
14. World of Color

PIXAR PIER
15. Incredicoaster
16. Pixar Pal-A-Round
17. Toy Story Midway Mania!

18. Jessie's Critter Carousel
19. Inside Out Emotional Whirlwind

CARS LAND
20. Luigi's Rollickin' Roadsters
21. Mater's Junkyard Jamboree
22. Radiator Springs Racers

AVENGERS CAMPUS
23. Guardians of the Galaxy—Mission: BREAKOUT!
24. WEB SLINGERS:
A Spider-Man Adventure

Getting Oriented

Disney California Adventure is a bit smaller than the nearby Disneyland Park, so most guests have little trouble covering all of it on foot—as long as they wear comfy walking shoes.

The main entrance area is known as Buena Vista Street. East of Buena Vista Street lies Hollywood Land. It's a mock studio backlot where guests can, among other things, say hello to Anna and Elsa, enjoy the lighthearted Monsters, Inc. Mike and Sulley to the Rescue!, and see Mickey's PhilharMagic.

West of Buena Vista Street is Grizzly Peak, home of the popular Soarin' Around the World attraction and a drenching, white-water rapids ride known as Grizzly River Run. San Fransokyo Square, a fictional mash-up of San Francisco and Tokyo, is a multicultural district of neighborhood restaurants and small businesses.

Pixar Pier and Paradise Gardens Park have nostalgic attractions with a modern twist, located around Paradise Bay. (If you want to minimize the wait time for Toy Story Midway Mania!, get there early.) The World of Color light show takes place right on the Paradise Bay. The show is best viewed from the Paradise Gardens Park side of the water.

The Avengers Campus area brings big thrills with WEB SLINGERS: A Spider-Man Adventure and Guardians of the Galaxy—Mission: BREAKOUT!

Finally, the impressively immersive Cars Land offers guests the opportunity to experience all the thrills of a trip to Radiator Springs. That's where to experience Mater's Junkyard Jamboree, Luigi's Rollickin' Roadsters, and the park's extraordinarily popular Radiator Springs Racers.

Guests may park vehicles in the six-level Mickey and Friends parking structure, the Pixar Pals parking structure, or the Toy Story parking area on Harbor Boulevard, which can be accessed from the I-5 freeway.

Parking Fees: Guests arriving in passenger vehicles or motorcycles pay about $35 to park. (The fee for over-sized vehicles, motor homes, or tractors without trailers is $40 [Toy Story parking area only]. The fee for buses or tractors with extended trailers is $45 at the Toy Story parking area only.) Preferred parking starts at $55. You may leave and return later the same day at no extra fee. Hold on to your parking stub as proof of payment.

Lost Cars: Even if you take careful note of where you park your car, you might have trouble remembering or recognizing the exact spot when you return hours later. (Hundreds more vehicles will likely be parked around yours!) To keep track of your vehicle, use the Car Locator feature in the Disneyland app. The free service uses Location Services to find and save your parking details.

GETTING AROUND

You'll have to depend entirely on your feet, as there is no transportation in this theme park. Stay hydrated and rest when needed!

Guests staying at Disney's Grand Californian hotel have their own exclusive entrance into Disney California Adventure park. (This entrance is reserved for guests of the Grand Californian. A valid hotel key card must be presented to use the private turnstiles.) Guests at Pixar Place Hotel have their own entrance to the park, too. (For details about the newly re-imagined Pixar Place Hotel, see page 46 and visit *disneyland.com*.) Other visitors must enter and exit Disney California Adventure through the park's main entrance, directly across the esplanade from the Disneyland park entrance. From there, trams or shuttles transport guests to parking areas. Since the area is quite pedestrian-friendly, guests may walk from the park along the esplanade to the three Disneyland Resort hotels and the Downtown Disney dining, shopping, and entertainment district.

HOT TIP

Attraction wait times and performance schedules may be tracked via in-park Tip Boards and by using the Disneyland app. Temporary closures, if any, will be listed there, too. This info comes in very handy while navigating through the parks.

Park Primer

BABY FACILITIES

Changing tables, baby-care products, and facilities for nursing can be found at the Baby Care Center. (It's next to Ghirardelli Soda Fountain and Chocolate Shop.)

DISABILITY INFORMATION

Many park attractions and nearly all shops and restaurants are accessible to guests using wheelchairs. Services are also available for those with visual or hearing disabilities. Ask about these services at Guest Relations in the park's Chamber of Commerce.

FIRST AID

Minor medical problems can be handled at the First Aid Center, at Chamber of Commerce inside the theme park's main entrance. *In case of medical emergency, alert a cast member and call 911.*

HOURS

Operating hours vary from about 10 A.M. until 8 P.M. to about 8 A.M. until 11 P.M., depending on the date and time of year. For the park's hours during your planned visit, use the Disneyland Resort app, *disneyland.com*, or call 714-781-4636. Guests with hopper tickets may hop to Disneyland starting at 11 A.M. Details are subject to change.

INFORMATION

Chamber of Commerce, near the park's main entrance, is equipped with guidemaps and a helpful staff. Maps may also be available at some of the park's shops. The Information Station, in Carthay Circle Plaza, is an excellent resource for attraction wait times and show schedules.

LOCKERS

Lockers are available near the park's main entrance. Fees range from $7 to $15 per day, depending on size.

LOST & FOUND

The Disneyland Resort's Lost & Found is on the left side of the Disneyland Park entrance. Report lost items there. If you find an item, kindly present it to the nearest cast member.

LOST CHILDREN

Report lost children to the closest Disney cast member (park employee) so security personnel can assist you. Children who become separated from their parents or guardians while in the park will be escorted to the nearest Baby Care Center by a cast member.

MONEY MATTERS

There's an ATM near Embarcadero Gifts. Currency may be exchanged at Guest Relations. Cash, credit cards, Apple Pay, Disney Visa Rewards redemption cards, and Disney gift cards are accepted for most purchases. Payment features in the Disneyland app may be used at many shops and eateries.

PARK RESERVATIONS

To enter a Disneyland Resort theme park, guests must have valid park admission *and* a park reservation for the day. Park reservations can (and should) be made in advance via the Disneyland app or *disneyland.com*. Details are subject to change at any time.

PARK RULES

To ensure a safe and enjoyable experience for all guests, visitors are asked to comply with all Park rules, including:
• Bags, clothing, and other items are subject to inspection.
• Proper attire is required.
• Smoking—including e-cigarettes and all types of vaping—is prohibited.
• Selfie sticks are not permitted in Disney parks.
• Weapons (including toys) are strictly prohibited.
• Marijuana is prohibited.
• Guests under age 14 must be accompanied by a guest age 14 or older to enter the park.
For a complete listing of Disney's theme park rules, visit Guest Relations or go to *disneyland.com/ParkRules.*

SAME-DAY RE-ENTRY

All guests have their picture taken upon initial entry to the park. The photos, which are linked to tickets, make for speedy and convenient re-entry, with the presentation of the respective park ticket.

SECURITY CHECK

All visitors entering Disney parks are subject to a thorough security check, including a metal detector screening. Bags purses, strollers, etc., will be checked by security personnel before guests may pass through the entrance.

STROLLERS & WHEELCHAIRS

Strollers, wheelchairs, and Electric Conveyance Vehicles (ECVs) can be rented just outside the Disneyland Park entrance. If you need a replacement, present a receipt. Strollers larger than 31 inches by 52 inches and wagons are not permitted. For pricing and other information, use the Disneyland app or visit *disneyland.com.*

PHOTO BY JILL SAFRO

BUENA VISTA STREET

When a young Walt Disney took the train from Kansas City to Los Angeles in 1923, he discovered a bustling metropolis teeming with pedestrian boulevards, shops, restaurants, and shiny red trolley cars. Buena Vista Street, inside the park's main entrance, sends guests back to this era—to an idealized version of a city beaming with optimism and opportunity.

Follow festive Buena Vista Street, which begins inside the turnstiles, to the Carthay Circle Restaurant—a replica of the theater where *Snow White and the Seven Dwarfs* premiered in 1937. (This version of the Carthay Circle houses a popular restaurant. For Carthay Circle details, see page 123.)

COMING ATTRACTIONS!

Three exciting new attractions will be added to the DCA lineup in the near future. The first will be based on the Pixar film *Coco* and its celebration of the Mexican holiday Día de los Muertos. Guests will join Miguel on a music-filled journey to the land of the dead! Walt Disney Imagineering plans to begin construction on this ride some time in 2026.

Avengers Campus will see the addition of two new attractions in the coming years: Avengers Infinity Defense and Stark Flight Lab. In the first, guests will join the Avengers—Black Panther, Ant-Man, Hulk, and more—as they fight King Thanos to save the universe. In the second, guests will be invited inside Tony Stark's lab to help him test some new gadgets. For updates on details and timing, check the Disneyland mobile app or visit *disneyland.com*.

HOLLYWOOD LAND

Lights! Camera! Action! The spotlight is on you in the glitzy Hollywood district of Disney California Adventure, where the action unfolds all around you. No motion pictures are actually filmed here, so you will have to keep waiting for your big break. You can think of this enchanting place as the "Hollywood that never was and always will be."

Turn onto Hollywood Boulevard and you'll enter Disney's interpretation of the legendary street. And it all fits neatly into a two-block strip. In contrast to the starstruck Hollywood Boulevard, the backlot area peels

TICKET PRICES

Although prices[†] will likely increase, the following should give an idea of what you will pay for tickets in 2025/2026. Note that 1-Day tickets purchased in 2026 must be used by 12/30/26. The first day of use of multi-day tickets must be on or before 12/30/26. Multi-day tickets must be used within 13 days of first use or by January 12, 2027, whichever occurs first. For updates, use the Disneyland mobile app or visit *disneyland.com*. All details are subject to change.

	ADULTS	CHILDREN*
1-Day Ticket		
(1 park)	$104/206	$98/196
1-Day Ticket (hopper)**	$169/281	$163/271
2-Day Ticket	$330	$310
2-Day Ticket (hopper)**	$415	$395
3-Day Ticket	$415	$390
3-Day Ticket (hopper)**	$505	$480
4-Day Ticket	$474	$444
4-Day Ticket (hopper)**	$569	$539
5-Day Ticket	$511	$476
5-Day Ticket (hopper)**	$616	$581
Enchant Key pass		$974
Believe Key pass		$1,374
Inspire Key pass		$1,749

† One-day prices represent the range in which you can expect to pay. Prices vary based on date. For dates, visit *disneyland.com*.
* 3 through 9 years of age; children under 3 free
** Guests with Park Hopper tickets and valid park reservations must enter the park as designated in their park reservation, and may hop between parks on the same day starting at 11 A.M. (subject to availability). After 11 A.M., guests with Park Hopper tickets who have a reservation for Disneyland park or Disney California Adventure, but have not yet entered that park, may enter either theme park (subject to availability).

There is a single price (for adults and children) for Enchant Key, Believe Key, and Inspire Key passes. Said passes are part of the "Magic Key" pass program that replaced traditional annual passes. There is a limited number of Magic Key passes available and sales may be suspended at any time. For more information on Magic Key passes, use the Disneyland mobile app or visit *disneyland.com*.

away the sparkly facade and takes a backstage look at Hollywood without its makeup. Alongside soundstage buildings, behind-the-scenes support departments do their unseen, essential work: Props are put into position, klieg lights are set to shine on the scene, and the crew is busy making sure every performer is on their mark before the director yells "Action!"

BIRNBAUM'S ★BEST★ MONSTERS, INC. MIKE AND SULLEY TO THE RESCUE!: MP A monster's-eye spin through Monstropolis, this colorful, slow-moving attraction was inspired by the Disney-Pixar animated film *Monsters, Inc.* It invites guests to follow affable monsters Mike and Sulley as they valiantly attempt to deliver Boo safely back to her room—all while dodging trucks, helicopters, and the occasional yellow-suited representative of the Child Detection Agency.

While this thoroughly enjoyable attraction is as family-friendly as it gets, there are some dark moments that may spook sensitive tots. Just a heads-up!

NEW DISNEY JUNIOR MICKEY MOUSE CLUB-HOUSE LIVE!: Fans of the Disney Junior show *Mickey Mouse Clubhouse* will flock to this new stage production at the Disney Theater. Mickey and Minnie, who host the show, welcome guests to Mickey's house. They are throwing a party! Expect plenty of music, dancing, and audience interaction. When Daisy, Goofy, and Pluto arrive at the party, it's time for an energetic finale. Little ones love to sing along with the characters. Check the Disneyland app for show times.

MICKEY'S PHILHARMAGIC: Mickey Mouse and a panoply of his pals (including Donald Duck, Simba, Miguel, Dante, and Ariel) strut their stuff in this snazzy 3-D production. The attraction, which debuted in 2019, has a new scene featuring the Disney-Pixar film, *Coco*.

The presentation is an amalgam of music, effects, and animation. Of course, this being Hollywood Land, the film is by no means ordinary. It's colorful, crisp, and to the delight of many a goggle-wearing guest, three-dimensional. The lively experience unfolds on a massive digital canvas. Special effects and silly surprises take place off the screen, too. Pay attention!

As with many Disney attractions, there are moments of darkness. If you are unsure as to whether your child might find this (or any attractions) unsettling, express your concern to an attendant. They will help you make the right decision. Note that all guests must wear 3-D glasses to enjoy the show.

BIRNBAUM'S ★BEST★ DISNEY ANIMATION: When you look around at all the attractions, themed hotels, and dozens of familiar animated faces that Disney has become famous for, it's almost impossible to remember it all started with a simple sketch of a mouse. This behind-the-scenes exploration invites guests to step into Disney's wonderful world of animation. Here, visitors get an insider's look at the process, the heritage, and, above all, the artistry of this world-renowned art form, along with a possible preview of an animated feature in progress.

The Animation Courtyard: This central area aims to make visitors feel as if they are stepping into an animated film. Sketches and artwork from Disney and Pixar movie classics are projected onto giant screens that encircle the colorful atrium as familiar melodies fill the air. From this central hub, guests progress to several interactive animation-inspired shows and activities.

Anna & Elsa's Royal Welcome: The beloved siblings welcome visitors in the Disney Animation building in Hollywood Land. The colorful experience pays tribute to Arendelle and the revered regal characters from the animated feature *Frozen.*

Anna and Elsa are popular, to say the least. Plan on a bit of a wait to see the regal duo. Try to get there early, or later in the day (after most tykes have run out of steam for the day). And don't forget to have a camera or mobile device powered up and ready to go.

Animation Academy: Do you want to draw a snowman? Or perhaps a famous mouse? Inspired by the animation art in the courtyard, this attraction lets guests take a crack at drawing favorite Disney characters. With step-by-step guidance provided by a Disney animator, you'll use basic shapes and simple techniques to create your own sketch, suitable for framing. Check with a cast member or check the schedule out front to see which character is being drawn during your visit. There's a new one every 30 minutes!

Sorcerer's Workshop: Budding animators and artists in particular get a kick out of these rooms. They are built around interactive exhibits featuring animation special effects and tricks of the trade.

Turtle Talk with Crush: If ever there were an attraction that left guests smiling and asking, "How do they do that?!"—this is it. The concept is simple enough:

a 10-minute, animated show starring the surfer-dude sea turtle from *Finding Nemo.* The amazing part? The cartoon critter actually interacts with the audience. In doing so, he imparts turtle-y wisdom, answers questions, and cracks more than a few jokes. Dory and friends may join in the fun. You have to see it to believe it. To do that, you may have to wait a bit—the show is popular with guests of all ages. It's totally awesome, dude.

Little humans are encouraged to sit up front, on the floor by the big screen. That'll make it easier for Crush to see them. Grown-up humans can take a load off on the theater's bench-style seating (note that the benches do not have backs). You can collect the wee ones at the conclusion of the performance.

AVENGERS CAMPUS

Avengers Campus brings together Earth's Mightiest Super Heroes for the common good, and they're calling all recruits to join them! The park's heroic neighborhood promises a host of high-flying adventures and close encounters of the Super Hero kind.

BIRNBAUM'S BEST **GUARDIANS OF THE GALAXY— MISSION: BREAKOUT!:** **MP** Inside this 183-foot, towering fortress is a collection of treasures, hoarded by one Taneleer Tivan, aka The Collector. Included in this trove are the Guardians of the Galaxy themselves. Your mission is to join forces with Rocket and break the Super Heroes out of their gilded cages.

The storytelling begins even before the ride does, with painted notes from Rocket scrawled throughout the queue area. (The attraction's story line expands on the film *Guardians of the Galaxy*—but even if you've never seen it, you'll have no trouble following along.)

The topsy-turvy ride experience is similar to this attraction's predecessor—The Tower of Terror. (If you have second thoughts about boarding the ride vehicle and following through with this daunting mission, simply ask the attendant to direct you toward the "chicken exit.") Once you take a seat in the gantry lift, the doors close and the room begins its ascent—and thus begins the chaotic and thrilling adventure.

Hang on—the gantry lift takes an immediate plunge (of about eight stories) before shooting up to the 13th floor. At the top (about 157 feet up), passengers can look out at the park below. Once the doors shut, you plummet 13 stories. The drop lasts about two seconds, but it seems a whole lot longer.

Just when you think it's over, the elevator launches skyward, barely stopping before it plunges again. And again. From the time you are seated, the mission takes about 5 minutes.

Note: You must be at least 40 inches tall to experience G.O.T.G.—Mission: BREAKOUT! The attraction is not recommended for pregnant women, or people with heart conditions, back and neck problems, or other medical issues. Though thrilling (and rather scary), the drops are surprisingly smooth. Still, if you are susceptible to motion sickness, sit this one out.

WEB SLINGERS: A SPIDER-MAN ADVENTURE: MP
The World Engineering Brigade, or WEB, is hosting an open house to show off some nifty new inventions—and you are invited! So are Peter Parker, Doreen Green, Lunella Lafayette, and other familiar faces. When the young inventors start to tinker, their technological wizardry goes a bit wonky. A self-replicating Spider-Bot (which seemed like a great idea at the time) suddenly multiplies and starts to run amok! As the hungry critters devour Peter Parker's lab, he calls on you for help.

Would-be Super Heroes (aka park guests) don 3-D glasses and board 8-person ride vehicles for a frenetic mission to catch or destroy the suddenly sinister Spider-

HOT TIP
Looking to improve your score at WEB SLINGERS: A Spider-Man Adventure? It helps to know that there's a hierarchy of value when it comes to blitzing 'bots. The gold ones yield the most points, followed by blue, red, and green! (Those that are a mix of red and blue are the least valuable.)

FOOD & WINE FESTIVAL

Every year, this park's dining scene expands exponentially in what's known as the Disney California Adventure Food & Wine Festival. The event, which usually runs from early March through late April, is a celebration of California's incredible bounty with vibrant cuisine and entertainment.

During the festival, guests may experience cooking demonstrations by top chefs, as well as wine and cooking seminars—and sample a smorgasbord of dishes from outdoor kiosks (fees apply).

In addition to the eats, the festival features live musical performances, merchandise themed to the event, and special activity zones for the little ones. The Food & Wine Festival is included with park admission, but some seminars and events may carry an additional fee. Space is limited for all such ticketed events; advanced reservations are recommended. For details or to book a special ticket event, visit *disneyland.com*. Make reservations as early as you can—this is a popular party.

Bots. The mission is accomplished with the help of virtual spider webs, conveniently (and somewhat miraculously) shot from guests' wrists. The attraction is fun for the whole family, with no height restrictions. Guests who are sensitive to motion or have back, neck, or other health issues should skip this web-slinging trip. Also? It's more than a tad strenuous. Consider warming up those web-slinging muscles before you ride.

ANCIENT SANCTUM: Doctor Strange, famous master of mystic arts, occupies a special section of Avengers Campus—in the ruins of an ancient sanctum. Surrounded by lush greenery, the doctor demonstrates illusions and sorcery for willing recruits. The quiet, shady enclave is especially atmospheric in the evening, when the trees and glowing ruins pulse with energy and special effects

GRIZZLY PEAK

The centerpiece of the Grizzly Peak recreation area (which includes the Grizzly Peak Airfield) is a bear-shaped mountain that juts 110 feet above the park floor. The eight-acre wilderness surrounding the Grizzly Peak mountain serves as a tribute to the Golden State's grandeur and natural beauty. The Grizzly Park Airfield area was inspired by California's aviation history. It pays tribute to famous flyers and their precious planes. A huge aircraft hangar, the focus of this section, is the site of a wildly popular attraction known as Soarin' Around the World.

BIRNBAUM'S ★BEST

SOARIN' AROUND THE WORLD: **MP**
Up, up, and away! On this smooth, high-flying attraction, you will be suspended in a hang-glider–like ride vehicle 45 feet in the air, above a giant IMAX projection dome, and treated to an aerial tour of majestic landscapes and treasured landmarks. Soarin' has been delighting park guests with its wraparound glory since 2001—but these days, instead of hovering over one state (California), visitors experience a much broader tour. (The original version of the show does return from time to time, much to the delight of Soarin' fans.)

Soarin' Around the World showcases some of the planet's most compelling sights: The Great Wall of China, the plains of Africa, the oceans of Fiji, the Grand Canyon, Egyptian pyramids, and much more. (Disneyland park veterans may notice a familiar mountain peak in the Swiss Alps. Yep, it's the Matterhorn!)

With the wind in your hair and your legs dangling in the breeze, the hang glider feels so real that you may even be tempted to pull up your feet for fear of tapping the rooftops and landscapes below.

The entire flight takes about 5 minutes and employs synchronized wind currents, scent machines, and a musical score set to a film that wraps 180 degrees around you. A Disney California Adventure original, there is a version of this ride in several Disney theme parks around the world. Soarin' is a hit with guests of all ages.

Note: You must be 40 inches tall and free of back problems, heart conditions, motion sickness, and any other physical limitations to ride. Afraid of heights? Skip this flight.

GRIZZLY RIVER RUN: **MP** Disney legend says that Grizzly Peak was once chock-full of gold—which made it a magnet for miners in search of riches, as is evidenced by the mining relics scattered about the mountain. But the gold rush has come and gone, and the peak has since been taken over by another enterprising group—the Grizzly Peak Rafting Company. They converted the area into a rafting expedition called Grizzly River Run.

Each round raft whisks eight passengers on a drenching tour of Grizzly Peak. The trip begins with a 45-foot climb, and it's all gloriously downhill from there. Fast-moving currents send adventurers spinning and splashing along the river, bumping off boulders and rushing through an erupting geyser field. Because the raft is perpetually spinning as it moves through the water, each rider's experience is slightly different, but one thing's for sure—everyone gets wet. During the expedition, intrepid rafters encounter a

HOT TIP

Don't bring cameras, mobile phones, or other valuables that must stay dry on Grizzly River Run. They will get soaked! Instead, leave them with a non-riding member of your party or in a nearby short-term locker. (These lockers are free of charge.)

couple of major drops. It's the 21-foot drop that earns Grizzly River the distinction of being one of the world's tallest, fastest raft rides.

As you exit the attraction, be sure to take another peek at the majestic mountain top—it looks like a Grizzly bear, the symbol of the state of California.

Note: To ride Grizzly River Run, passengers must be free of back and neck problems, heart conditions, motion sickness, and other physical issues to ride. Pregnant women and guests not meeting the 42-inch height requirement will not be permitted to board. Finally, if you prefer to stay dry, plan to bypass this ride—or do as many guests do: Wrap yourself in a rain poncho and hope for the best!

REDWOOD CREEK CHALLENGE TRAIL: Lace up your trusty sneakers and test your skills at this rustic adventure zone near the eastern slope of Grizzly Peak. Some of the highlights include the Cliff Hanger Traverse Rock Climb, Boulder Bear rock formations, and a trio of wooden lookout towers featuring authentic ranger gear, rope bridges, and hidden surprises to keep guests on their toes.

Of course, even the most intrepid explorers may need directions. Fortunately, there are handy maps at the trail's entrance. Need a hand to assist you through the course? Just whistle for one of the workers outfitted in ranger gear. They're always happy to help.

There is a special cave hidden here, too. Find it and you will discover which noble creature—bear? salmon? skunk?—is your animal spirit.

Most areas of the Redwood Creek Challenge Trail are available to guests of all sizes. However, the following zones have height requirements: Cliff Hanger Traverse Rock (guests must be at least 42 inches tall); Hoot n' Holler Log Slides (32 inch height requirement); and Sequoia Smokejumpers Training Tower (guests must be between 42 and 63 inches tall and under 13 years of age to participate).

Note: Redwood Creek Challenge Trail keeps shorter hours than the rest of the attractions in the park. Check *disneyland.com* or use the Disneyland mobile app for current operating hours.

PHOTO BY JILL SAFRO

CARS LAND

Ladies and gentlemen, start your engines—there's a real-life Radiator Springs in this theme park! This 12-acre *Cars*-themed town invites guests to enjoy the following attractions:

LUIGI'S ROLLICKIN' ROADSTERS: Luigi's Flying Tires has, well, flown away. But Luigi fans, fear not! The mechanically inclined Radiator Springs resident has a fun-filled (or is that fun-fueled?) experience for guests to enjoy. The attraction, which sits behind Luigi's Casa Della Tires, takes guests for a silly ride as Luigi's cousins demonstrate dances from their native Italy. It's a "wheel" hoot! Guests must be at least 32 inches tall to ride. The experience involves quite a bit of motion, including spinning. Just a heads-up.

MATER'S JUNKYARD JAMBOREE: This attraction is a tractor-pulling square dance party hosted by a friendly, familiar tow truck. As baby tractors pull the junkyard cart (with you in it), the cart gets whirled and twirled

in time to tunes pumped through Mater's junkyard jukebox. Those tunes—all seven of 'em—are original songs performed by Disneyland legends, Billy Hill and the Hillbillies. To ride, guests must be at least 32 inches tall. Don't ride on a full stomach.

PHOTO BY MIKE CARROLL

BIRNBAUM'S ★BEST★ **RADIATOR SPRINGS RACERS:** Fasten your seat belts—this bona fide "E-Ticket" attraction will set your heart racing as you compete with other speed seekers. Using technology similar to that of EPCOT's beloved Test Track attraction, Imagineers have devised a thrilling experience for guests: a high-speed tour of Ornament Valley, featuring hairpin turns, steep banks, and a head-to-head race to the finish. Sally, Luigi, Guido, Ramone, and other familiar *Cars* friends zoom around this revved-up racetrack.

At press time, this attraction was available via traditional standby line (included with park admission) or via Lightning Lane Single Pass. For additional information about this attraction (including Lightning Lane status updates), visit *disneyland.com*, or use the Disneyland mobile app.

Note: To ride, guests must be at least 40 inches tall and without health conditions. Expectant mothers are advised to sit out this race.

PIXAR PIER

It's all about fun in the sun at Pixar Pier, a colorfully themed neighborhood featuring high-flying adventures with popular Pixar pals. Attractions here line a boardwalk amusement pier wrapped around a scenic lagoon.

At night, the district undergoes a dazzling transformation. Thousands of tiny lights illuminate the rides and building facades, creating a magical display—especially as you soar past them on one of Pixar Pier's most thrilling attractions: Incredicoaster. This area used to be known as Paradise Pier.

BIRNBAUM'S ★BEST★ **INCREDICOASTER:** **MP** Like many classic boardwalks, the centerpiece of Pixar Pier is a gleaming roller coaster. A steel structure, Incredicoaster is designed to look and sound like an old-fashioned wooden coaster, but the thrills are as modern as they get. The ride starts at lagoon level, where the long car bursts up the track as if catapulted up by a crashing wave. The car goes from zero to 55 miles per hour in 4.7 seconds—before reaching the first hill. Several lengthy drops are combined with an upside-down loop, plus a blasting soundtrack. The result is the longest and fastest roller coaster ride in the entire Disneyland Resort.

Along the way, vehicles travel through bright red tubes that trap guests' screams as they test their vocal cords on the big drops, magnifying all the hoots and hollers and adding to the excitement. Every time you approach a tube, you know you're in for a very big thrill, so brace yourself and be prepared to scream! Daredevils should be sure to enjoy this attraction after the sun goes down, when the night sky is speckled with the pier's glowing lights, and the topsy-turvy twists and turns of the roller coaster just may prove even more disorientingly exciting—and scary!

Note: On select nights, this attraction may close early to accommodate World of Color performances. Passengers must be at least 48 inches tall and free of back problems, neck problems, heart conditions, motion sickness, and other health concerns to ride. Pregnant guests should skip this attraction.

INSIDE OUT EMOTIONAL WHIRLWIND: This attraction may trigger memories of the cherished Flik's Flyers from the now-defunct "A Bug's Land." If that is not enough to get your emotions churning, *Inside Out's* Joy, Sadness, Disgust, Anger, and Fear will get the job done. The simple ride—which tends to be a big hit with fans of Disneyland park's Dumbo the Flying Elephant—lasts about a minute and a half.

JESSIE'S CRITTER CAROUSEL: Yee-ha! Get ready to saddle up with one of the 56 cuddly critters on this carousel. Jessie's roundabout ride was inspired by the *Woody's Roundup* TV show in *Toy Story 2*. It features a twirling herd of wilderness creatures such as bunnies rams, armadillos, turtles, snakes, and one super silly skunk. There are two stationary logs in which guests may ride, too (both logs are inhabited by owls). This attraction is fun for the young and the young at heart. On select nights, the carousel closes early to accommodate World of Color (see page 114) performances.

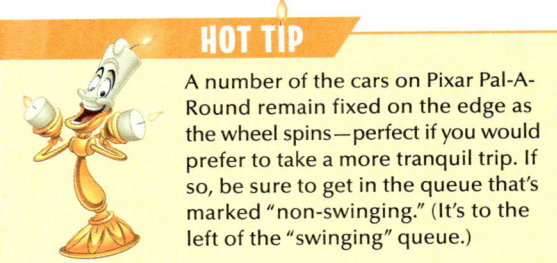

HOT TIP

A number of the cars on Pixar Pal-A-Round remain fixed on the edge as the wheel spins—perfect if you would prefer to take a more tranquil trip. If so, be sure to get in the queue that's marked "non-swinging." (It's to the left of the "swinging" queue.)

PIXAR PAL-A-ROUND: A modern loop-de-loop, this gleaming Ferris wheel, centered by a huge Mickey face, takes guests on a head-spinning trip. If you think this is a run-of-the-mill Ferris wheel, you're in for a surprise: While the wheel turns, most of its cabins swing in and out along the interior edges of the wheel's colossal frame—which creates a dizzying effect. At 150 feet, this is one of the park's tallest attractions, and while it may wreak havoc on sensitive stomachs, thrill-seekers rave over its ride within a ride. For a tamer experience, board a non-swinging gondola. (There may be a longer wait involved.) This attraction closes early on days when World of Color is presented.

Pixar Pal-A-Round is one of only two Ferris wheels that combine fixed and swinging gondolas. The other one is the Wonder Wheel at New York's Coney Island.

Note: Passengers must be free of back problems, heart conditions, motion sickness, and other physical limitations to ride. Afraid of heights? We *highly* recommend skipping this one!

HOT TIP

Want to up your score at Toy Story Midway Mania!? Aim for the hard-to-hit and moving targets—they yield the most points. We recommend skipping the practice round, too. That'll conserve precious arm-strength and help you clinch that highly coveted "high score" of your ride vehicle!

BIRNBAUM'S ★BEST★ TOY STORY MIDWAY MANIA!: MP A beloved attraction, Toy Story Midway Mania! is an energetic, interactive toy box tour with a twist: Guests wear 3-D glasses as they take aim at animated targets with spring-action shooters. The high-tech adventure is rooted in classic midway games of skill. As points are scored, expect effusive encouragement from a colorful cast of characters—Toy Story's Jessie, Woody, Buzz, Hamm, Wheezy, Rex the Dinosaur, and, of course, the Little Green Men.

Fans of Disneyland's Buzz Lightyear Astro Blasters will no doubt delight in this adventure, which takes the experience of the interactive attraction into a new dimension. As far as skill level goes, there's something for everyone—from first-timers to seasoned players alike. (Most folks up their score with practice.) And don't worry about your accuracy score—it's all about the point total.

Toy Story Midway Mania! is a very popular destination with guests of all ages—make a beeline for it when the park first opens for the day. The 6-minute adventure is quite kinetic—guests who are prone to motion sickness may want to sit this one out. Note that there are stairs to climb at the exit of the attraction. If that is a concern for anyone in your party, please alert a Cast Member.

PARADISE GARDENS PARK

A colorful celebration of the Golden State (California), Paradise Gardens Park hugs the shores of Paradise Bay, a shimmering lagoon in the heart of Disney California Adventure park. Here you'll find a dynamic lineup of shows and attractions:

HOT TIP

World of Color—ONE, this theme park's nighttime spectacular, is a wildly popular show. Get there early, or reserve a spot in the "virtual queue." You can do so via the Disneyland app beginning at 12 P.M. (You must be inside the park to do so). If you're lucky enough to snag a spot in the virtual queue, you will get a notification to enter the viewing area approximately 45 minutes before the show begins. Note that all reserved viewing areas are "standing room only." Details are subject to change.

SILLY SYMPHONY SWINGS: This fanciful attraction pays tribute to some of Walt Disney's earliest animated triumphs—the Silly Symphonies. The specific symphony highlighted here is the 1935 animated short called *The Band Concert*. Riders take flight in swings, while Mickey Mouse and his barnyard band serenade them with a rousing rendition of the William Tell Overture.

As the attraction's momentum picks up, a cyclone reveals itself as guests swirl higher and higher. Avoid it if you fear heights.

Note: Riders must meet the Silly Symphony Swings height requirement of 48 inches to ride solo. (Guests between 40 and 48 inches may ride in a double swing. Children under the age of 7 must be accompanied by a responsible person over age 14. Those under 40 inches are not permitted to take this flight.) All guests must be free of back problems, heart conditions, motion sickness, and other physical limitations to experience this attraction.

Silly Symphony Swings may close early to accommodate World of Color performances.

F.Y.I.: When this attraction first opened, it was known as the Orange Stinger and it looked like—you guessed it—a gigantic orange!

GOOFY'S SKY SCHOOL: **MP** At this miniature roller coaster, guests of most sizes can climb into crop dusters and follow the same fluky flight path taken by the Goof himself. The planes zip through a farm and crash through a barn, causing quite a ruckus among the chickens. Don't let the size fool you. This roller coaster proves that big thrills definitely can come in small packages. Although guests as young as age 3 are permitted to ride, it may be too turbulent for some.

PHOTO BY JESSICA WARD

Note: Although it is small as roller coasters go, the ride's sudden stops and herky-jerky motion during turns may prove too scary for riders not used to more strenuous coasters. Riders must be at least 42 inches tall and free of back problems, neck problems, heart conditions, motion sickness, and any other physical limitations to take this jolting ride.

JUMPIN' JELLYFISH: A dense kelp bed tops this sea-themed attraction, from which riders sitting in brightly colored jellyfish seats are lifted about 40 feet straight up in the air. When you reach the top, hang on to your tentacles! A jellyfish acts as a parachute, and fish and friends float safely back down to the ground. While the trip is a rather gentle one with special appeal for younger riders, it might take a few minutes for guests with the most sensitive of stomachs to get their land legs back. Folks who are highly susceptible to motion may want to save the heavy snacking for after they jump like a jellyfish.

Note: All guests must be at least 40 inches tall and free of back problems, heart conditions, motion sickness and any other physical limitations to ride.

PHOTO BY JILL SAFRO

On nights when World of Color (see page 114) is presented, Jumpin' Jellyfish closes early to accommodate the evening's performances of the park's popular fountain and light show.

GOLDEN ZEPHYR: Disney Imagineers took the rocket ride to new heights with the launch of Astro Orbitor in Disneyland. But long before those space-age ships took off, riders were taking flights in rocket-shaped swings on boardwalks and amusement piers across America. Disney pays homage to those old-fashioned attractions with rocket ships that take guests for a spin beneath the Golden Zephyr tower. As speed picks up, the rockets lift into the air and fly over the lagoon several times before touching down for a landing. The high-flying ride lasts approximately a minute and a half.

Note: All passengers must be free of back, neck, and heart issues, motion sickness, and other physical limitations to ride. This attraction closes for World of Color

presentations (see page 114 for details on this park's nighttime spectacular) and during inclement weather (including, but not limited to, high winds). While there is no height minimum, young guests must be able to ride without assistance. Do you tend to have an unpleasant reaction to heights? Skip this attraction.

THE LITTLE MERMAID—ARIEL'S UNDERSEA ADVENTURE: MP In the first theme park ride to have featured everyone's favorite Disney mermaid, guests are invited to climb aboard (continuously moving) clam-mobiles and embark on a jolly journey above and below sea level. (Be sure to notice the beautiful

86-foot-long, hand-painted mural in the boarding area.) Along the way, voyagers join Ariel, Flounder, Sebastian, and all of their aquatic acquaintances and enjoy major musical moments and pivotal plot points from the classic feature. It's fun for the whole family—though some tots may be spooked by the larger-than-life Ursula (see above). She's 12 feet wide!

A wheelchair-access ride vehicle is available for this "undersea" attraction. Ask a cast member for assistance.

BAKERY TOUR: Mmmmmmmmm . . . when you catch a whiff of freshly baked sourdough bread, you have stumbled upon the local outpost of San Francisco's oldest continuously operating business: Boudin Bakery! Nested within Aunt Cass Café, the San Fransokyo Square outlet of the historic sourdough-maker offers a nifty "behind the scenes" tour. In it, guests may enjoy a free sample as they spy on bakers whipping up fresh batches of the world-famous bread in a replica of the company's Fisherman's Wharf location. At tour's end, visitors may explore the adjacent Aunt Cass Café—which proudly serves (among other things) Baymax-shaped sourdough bread. Fun!

San Fransokyo Square

The city of San Fransokyo—home to everyone's favorite inflatable health care robot—has popped up in the heart of Disney California Adventure! As Baymax fans know, the futuristic metropolis is a mash-up of San Francisco and Tokyo—and, like those cities, the former fishing village of San Fransokyo Square is a celebration of the many cultures that thrive there. The new neighborhood (which replaced Pacific Wharf in 2023) offers a vibrant variety of shops, eateries, and experiences (including a Bakery Tour). The one-and-only Baymax greets visitors, too!

NEW

HAMADA BOT SHOP: The *Big Hero 6* team builds high-tech gear in a colorful, converted warehouse beside the San Fransokyo Maker's Market. While guests can peruse and purchase items featuring Baymax and Hiro at the Maker's Market, they can actually *meet* the heroic duo at the Bot Shop! The two take turns meeting, chatting, and posing for photos with guests throughout the day. (They may even appear together from time to time.) Hiro Hamada is happy to sign autographs for folks, but Baymax sticks to photo ops. (Those puffy fingers of his make it challenging to grip a pen.) Hiro Hamada and his buddy Baymax are quite popular, so the line to meet them can get a bit long—so get there early if you can. Check a park Tip Board or the Disneyland mobile app for their appearance schedule.

HOT TIP

There's no shortage of sustenance spots in San Fransokyo Square—and many offer the time-saving service known as Mobile Ordering (visit *disneyland.com* for details). A duo of destinations have been known to offer free samples, too. Visit the Ghirardelli Soda Fountain and Chocolate Shop and/or the Bakery Tour to nosh on an "on the house" nibble!

Shopping

HOT TIP

Disney California Adventure occasionally offers special, reservation-only shopping experiences. (Note that valid same-day park admission and a DCA park reservation are required, too). For additional information, visit *disneyland.com*.

BUENA VISTA STREET

ATWATER INK AND PAINT: Shoppers enjoy the quaint ambience of a 1930s Hollywood-style market house as they eyeball collector pins, seasonal merchandise, kitchen gadgets, towels, mugs, dinner plates, flatware, and much more.

BIG TOP TOYS: Teeming with playthings, Big Top Toys sells innovative and interactive toys and games, plus a plethora of plush character merchandise. You may also find Star Wars–themed toys and souvenirs (action figures, lightsabers, and other selections).

ELIAS & CO.: Paying tribute to the Art Deco–style buildings of yesteryear, this emporium features an array of fashion finery for the whole family—it rivals Disneyland Park's Emporium shop in size. It stocks clothing (hats, shirts, shoes, jackets, and more), snacks, accessories, and wristwatches.

    F.Y.I.: Elias was Walt Disney's middle name and his dad's first name.

JULIUS KATZ & SONS: Adorned with old-timey clocks, radios, and assorted memorabilia, this cozy shop is a hot spot for Disney shoppers. Among its wares: kitchen items, mugs, frames, and Christmas ornaments. The store's name was inspired by Julius the Cat, a featured character in Walt Disney's classic Alice Comedies.

KINGSWELL SHOP: Stop here to peruse, purchase, and personalize mouse ear hats. The shop's name comes from Walt Disney's first California address. When he arrived in Los Angeles in 1923, he rented a room from his Uncle Robert on Kingswell Avenue. It's where The Walt Disney Company was born.

LOS FELIZ FIVE & DIME: In addition to attraction- and themed clothing and souvenirs, there is a selection of Disney character items. It's possible to have some items personalized (for a fee).

OSWALD'S: Head here for autograph books, hats, bags, and souvenirs themed to the park, Oswald the Lucky Rabbit, and more. It's located just inside the park's main entrance. (Fittingly, Oswald was the first Disney character to generate merchandise. Nearly a century ago, there was a pen, a stencil set, and a pin featuring Walt's very first animated star.)

TROLLEY TREATS: If the thoughts of "mountains of candy" and "rivers of fudge" make you smile, this is the shop for you. Tasty temptations may include caramel apples, toffee, chocolate-dipped cookies, fudge, and seasonal selections such as house-made marshmallows.

PLAY DISNEY PARKS APP

When it comes to visiting a Disney park, the name of the game is fun—and lots of it! And thanks to the Play Disney Parks App, there's another layer of digital fun for guests to enjoy in Disneyland Resort theme parks. The free app lets you test your Disney trivia smarts and play games while waiting in lines for several theme park attractions. At press time, that list included Toy Story Midway Mania! (at Disney California Adventure) and Disneyland Park's Space Mountain and Peter Pan's Flight. The app also lets you interact with Disneyland Park's famous Fortune Tellers: The Great Esmeralda on Main Street, and Fortune Red in New Orleans Square. Perhaps the most impressive feature of the trusty app is its power to transform your smart device into a "Star Wars: Datapad" in Star Wars: Galaxy's Edge. With it, you can decrypt messages in Aurebesh (the native tongue of Batuu), discover hidden items in the land, hack into droids, and much more.

   We recommend downloading the app prior to arriving at the Disneyland Resort theme parks. And pack an extra battery pack for your mobile device. You'll need it.

PHOTO BY MIKE CARROLL

Choose from packaged candy or items made fresh in the display kitchen. It's fun to watch the candymakers hard at work—and it's even more satisfying to gobble up their creative confections.

OFF THE PAGE: The magic of Disney animation leaps off the page at this shop that showcases collectible Disneyana pieces. Cels, limited-edition prints, books, and figurines are sold here, as are attraction-inspired items. Guests may interact with artists as they sketch classic Disney characters.

GRIZZLY PEAK

HUMPHREY'S SERVICE & SUPPLIES: When you see the large selection here, you know this is a "beary" serious shopping spot (sorry, we couldn't resist). The grizzly bear–inspired merchandise includes hats, souvenirs, toys, pins, items with a Soarin' theme, and glow merchandise. This souvenir shop is across from the park's perennially popular Soarin' Around the World attraction.

RUSHIN' RIVER OUTFITTERS: This outpost is the perfect place to gear up for an outdoor adventure. Expect to find a variety of apparel, headwear, towels, rain ponchos, plush toys, and other items.

HOLLYWOOD LAND

GONE HOLLYWOOD: A cheerful boutique, Gone Hollywood celebrates Hollywood blockbusters. Expect to find apparel, books, toys, collectibles, and seasonal items—many with a Star Wars or Avengers twist.

CARS LAND

RADIATOR SPRINGS CURIOS: Hit the brakes and make a quick stop at this country-style mercantile. You may be tempted to fill the trunk with collector pins, *Cars*-themed paraphernalia, and other accessories. There is also a substantial supply of souvenirs celebrating the revered roadway Route 66.

RAMONE'S HOUSE OF BODY ART: Ramone stocks all manner of items with a *Cars* theme (hey, this *is* Cars Land). Look for T-shirts, hats, toys, and other wares with a Radiator Springs vibe.

SARGE'S SURPLUS HUT: Young (and young at heart) racers, rejoice: Sarge has a super supply of clothes and toys that were designed with you in mind. For many *Cars* fans, it's well worth making the pit stop—even if it is just to sneak a peek at the scale model of Radiator Springs. It's super cool.

PIXAR PIER

BING BONG'S SWEET STUFF: This super sweet spot specializes in sugary treats and colorful merchandise celebrating familiar friends from the film *Inside Out*: plush toys, baseball caps, shirts, mugs, and assorted accessories. It is located on the boardwalk, across the way from Pixar Pal-A-Round.

PHOTO BY JILL SAFRO

KNICK'S KNACKS: The snow globe snowman (from the classic Pixar short *Knick Knack*) stocks items themed to Disney/Pixar films. Look for items featuring *Finding Nemo*, *Up*, *Inside Out*, *Coco*, *WALL-E*, and more. The shop's on the boardwalk, across from Lamplight Lounge.

MIDWAY MERCANTILE: Conveniently located next to *Toy Story Midway Mania!*, the shelves at this shop are lined with items featuring a *Toy Story* theme. Expect to see spirit jerseys, T-shirts, hats, toys, costumes, and other similarly themed merchandise.

PARADISE GARDENS PARK

SEASIDE SOUVENIRS: A 1930s-style, open-air stand, Seaside Souvenirs offers character items, hats, shirts, toys, sunglasses, and more.

SAN FRANSOKYO SQUARE

GHIRARDELLI SODA FOUNTAIN AND CHOCOLATE SHOP: In addition to a decadent lineup of ice cream treats and soda fountain specialties, Ghirardelli offers a sweet array of their famous chocolates (available in every flavor), plus chocolate gifts and limited-edition packaging unique to this location, and an assortment of bulk snacks, including chocolate covered almonds and cashews. There's always the possibility of a free sample, too. Sweet!

SAN FRANSOKYO MAKER'S MARKET: Stroll over to this salvage yard to bond with bots from the *Big Hero 6* movie and animated series. Items available include toys, collectible pins, and clothing.

AVENGERS CAMPUS

AVENGERS VAULT: Park guests have been granted special clearance to enter the Avengers Vault! Stop by to peruse and/or acquire Avengers-related apparel, accessories, art, collectibles, and assorted souvenirs.

CAMPUS SUPPLY POD: A somewhat self-explanatory spot, the supply pod specializes in Avengers-inspired treasures such as T-shirts, backpacks, accessories, jackets, and action figures.

THE COLLECTOR'S WAREHOUSE: The exit lobby of Guardians of the Galaxy—Mission: BREAKOUT! does double duty as a nifty gift shop. It sells souvenirs themed to the attraction, plus shirts, comic books, and toys. This is also the place to purchase the photo that's taken of your party on the attraction. Say cheese!

WEB SUPPLIERS: This "one-stop hero shop" supplies everything arachnid—Spider-Bots (those remarkably rascally remote-controlled critters known for causing a commotion at WEB SLINGERS: A Spider-Man Adventure), special Spider-Bot backpacks, spider light-up goggles, web shooters, and other cutting-edge inventions ostensibly developed by the Worldwide Engineering Brigade (aka WEB). Other merchandise selections may include head-wear, shirts, key chains, collector pins, notebooks, and assorted souvenirs.

Entertainment

Disney California Adventure boasts a boisterous lineup of live entertainment. For updates and Disney character greeting locations go to *disneyland.com*. Check a park Tip Board or the Disneyland app for schedules. Details are subject to change at any time.

AVENGERS HEADQUARTERS: Encounter some of Earth's mightiest heroes and watch them spring into action to defend the Avengers command center. You will find it in the Avengers Campus area of the park.

FIVE & DIME: This singing group travels Buena Vista Street in their jalopy, hoping to get their big break in the music world. A fleet-footed Goofy joins in the jazzy fun.

GUARDIANS OF THE GALAXY: AWESOME DANCE OFF!: Gather around as Peter tries to get Gamora to crack a smile by playing his legendary mixtape. Help him out by showing off your own epic dance moves!

MARIACHI DIVAS: Guests are invited to sing along as this talented, Grammy award–winning quintet performs pop music and traditional Mexican folk songs.

OPERATION PLAYTIME!—FEATURING THE GREEN ARMY PATROL: A rhythmic squad of *Toy Story's* Green Army soldiers is on a mission to serve, protect, and entertain! The plastic platoon engages guests with games and percussive shenanigans.

PARADISE GARDEN BANDSTAND: Sit back, relax, and enjoy a variety of live musical acts in a lovely garden setting. Shows usually last about 25 minutes.

BIRNBAUM'S  **WORLD OF COLOR—ONE:** Arrive early and prepare to smile. This 24-minute nighttime spectacular, shown on Paradise Bay, is a kaleidoscopic journey of music, animation, water, special effects, and, of course, brilliant color. The show is best viewed from the esplanade near The Little Mermaid—Ariel's Undersea Adventure.

World of Color is intended for all audiences, but it does feature loud noises, fire, and other effects that may be too intense for some tykes. Guests closest to the water's edge will get spritzed.

An extra-festive version of this show—World of Color Season of Light—may be offered during the end-of-year holiday season. Details are subject to change.

HOT TIPS

Favorite characters (including Mickey Mouse) make appearances throughout the day. Check a park Tip Board or the Disneyland app for appearance schedules.

As a rule, Disney's Single Rider lines involve a shorter wait than the standby line. Soarin' Around the World, however, tends to be an exception to that rule. The good news is the wait time for this attraction tends to dwindle as the day wears on.

Curious about showtimes or wait times? Stop by the Information Station on Buena Vista Street or use the Disneyland app. Guest Relations kiosks in Cars Land and Paradise Gardens Park can help, too.

Shops on Buena Vista Street usually stay open about a half hour after the park closes.

Ready for a break from the park? Head to Downtown Disney District to shop or grab a bite to eat. There are several (relatively) cost-efficient spots to try (i.e., Wetzel's Pretzels, Napolini Pizzeria, Blue Ribbon Corn Dog, Jamba, and Beignets Expressed).

Many attractions have height requirements—measure the kids before you leave home.

Radiator Springs Racers has a fervently devoted fan base. To minimize your wait, get to the park as it opens, and head to this attraction after passing through the turnstile—or take advantage of the Single Rider line. If budget allows, consider booking an à la carte Lightning Lane reservation (fees apply).

Don't risk water-logging your valuables while riding Grizzly River Run. We recommend using zip-top bags to protect mobile phones and cameras while you ride. Better yet, stash your items in a short-term complimentary locker (conveniently located by the drenching attraction's exit).

Guests begin queueing up long before the park's posted opening time, so we always aim to arrive at the gate about 40 to 45 minutes early.

For a sweet retreat, visit Ghirardelli Soda Fountain and Chocolate Shop in the San Fransokyo Square neighborhood of Disney California Adventure. You may even score a free sample. Now that is sweet!

GOOD MEALS, GREAT TIMES

Dining at the Disneyland Resort is definitely an adventure—and not just in Adventureland. There's more to any meal in a theme park, Downtown Disney, District, or a Disneyland Resort hotel than just food. Disney friends such as Mickey, Minnie, Goofy, Chip and Dale, Donald Duck, or Disney princesses might pass by your table to say hello. A colorful parade or a romantic paddle wheeler could drift by. Or you just might find yourself surrounded by twinkling stars (in the middle of a sunny day!) as you savor some Cajun cooking in an elaborate bayou setting.

In this chapter, the Disneyland Resort restaurant section is divided by location (Disneyland park, Disney California Adventure park, the Disney hotels, and the Downtown Disney District). Within the theme parks, eateries are arranged by area, and then by category—table service or fast-food and snack facilities, including food courts; individual listings include an approximate price range for eateries within each respective category.

If you're hankering for something to do after dinner, or you just need to take a break from the theme parks, you will find plenty of suggestions at the end of the chapter. Downtown Disney, the property's dining and entertainment district, is party central. Or for a more relaxed atmosphere, chill out in a lounge at one of the Disneyland Resort hotels.

Dining In Disneyland Park

One of the most popular noshes in Disneyland is the burger, followed closely by churros (sticks of deep-fried dough rolled in cinnamon and sugar) and ice cream. But healthy-minded eaters will be happy to find fish, grilled veggie skewers, salads, grilled chicken, and vegetable soup, plus fruit and smoothies. Disneyland's table-service spots (Blue Bayou, Café Orleans, River Belle Terrace, and Carnation Café) provide hearty meals and lighter fare, plus a welcome break from long lines and the California sun. Reservations are highly recommended. All details are subject to change.

Main Street, U.S.A.

TABLE SERVICE

CARNATION CAFE: On the west side of Main Street, near Town Square, this indoor/outdoor cafe is exceptionally pleasant, especially in springtime, when its planters are bursting with seasonal flowers. Stroll into the courtyard dining area that's filled with umbrella-shaded tables and surrounded by a cast-iron fence; from your table you'll hear the melodies from any passing parade. Breakfast choices include Mickey-shaped waffles; pancakes; oatmeal; breakfast sandwich (served with potatoes); and a breakfast skillet (including three-cheese scrambled eggs, potatoes, applewood smoked bacon, and sliced smoked sausage), along with coffee, tea, and orange juice.

Lunch and dinner feature comfort foods, including fried pickles with dipping sauce, "Walt's chili," baked potato soup, and wedge salad. Popular entrées include braised short rib, cheeseburgers, veggie burgers, patty melts, and chicken fried chicken. There are special selections for kids, too. Finish off the meal with a house-made dessert (pie à la mode, perhaps?) and specialty coffees. This cafe is one of four restaurants in Disneyland park that offers table service for lunch and dinner. (River Belle Terrace, Blue Bayou, and Café Orleans are the others). **BLD/$–$$**

HOT TIP

For a jolt of java, head to Market House (aka Starbucks) or Jolly Holiday Bakery Cafe on Main Street, U.S.A. The iced and hot specialty coffees are sure to please. Specialty cold brew drinks are offered at various park locations, including Oga's Cantina in Star Wars: Galaxy's Edge.

RESTAURANT PRIMER

The eateries in this chapter have been designated inexpensive (lunch or dinner under $15), moderate ($15 to $36), expensive ($36 to $60), and very expensive ($60 and up). Prices are for an entrée, a soft drink, and either soup, salad, or dessert for one person, excluding tax and tip. Some prices may be higher during peak-attendance times throughout the year. The letters at the end of each entry refer to the meals offered: breakfast (B), lunch (L), dinner (D), and snacks (S).

Cash, credit cards, traveler's checks, and Disney gift cards can be used at all of the eateries described on the following pages. (Foreign currency may be exchanged at City Hall in Disneyland Park and at the Chamber of Commerce in Disney California Adventure theme park.) Disneyland Resort hotel guests can charge meals from select theme park eateries to their rooms (with use of the Disneyland Resort app).

While a few theme park restaurants and lounges (Disneyland's Blue Bayou, Oga's Cantina, River Belle Terrace, Café Orleans, Carnation Café, and Plaza Inn [breakfast only], plus Wine Country Trattoria, Lamplight Lounge, and Carthay Circle [restaurant and lounge] in Disney California Adventure) accept reservations, you can book a table at most Downtown Disney spots and at the Disneyland hotels. Unless otherwise noted, **make reservations 60 days ahead** via *disneyland.com*, or the Disneyland app—starting at 6 A.M. Pacific time for most eateries and as early as 3 A.M. for some.

FAST FOOD & SNACKS

GIBSON GIRL ICE CREAM PARLOR: A perennially popular place, with a polished-wood soda fountain, the parlor serves up a delightful array of scoops and toppings in paper cups, handmade waffle cups, and cones (plain and peanut- or rainbow sprinkle-dipped). Choose from nine flavors, including cookie dough, mint chocolate chip, and no-sugar-added butter pecan. We're quite fond of the Firehouse Dalmatian Mint Sundae (hold the cherry). Don't be daunted by the (usually) long line; it tends to move rather quickly. (It helps to commit to your treat order *before* jumping into the queue.) **S/$**

JOLLY HOLIDAY BAKERY CAFE: A festive tribute to Disney's *Mary Poppins*, the Jolly Holiday is at the far end of Main Street. There is always a steady supply of pastries here, including croissants, cupcakes, and Mickey-shaped cookies. Specialty coffee drinks are available all day (hot and iced). Also on the menu (which changes seasonally): breakfast sandwiches, yogurt parfait, and (after 10:30 A.M.): soups, salads, and sandwiches. Kids' meals are available as well. **BLDS**/**$–$$**

LITTLE RED WAGON: This wagon, near the Plaza Inn, is a throwback to the delivery trucks of the early 1900s, with ornate beveled and gilded glass panels. Step right up and order your freshly hand-dipped corn dogs, the specialty of the wagon. A selection of soft drinks and chips is also served. **LDS**/**$**

MAIN STREET FRUIT CART: Parked between Disney Clothiers Ltd. and Market House, this old-fashioned cart is stocked with fresh fruit, chilled juices, bottled water, and other soft drinks. Other snack options may include pickles, chips, and fresh vegetables. It's the perfect pit stop for a (relatively) healthy snack. **S**/**$**

WHERE TO DINE WITH CHARACTERS

Meals with Disney characters take place daily at Disneyland Park's Plaza Inn (breakfast with Minnie Mouse and her friends) on Main Street, U.S.A.; Storytellers Cafe (breakfast with Mickey Mouse and his pals) and Napa Rose (breakfast with princesses) in the Grand Californian Hotel; and Goofy's Kitchen at the Disneyland Hotel (breakfast and dinner with Goofy and friends). For details and to make reservations, visit *disneyland.com* or use the Disneyland app. Note that Disneyland Resort character meals are wildly popular. We recommend setting your alarm to make reservations when the 60-day advance booking window opens—starting at 6 A.M. Pacific time for most restaurants, but as early as 3 A.M. for some!

HOT TIP

Do you spend a lot of time visiting the Disneyland Resort each year? If so, we recommend the purchase of a Magic Key pass. It could net you a 10 to 15 percent discount (depending on the type of pass) at many eateries and shops property-wide. Note that passes are limited and may not always be available for purchase or renewal.

MARKET HOUSE: Visit this Victorian-style market for a fresh-baked or brewed treat. It sells sweet and savory snacks and a cornucopia of tea and coffee concoctions, courtesy of Starbucks. Breakfast wraps and sandwiches, fresh fruit, and pastries are served all day. **BLDS**/**$**

PLAZA INN: On the east side of Main Street's Central Plaza, this eatery is the one Walt Disney was most proud of, and with good reason. Tufted velvet upholstery, gleaming mirrors, and a fine, ornate floral carpet elevate this cafeteria above similar eateries. Two ceilings are stained glass framed by elaborate painted moldings. Sconces of Parisian bronze and Baccarat crystal are mounted on the walls, and two dozen basket chandeliers hang from the ceiling.

The setting, including front-porch and terrace dining (with heat lamps to keep guests toasty at night), creates a lovely backdrop for the food—pasta; seasonal fish; fried chicken served with mashed potatoes and mixed vegetables; pot roast served with fresh veggies and mashed potatoes; salads; and desserts.

An extremely popular character breakfast is held here daily, from park opening until 11 A.M. Minnie Mouse and her pals make appearances. A fixed-price buffet features made-to-order omelets, eggs, Mickey-shaped waffles, sausage, bacon, breakfast potatoes, fresh fruit, pastries, and more. **BLD**/**$$$**

REFRESHMENT CORNER: Better known as Coke Corner, this eatery at the northern end of Main Street is presided over by a ragtime pianist who tickles the ivories periodically throughout the day while visitors nibble hot dogs, chili cheese dogs, or chili in a sourdough bread bowl. Mickey-shaped pretzels, jalapeño cheese-stuffed pretzels, soft drinks, and coffee are sold, too. **LDS**/**$**

Adventureland

PHOTO BY JILL SAFRO

FAST FOOD & SNACKS

BENGAL BARBECUE: This top-notch alfresco stand is a popular place to munch on a skewered snack of bacon-wrapped asparagus, chicken, beef, grilled pork belly, or grilled veggies. It's possible to have skewers served on a bed of rice with citrus slaw. Other choices include pickles, pineapple spears, tiger tails (breadsticks baked with garlic,

DINING PACKAGES

The Disneyland Resort offers "dining and a show" experiences—pairing nibbles and sips with reserved viewing for the popular Magic Happens Parade (in Disneyland), World of Color, and Fantasmic! Here are two recent offerings:

1. Plaza Inn (in Disneyland Park): A table-service lunch package comes with reserved seating for the Magic Happens parade. Cost for lunch starts at about $55 for adults, $28 for kids.

2. World of Color Dessert Party (in Disney California Adventure): At this soirée, guests enjoy sweet treats and cheeses as they view the evening's presentation of World of Color from a dedicated waterfront area. The package includes unlimited soft drinks and two alcoholic beverages (for guests 21 years of age and older). The cost is $89 per guest.

Space is limited for these experiences, so reservations are recommended. For details on these and other dining packages, or to make reservations up to 60 days ahead, visit *disneyland.com*, or use the Disneyland app. Reservations require a credit card guarantee. Check your confirmation email for info about the dining package cancellation policy.

herbs, and cheddar cheese), and house-made hummus served with vegetables. There is a large indoor seating area in which to savor your skewers. **LDS**/**$**

TIKI JUICE BAR: Located at the entrance to Walt Disney's Enchanted Tiki Room, this popular thatched-roof kiosk sells pineapple juice and bottled water, but the biggest draw here is the classic Dole Whip soft-serve—a frozen, non-dairy, pineapple treat. **S**/**$**

TROPICAL HIDEAWAY: An alfresco courtyard behind the Tiki Room, this enchanting hideaway has two counters from which to order sweet and savory selections. The menu offers steamed bao buns (lime chicken, pork, and spiced veggie), fruit, chips, and (frozen non-dairy) Dole Whip desserts. (In addition to traditional pineapple, this spot sells strawberry, mango, and other specialty Dole Whip flavors.) Diners are entertained by talented Tiki Bird, Rosita—who tells tales and cracks one-liners worthy of the nearby Jungle Cruise attraction. **LDS**/**$**

TROPICAL IMPORTS: A close neighbor of Bengal Barbecue, this stand offers whole fresh fruit, pineapple spears, cheese, pickles (regular or spicy), assorted chips, bottled water, and soft drinks. This is also the place to get your fortune told by Shrunken Ned (for 50 cents). **S**/**$**

Bayou Country
FAST FOOD & SNACKS

BAYOU COUNTRY FRUIT CART: It may be a modest peddler's cart, but it's filled with refreshing selections—including dill pickles, chilled bottled water, and soft drinks. (It's handy if you need some fortification after taking the big Bayou Adventure plunge.) **S**/**$**

HARBOUR GALLEY: This tiny place, tucked into the shanties that line the docking area for the *Columbia*, has offered fresh-baked sourdough bread bowls filled with New England clam chowder or vegetable stew; tuna salad sandwiches; lobster rolls; kids' "power packs" (snack packs with mini yogurt smoothie, fruit, whole grain "fish" crackers, and low-fat milk or water); soft drinks (including frozen lemonade); and fresh fruit. **LDS**/**$**

HUNGRY BEAR RESTAURANT: A rustic, waterside fan-favorite, this alfresco locale serves classic cheeseburgers, plant-based cheeseburgers, barbecue chicken salads, honey-spiced chicken sandwiches, french fries, and onion rings. For youngsters, there are hamburgers, chicken nuggets, or mac and cheese (kids' meals come with applesauce, fruit, and a choice of milk or water). Hungry Bear's dessert options include strawberry fruit bars, ice cream sandwiches, and funnel cakes topped with powdered sugar. **LDS/$**

New Orleans Square
TABLE SERVICE

BLUE BAYOU RESTAURANT: The lure of this eatery is as much the atmosphere as it is the menu. Occupying a terrace alongside the bayou in the Pirates of the Caribbean attraction, the eatery is perpetually moonlit—stars shine through Spanish moss draped languidly over the big, old live oaks. Off in the distance, an old settler rocks away on the porch of a tumbledown shack.

The menu features starters such as blackened shrimp, chicken gumbo, and Brussels sprout and tasso salad. Entrée options may include sustainable catch of the day, Creole roasted chicken, sunchoke and pistachio pesto pasta, plus prime rib. A sweet finish to the meal may come in the form of a petite sundae, seasonal sorbet, cheesecake, assorted macarons, or crème brûlée tart. Specialty beverages include (alcohol-free) mint juleps and Louisiana lemonade, plus cocktails, wine, and sparkling wine. Kids' menu selections may include roasted chicken, prime rib, sautéed shrimp, and whole grain pasta. Children's meals come with two sides (choose from vegetables, rice, mashed potatoes, and fruit), plus bottled water or small low-fat milk.

The busiest periods are from about noon to around 2 P.M. and from about 5 P.M. until 9 P.M. Reservations are recommended. **LDS/$$$–$$$$**

CAFE ORLEANS: An authentic Cajun-Creole spot, Café Orleans offers starters such as burrata and prosciutto (with fig, pear, crispy quinoa, and balsamic reduction), gumbo (with rice, ham, and andouille sausage), plus seasonal soup and Caesar salad. Among the entrées, look for squash and farro risotto, chicken jambalaya pasta, beef Bourguignon; and two versions of the Monte Cristo sandwich. For dessert, there's cheesecake, crème brûlée tart, and macarons. The kids' menu offers roasted chicken, cheesy macaroni, short rib, and sautéed shrimp. Guests may nosh inside or out overlooking Tom Sawyer Island, the *Columbia* and the *Mark Twain* resting on the Rivers of America. Reservations are recommended. **LDS/$$$–$$$$**

FAST FOOD & SNACKS

MINT JULEP BAR: Beside the New Orleans Square train station, this recently refreshed spot serves Mickey-shaped beignets, hot chocolate, hot tea, and coffee. The alcohol-free mint juleps taste a bit like lemonade spiked with mint syrup (an acquired taste for some); regular lemonade is also on tap. Seasonal specials may grace the menu. Enjoy your snack at one of the tables at Tiana's Palace or the Hungry Bear Restaurant. **BS/$**

ROYAL STREET VERANDA: Across the esplanade from Café Orleans, this counter-service spot has fresh-baked sourdough bread bowls filled with creamy clam chowder, sandwiches, seasonal fritters, and assorted drinks. In the morning, look for "waffle cristos." Check out the wrought-iron balustrade above Royal Street Veranda's patio. The initials at the center are those of Roy and Walt Disney (this balcony belonged to an apartment that was being built for Walt himself). **BLDS/$–$$**

HAPPY BIRTHDAY, DISNEY STYLE

For starters, it is always a good idea to inform Disney cast members when you are celebrating a special occasion, no matter where you are at the Disneyland Resort. But it also helps to plan ahead. Mickey-shaped cakes can be delivered to many full-service restaurants. Each one serves 4 to 6 people and costs about $45 (plus tax and tip). They can be "added on" when making a reservation via *disneyland.com* or the Disneyland app.

Finally, be sure to pick up (and wear!) a special Happy Birthday button. The buttons are complimentary and available at City Hall in Disneyland Park, at the Chamber of Commerce in Disney California Adventure, and at select shops within the aforementioned theme parks.

SWEET TREATS

Sweet teeth may be satisfied at a plethora of places in Disneyland Park. After passing through the turnstiles, make a beeline for Jolly Holiday Bakery Cafe, Mint Julep Bar, Gibson Girl Ice Cream Parlor, or Candy Palace. By all means, try a churro (fried dough rolled in cinnamon and sugar) from a food cart. Finally, no trip to the "Happiest Place on Earth" is complete without savoring the classic frozen pineapple treat known as the Dole Whip (available at the Tiki Juice Bar and Tropical Hideaway). The line at the Tiki Juice Bar is often quite long, but for many a Dole Whip aficionado, it's well worth the wait.

TIANA'S PALACE RESTAURANT: A short stroll from the crowd-pleasing Tiana's Bayou Adventure attraction, this eatery is a destination in its own right. Within its peach-colored walls and fancy green wrought-iron balconies, are elegant fixtures and appointments reminiscent of Tiana's life and friendships. On a pleasant day, nothing beats relaxing on the open-air terrace, savoring seasonal flavors and classic dishes from New Orleans. Look for menu items such as shrimp and grits, muffaletta sandwiches, beef po 'boy sandwiches, red beans and rice, gumbo, and cornbread. Dessert may be a lemon-glazed beignet bursting with lemon icebox pie filling. Coffee (including chicory cold brew with sweet cream), milk, and assorted fountain beverages are served. Kid-centric selections are available, too. **LDS**/**$$–$$$**

Frontierland
TABLE SERVICE

RIVER BELLE TERRACE: The terrace, between Golden Horseshoe Saloon and the Pirates of the Caribbean, offers one of the best views of the Rivers of America and of the passing throng—and the food is wholesome and hearty. Walt Disney himself used to dine here most Sundays. For brunch, consider pancakes, biscuits & gravy, fried chicken sandwich, or the brunch platter (pancakes, scrambled eggs, biscuit & gravy, and house slaw). Start the afternoon or evening meal with loaded house fries or warm bacon and spinach salad. Choose from hearty entrées such as BBQ burnt ends pasta, pork chop (with mashed potatoes and veggies), or blackened sustainable fish. For dessert, there's house-made pudding, red velvet cake, and Rocky Road brownie skillet. Kids' selections include chicken skewer, meatballs, and mac & cheese. Lunch and dinner may include a ticket for same-day, premium viewing of Fantasmic!—as part of a dining package. (For more info about Fantasmic! dining packages, visit *disneyland.com*.) With a lovely interior, it's just as pleasant to dine inside as it is out. **Brunch D**/**$$–$$$**

FAST FOOD & SNACKS

RANCHO DEL ZOCALO RESTAURANTE: Big Thunder Mountain Railroad's neighbor, this eatery features south-of-the-border specialties. Several of the usual Mexican dishes, including street tacos and burritos, along with selections such as fire-grilled half chicken, cauliflower

PHOTO BY JILL SAFRO

tacos topped with cabbage slaw, chips and salsa, and tostada salad are sure to hit the spot. For dessert, try some sweet cinnamon crisps. **LDS/$$**

F.Y.I.: Rancho del Zocalo is in an area of Frontierland that was once called "El Zocalo," or "town square." The eatery's name translates to "Ranch of the Square."

PHOTO BY JILL SAFRO

GOLDEN HORSESHOE: Head to this (dry) saloon for chicken tenders, fish and chips, mozzarella sticks and fries with marinara sauce, and salad with grilled chicken. Wash it down with a soft drink. The kids' menu offers chicken tenders. Cap off the meal with an ice cream sundae, bowl of ice cream, or an ice cream float. Seating is on a first-come, first-served basis. Disneyland purists may remember that the Golden Horseshoe Revue was one of Disneyland's original 18 attractions and was the world's longest-running stage show (July 17, 1955–October 12, 1986). Walt Disney was a big fan and had his favorite box right next to the stage. **LDS/$$**

SHIP TO SHORE MARKETPLACE: Neatly nestled near the shores of the Rivers of America, this satisfying snack stand sells turkey legs, buttered corn on the cob, chimichangas, pickles, fruit, cheese, frozen lemonade, soft drinks, tea, coffee, and hot cocoa. **BLDS/$**

GOT I.D.?

The legal drinking age in the state of California is 21. However, just being 21 is not enough to get you served—you have to prove it. To do so, you must present a valid government-issued photo ID that includes your date of birth (U.S. driver's license, active U.S. Armed Services ID, or passport). Non-U.S. citizens must present a valid passport. Otherwise, you'll have to stick to soft drinks.

STAGE DOOR CAFE: Are you in the mood for one of Disneyland's famous hand-dipped corn dogs? Head here. This small stand, which adjoins the Golden Horseshoe Stage, also serves fish and chips, chicken tenders, fries, mandarin oranges, funnel cakes, and soft drinks. Grab a seat at an outdoor table. **LDS/$$**

Fantasyland
FAST FOOD & SNACKS

EDELWEISS SNACKS: Next door to the Matterhorn, this chalet-style kiosk can supply a quick pick-me-up in the form of bratwurst with sauerkraut, jumbo turkey legs, cheesy garlic pretzel bread, and soft drinks (including frozen slushes). Souvenir sippers are sold, too. **S/$–$$**

TROUBADOUR TAVERN: Located beside the Fantasyland Theatre, this spot has been known to dispense potato sambusas, loaded baked potatoes, spiced popcorn, kids power packs (with whole fruit, carrots, fish crackers, a beverage, and more), frozen treats, tea, coffee, cocoa, and other assorted soft drinks. **S/$–$$**

RED ROSE TAVERNE: This eatery, with its gables, pointy roof, and wavy-glass windows, could easily have been relocated to Fantasyland from that small provincial town in Disney's *Beauty and the Beast*. Breakfast items include Mickey pancakes, breakfast sandwiches, scrambled egg platters, potato bites, and plant-based bowls. The lunch/dinner menu offers cheeseburgers, veggie burgers, fried chicken sandwiches, garden salads, chicken tenders with potato bites, flatbread (plain, pepperoni, or spiced lamb sausage), seasoned potato bites, and assorted soft drinks—including Taverne Cold Brew (caramel, vanilla, and cinnamon coffee with cream). Kids' selections include hamburgers and chicken breast nuggets served with packaged yogurt smoothie, fresh fruit, and lowfat milk, or bottled water. **BLDS/$$**

Mickey's Toontown
FAST FOOD & SNACKS

CAFE DAISY: Brought to you by acclaimed culinary expert Daisy Duck (she is quite the versatile bird!), this sidewalk cafe can hit the spot with pizza flop-overs (pepperoni or cheese), hot dogs (plain or "dressed up"), chips with chili cheese sauce, and spring garden wraps. For dessert, try Daisy's Goody-Goody mini donuts. Soft drinks, cold brew coffee, and specialty drinks such as watermelon lemonade round out the menu. **LDS/$$**

GOOD BOY! GROCERS: A friendly roadside snack stand, Good Boy! offers grab-and-go items such as picnic supplies, fruit, cheese, cookies, pickles, frozen slush drinks, water, and bottled beverages. **LDS/$-$$**

Tomorrowland
FAST FOOD & SNACKS

ALIEN PIZZA PLANET: Similar to *Toy Story's* Pizza Planet (minus the arcade), this brightly hued dining destination specializes in pizza, plus pasta, salads, snacks, and soft drinks. The claw-free environment supplies diners with slices of freshly prepared cheese or pepperoni pizza, chicken fusilli, Caesar salad, mixed green salad, and garlic bread. The set-up is classic cafeteria-style—fill a tray as you slide past the serving stations. Little aliens may order space-ghetti with meatballs or kid-size pizza. Situated near the Space Mountain entrance, this no-frills food court neighbors the Moonliner. Soft drinks, milk, coffee, and cocoa are served. **LDS/$$**

GALACTIC GRILL: This is one of Disneyland's largest dining areas. For breakfast there's a choice of breakfast burritos, sandwiches, and breakfast potatoes. At lunch and dinner, choose from burgers, cheeseburgers, veggie wraps, chicken tenders, chopped salads, fries, and pickles. Kids' selections include burgers and mac & cheese. For dessert, there are ice cream sandwiches, strawberry fruit bars, and Mickey ice cream bars. Coffee, tea, milk, juice, and assorted soft drinks are served. Seasonal selections may be offered. **BLD/$-$$**

TOMORROWLAND FRUIT CART: Fruit may not sound especially futuristic, but it's a healthy way to snack today and tomorrow. Stop here for fresh fruit, pickles, soft drinks, and more. **S/$**

HOT TIP

Relatively well-balanced dining options are available throughout the Disneyland Resort—and kids' meals are no exception. Children's meals tend to include a small entrée, side dish, and drink, and are served in youngster-pleasing shapes and sizes. All kids' meals come with a healthy side and a choice of low-fat milk or water. Toddler meals are available in some spots, too. If you don't see a kids' menu, just ask!

Star Wars: Galaxy's Edge
FAST FOOD & SNACKS

DOCKING BAY 7 FOOD & CARGO: Chef Strono "Cookie" Tuggs has docked a food freighter loaded with fresh supplies and he appeases appetites with an array of savory offerings: Endorian fried chicken tip yip, Dewback chili noodles, and Felucian kefta and hummus garden spread. Dessert, soft drinks, and specialty soft drinks (try the Moof Juice—it's delicious!) are served. Kids' selections are available. **LDS/$$**

KAT SAKA'S KETTLE: Pop over to this stand for Outpost Mix—a sweet and savory popcorn-based treat. Kat Saka may add items on a seasonal basis. **S/$-$$**

MILK STAND: Vendors at this stall offer travelers a drink that's a favorite among residents of Batuu—and Luke Skywalker himself (though for many Earth residents, it's definitely an acquired taste). The plant-based (non-dairy) frosty beverage comes in blue or green. **S/$-$$**

OGA'S CANTINA: Come to the cantina to quench your thirst and rub elbows with revelers from around the galaxy (guests pack into this place like proverbial sardines). As folks quaff spirited beverages such as the Jedi Mind Trick, Bad Motivator IPA, or Toniray wine, they're treated to bold musical entertainment courtesy of droid DJ R-3X, a former Starspeeder 3000 pilot. Non-alcoholic specialty drinks are served, too. Guests of all ages are welcome to enjoy Oga's hospitality, but valid ID is required for alcohol. Reservations are highly recommended. **S/$-$$$**

RONTO ROASTERS: To find this stand, just follow your nose—aromas of spit-roasted specialties fill the air. The menu features the Ronto Wrap (grilled sausage and roasted pork), plant-based sausage wraps, and Meiloorun Juice. The aforementioned spit, incidentally, is operated by a pit-master droid. **BLDS/$$**

In Disney California Adventure Park

With a winery and an elegant bay-side eatery, the tastes at Disney California Adventure park are clearly grown-up. But fast-food spots and snack stands also supply theme park fare with an entertaining flair—retro Hollywood decor or a seaside boardwalk setting. Just don't gorge before experiencing thrill rides.

Full-service eateries—including Lamplight Lounge, Carthay Circle Restaurant, and Wine Country Trattoria—accept reservations. Use the Disneyland mobile app or visit *disneyland.com* to book a table. Details are subject to change.

Buena Vista Street
TABLE SERVICE

CARTHAY CIRCLE RESTAURANT: The original Carthay Circle Theatre was one of the best known and revered movie palaces in Hollywood history. It also happens to be where Walt Disney's *Snow White and the Seven Dwarfs* made its dazzling debut. The theatre has been re-created at Disney California Adventure. But don't go expecting to catch a flick—this version of Carthay Circle Theatre is actually an upscale restaurant. Menu items such as Spanish potato croquettes, Mediterranean mussels and bay scallops, citrus marinated ceviche, sautéed fish of the day, slow-braised lamb shank, seasonal salad, pork chop, and chocolate cheesecake earn Carthay Circle rave reviews. Reservations are recommended. Walk-ins may be accommodated in the lounge area. **D**/**$$$$**

FAST FOOD & SNACKS

CLARABELLE'S HAND-SCOOPED ICE CREAM: Cones and sundaes are among the frosty treats served here. The specialty of the house is hand-dipped ice cream bars. Simply select your bar flavor, milk or dark chocolate for dipping, and a topping. Sweet! Clarabelle offers spirited treats such as hard floats, too (for guests ages 21 and older and willing to prove it). **S**/**$**

FIDDLER, FIFER & PRACTICAL CAFE: Named for the notoriously wolf-averse trio of house-building pigs, this is a great spot to quell hunger pangs and enjoy a Starbucks beverage. Breakfast items, pastries, salads, sandwiches, and snacks are served all day. **BLDS**/**$**

MORTIMER'S MARKET: Stop here for "the freshest fruit in town." In addition to produce, there are other healthy snacks and soft drinks from which to choose.

   F.Y.I.: Mickey Mouse was almost named Mortimer. Fortunately, Lillian Disney talked her husband into naming him Mickey. **S**/**$**

Hollywood Land
FAST FOOD & SNACKS

AWARD WIENERS: All-beef dog, Bacon Street Dog, and Uptown Chili dogs are the specialties here. Plant-based Philly dogs and asada (grilled meat) fries round out the menu. A "power pack" snack box may be ordered for wee ones. A nearby seating area provides shaded tables. **LDS**/**$–$$**

FAIRFAX MARKET: Inspired by the historic Farmers Market in Los Angeles, this stand serves assorted whole fresh fruits, fresh vegetables with ranch dip, dill pickles, hummus with snap peas and tomatoes, chips, applesauce, and soft drinks. **S**/**$**

SCHMOOZIES!: Smoothies made with ice cream or lowfat yogurt are the specialty of the house: Strawberry Banana Sensation, Mango Madness, and Make Mine Mocha. Iced cold brew coffee, spirited drinks, "extreme" refreshers such as ice cream topped with espresso, and bottled water are also available. **S/$**

Avengers Campus
FAST FOOD & SNACKS

PYM TEST KITCHEN: Ant Man and The Wasp used PYM Particles to shrink or supersize menu items in this futuristic food factory. Start the day with Ever-expanding Cinna-Pym Toast (pictured above), eggs two ways with bacon and crispy potato bites, or a plant-based folded omelet. Later in the day, sample salad with shrimp, Bigger than Buffalo (turkey) wings, and savory sandwiches such as Not So Little (fried) Chicken and Pym-iny (salami, ham, and provolone). Kids selections include PB&J sandwich or pasta with plant-based meatballs with tomato sauce. Other menu items of note: ginormous soft pretzels and "choco smash cake." Wash it all down with some Proton Punch, cold brew coffee, beer, or a fizzy soft drink. **BLDS/$$–$$$**

PYM TASTING LAB: Connected to PYM Test Kitchen, this casual lounge offers a full bar, wine, craft beers, non-alcoholic sips, and creative concoctions such as the Regulator (beer cocktail with tequila and mango and habañero syrups) and Honey Fusion (beer with gin, honey syrup, and a mint sprig). Enjoy any of the afore-mentioned beverages with fare from PYM Test Kitchen or the solo selection on the Lab menu: Zarg-Bits (a savory mix of crispy rice paper, corn chips, veggie chips, and seasoned roasted pistachios). **S/$–$$**

SHAWARMA PALACE: You ever tried shawarma? The Avengers invite you to enjoy their go-to New York City shawarma spot—which has opened a second location right here in Disney California Adventure park. There's a breakfast wrap with plant-based sausage and egg, plus New York's Tastiest (chicken shawarma wrap) and a falafel and cauliflower wrap. Bottled soft drinks are also served at this stand. **BLDS/$$–$$$**

Grizzly Peak
FAST FOOD & SNACKS

SMOKEJUMPERS GRILL: Paying tribute to the brave souls who parachute into forest fires, this spot serves breakfast sandwiches and burritos, double cheeseburgers, plant-based burgers, spicy chicken sandwiches, grilled chicken salad, fish & chips, crinkle-cut french fries, and onion rings. For dessert, there are frosty shakes (vanilla or chocolate). **BLDS/$$–$$$**

Paradise Gardens Park
TABLE SERVICE

WINE COUNTRY TRATTORIA: On the lower level of the mission house at the Golden Vine Winery, this bright spot offers Mediterranean fare that blends well with the wine list. (Wines are available by the glass or bottle.) Menu favorites include tomato salad, roasted vegetable lasagna, fried calamari, pasta, salmon, and steak. There is a children's menu, too. Outdoor dining in the plaza features a fountain surrounded by herbs and flowers, conjuring images of Napa Valley. Inside, the dining room is reminiscent of an Italian villa, with plastered walls, terra-cotta tiles, and arched doorways. Reservations are recommended. **LDS/$$–$$$$**

PHOTO BY JILL SAFRO

FAST FOOD & SNACKS

BOARDWALK PIZZA AND PASTA: This eatery serves Italian dishes, including pizzas, pastas, and salads. Kids' meals include spaghetti with turkey meatballs, cheesy macaroni, pizza, and turkey meatball sandwiches. Wee ones enjoy the breadsticks with marinara sauce side dish. For dessert, consider cheesecake, tiramisù, or fruit. Meals may be enjoyed alfresco, on the shaded patio. As an added treat, live entertainment is often provided at the nearby Paradise Garden Bandstand. **LDS/$$**

CORN DOG CASTLE: Corn dogs, deep-fried to a golden brown and served on a stick, reign supreme. Also served: fried cheddar cheese sticks dipped in corn batter and assorted soft drinks. **LDS/$-$$**

PARADISE GARDEN GRILL: Despite its name, this spot offers little from the grill. Though the menu changes seasonally, it has been known to serve burritos, tacos, and loaded baked potatoes. Beer, wine, and soft drinks are served year-round. **LDS/$-$$**

San Fransokyo Square
FAST FOOD & SNACKS

NEW **AUNT CASS CAFÉ:** Guests who visit this newly re-imagined extension of Boudin's display bakery have the chance to sample some sourdough bread (from a secret family recipe dating back to 1850). American and Asian-inspired dishes are specialties of the house. The menu features creamy clam chowder, curry beef, soba noodle salad, and sandwiches (shrimp katsu, turkey pesto, and others). They have bread shaped like Baymax, too! **LDS/$$**

COCINA CUCAMONGA MEXICAN GRILL: Come here for street-style Mexican cuisine, inspired by family favorites of Mexico and Southern California. Street tacos are the stars of the menu: steak, chicken, braised beef. Augment your meal with frijoles charros (chorizo and bacon stewed pinto beans) or lime-cilantro rice. Kids' taco meals are available, as are soft drinks, chocolate milk, beer, margaritas, and other spirits. **LD/$-$$**

GHIRARDELLI SODA FOUNTAIN: San Francisco's famous sweet-maker also calls Disney California Adventure home. Stop by this soda fountain for a banana split, chocolaty treat, or root beer float. There's no better place to please a sweet tooth. (And there's always the possibility of a free sample.) The coffee is tops, too. **S/$-$$**

BABY NEEDS

Babies. They're a needy lot. Fortunately, most of the requisite supplies can be found somewhere at Disneyland—if you know where to look. Formula and jarred food are sold at Baby Care Centers in both theme parks and at the three Disneyland Resort hotels. Most restaurants offer kids' menus with toddler-friendly food (mac and cheese, chicken tenders, and the like).

If your baby is partial to a specific formula or food, consider shipping a box of it to your hotel before you leave home. (Note that a delivery fee will be charged to your room for each parcel handled by Front Desk personnel.) Keep in mind that there are several grocery/convenience stores near Disneyland property. If you have a car, it is worth the trip (a Guest Relations clerk can help with directions). Selections are more varied, as are the prices. Stash perishables in an in-room mini fridge. Some additional points of interest regarding baby diners at Disneyland Resort:

• Most table-service eateries have high chairs for little diners. Request them when you make your reservation. Quick-service spots offer high chairs on a first-come, first-served basis. Ask a cast member (park worker) for assistance if you need help finding or transporting one to a table.

• To make your dining experience a little less harried, consider feeding your baby before you arrive at a restaurant for your meal.

• Stroller use inside restaurants is not permitted due to fire safety codes. Kindly park it outside the eatery. Safety codes require that tots be included in restaurant reservations, too.

• Be it a fast-food or table-service restaurant, take (quiet) toys to keep youngsters busy.

• If you'd like a comfortable, distraction-free spot to nurse an infant, head to a Baby Care Center in Disney California Adventure or Disneyland park. They have rooms with rocking chairs.

• In addition to bottle warmers and microwaves (for select use only), theme park Baby Care Center vending machines offer formula, baby food, juice, diapers, wipes, sunscreen, pacifiers, and over-the-counter medication—all available for purchase with a major credit card.

• If you're headed for a long day in a park, pack simple, healthy snacks for hungry toddlers. And look for the Disney check symbol on menus (it marks somewhat healthier options).

LUCKY FORTUNE COOKERY: This counter-service spot serves savory selections such as teriyaki chicken, beef birria ramen, wings, crispy chicken sandwiches, yaki udon, burritos, and crispy veggie/chicken pot stickers. Dessert can be a Baymax macaron (filled with chocolate-hazelnut spread and buttercream). A slew of soft drinks (including lychee, Thai, and hot green teas) and spirits are served. There are selections for kids, too. **LD**/**$–$$**

MENDOCINO TERRACE: Take a break beside a hand-carved stone fountain in this alfresco lounge at the Golden Vine Winery. The sipping menu includes reds, whites, rosés, ports, sparkling wines, bottled beer, and hard cider from around the world. Cheese plates, alcohol-free sparkling cider, and other soft drinks round out the menu. **S**/**$$**

Pixar Pier
TABLE SERVICE

LAMPLIGHT LOUNGE: A charming waterside retreat, Lamplight is a breezy celebration of storytelling—with a spotlight on the folks who bring Pixar stories to life. The California casual gastro-pub offers a panoramic perspective of Pixar Pier's amusements and the Paradise Bay lagoon. The area is quite festive in the evening, when the boardwalk is aglow with twinkling lights. Lamplight's brunch menu

LET 'EM EAT CAKE

What could possibly make celebrating a special occasion at Disneyland Resort even more special? How about a Mickey Celebration Cake? You can have one sent to your table at select Disneyland eateries. Simply add it to your dining reservation via *disneyland.com* or the Disneyland app at least 3 days in advance.

If you miss the advance ordering deadline, don't despair—no one has to go cake-less at Disneyland (perish the thought!). Spontaneous cake delivery is a possibility, provided you request one at the podium when you check in at a restaurant.

Each Mickey Celebration Cake serves 4 to 6 guests and comes in chocolate or white chocolate flavor. It will add about $45, plus tax, to the total tab (charged at the end of the meal). At press time, the following restaurants could grace your table with a Mickey cake: Blue Bayou, Café Orléans, River Belle Terrace, and Carnation Café in Disneyland Park, plus Lamplight Lounge and Wine Country Trattoria at Disney California Adventure park. All details are subject to change at any time.

includes spiced-ham Benedict, burgers, chilaquiles, French toast, and avocado toast. For lunch and dinner, savor small and large bites. Items of note may include lobster nachos, salmon poke, potato skins, lemon-rosemary chicken, salad, grilled salmon, pork chop, cheddar burgers, and more—plus a crowd-pleasing dessert of warm fluffy doughnuts with dipping sauces. "Budding artists" can enjoy mini cheeseburgers, chicken tenders, and cheesy pasta. Also served at Lamplight Lounge: soft drinks, beer, wine, and signature cocktails (with and without alcohol). Reservations are recommended. **Brunch LD**/**$$$**

LAMPLIGHT LOUNGE—BOARDWALK DINING: This alfresco, waterside gem is easily confused with its nearby indoor counterpart, Lamplight Lounge. This spot offers equally impressive cuisine, but it has its own menu and does not accept reservations. Use the Disneyland app to join the mobile walk-up list and you'll be notified when your table is ready. Once that happens, settle in for tasty temptations such as Kung Pao bao buns, salmon poke bowls, potato skins, and the perennially popular lobster nachos (warm lobster with black beans, cheddar and Monterey Jack, pico de gallo, serrano chiles, and chipotle crema), house specialty salad, cheddar burgers, and plant-based burgers. Kids' selections include corkscrew pasta, grilled chicken tenders, and mini cheeseburgers.

The Lounge has a nice selection of alcohol-free drinks, including Goofball Island (fruit punch, lemonade, and raspberry purée) and Mint to Be (limeade with watermelon and berry puree with fresh mint and soda water), plus a full bar, craft beers, local and imported wines, and a variety of specialty cocktails. **LDS**/**$$–$$$**

FAST FOOD & SNACKS

ADORABLE SNOWMAN FROSTED TREATS: Frozen treats are ostensibly doled out by the not-so-abominable snowman from *Monsters, Inc.* The non-dairy soft-serve (lemon, mango, and more) offerings come in cones or cups. A duo of spiked treats and bottled water round out the menu. Helping guests cool off during a day of fun in the sun makes the snowman feel warm and fuzzy. **S**/**$**

ANGRY DOGS: It seems Anger, from *Inside Out*, is channeling his rage into cooking. Head to his snack stand for hot dogs and other blazing bites. **LDS/$**

JACK-JACK COOKIE NUM NUMS: Among the various num nums that Jack-Jack is willing to share (for a price) are warm chocolate chip, shortbread, and gluten-free jam-filled cookies—which may be washed down with milk or bottled water. **S/$**

POULTRY PALACE: Chicken drumsticks box (three seasoned drumsticks with coleslaw), jumbo smoked turkey legs, corn on the cob, and bags of chips are served at this waterside walk-up window. **LDS/$–$$**

SEÑOR BUZZ CHURROS: Stop at this stand for some Cinnamon Super Galaxy Churros (with cinnamon and sugar) and assorted soft drinks. **S/$**

Cars Land
FAST FOOD & SNACKS

COZY CONE MOTEL: Sally's cozy motel has been converted to a colorful eatery in Radiator Springs. Here guests may find items such as bacon mac and cheese cones, soft-serve ice cream cones, pop "cone," and chili "cone" queso. Beer and specialty cocktails are served. Soft drinks of note include Ramone's "Pear of Dice" Soda and Fillmore's Fuelin' Groovy Lemonade. **LDS/$–$$**

MOBILE ORDER MAGIC

Quietly introduced a few years back, Mobile Ordering has surged in popularity and many a Disneyland Resort quick-service eatery has jumped aboard the bandwagon. While you can still place an order with a cheery cast member, you may opt to order and pre-pay for your vittles with the Disneyland mobile app.

If you've made it this far in this book, chances are you have already downloaded the app. If not, be sure to do so *before* you find yourself exploring Disneyland with your stomach growling.

When it's time to enjoy a meal or snack, open the Disneyland app on your smartphone. Hit the plus sign (+) on the home page. Then tap "Order Food." (You will be asked to sign in at some point, so make sure you know your user name and password for the app.)

After you hit Order Food, a list of available restaurants will pop up, along with possible pick-up times. Choose your eatery and select a pick-up time. Now it's time to place your order! You can even customize certain menu items to your taste. After you have reviewed your details, pay for your order using a credit card, debit card, Disney Gift Card, Disney Rewards Redemption Card, Apple Pay, or stored payment method. (If you qualify for a discount as an eligible Disney Vacation Club Member, it will automatically be applied to your total bill.)

As it gets close to your pick-up time, make your way toward the restaurant. When your order is ready, find the Mobile Pick-up sign, grab your grub, and chow down. *Mangia!*

Specifics are subject to change at any time. For a complete list of Disneyland Resort eateries that currently offer Mobile Order service, check the Disneyland app or visit *disneyland.com*.

FILLMORE'S TASTE-IN: Guests here fuel up on snacks such as pickles, whole fruits, cheese, assorted chips, and soft drinks. It's the perfect place for a speedy and refreshing pit stop. **S/$**

FLO'S V8 CAFE: Inspired by classic roadside diners, Flo serves comfort food along the lines of fried chicken, turkey club sandwiches, Cobb salad, cheeseburgers, plant-based burgers, steak fries, and shakes (vanilla, chocolate, or strawberry). There's indoor and outdoor seating. **LDS/$$–$$$**

In the Disneyland Resort Hotels

DISNEYLAND HOTEL

The diverse dining possibilities at the Disneyland Hotel range from grand to Goofy. To make reservations up to 60 days in advance, use the Disneyland mobile app or visit *www.disneyland.com.*

THE COFFEE HOUSE: Order bagels, muffins, pastries, fruit, yogurt, cold cereal, sandwiches, salads, and coffee in this small but busy shop. As the name indicates, this place specializes in fresh-brewed coffee—with everything from a simple cup of decaf to a cafe mocha and ice-blended latte. Outside seating only. Be prepared for long lines early in the morning. **BLS/$–$$**

GOOFY'S KITCHEN: This whimsical dining room features popular meals and happy encounters with Goofy and other Disney characters. Special seasonal selections

may be offered. The fare here is presented buffet-style, so fill your plate as high and as often as you please. Just be sure to clean that plate!

Highlights at brunch include Mickey Mouse–shaped waffles, made-to-order omelets, and Goofy's famous peanut-butter-and-jelly pizza (a favorite with youngsters and Birnbaum editors alike). Dinner offers a carving station, catch of the day, macaroni and cheese, pizzas, salads, breads, fruit, and desserts. Don't forget a camera—Disney characters provide prime photo ops. Reservations are required. (Same-day reservations may be secured via *disneyland.com* or the Disneyland app up to 20 minutes in advance, based on availability.) **BD/$$–$$$$**

BROKEN SPELL LOUNGE: Themed to the film *Sleeping Beauty*, this spot neighbors the always bustling Goofy's Kitchen—and is differentiated from its whimsical neighbor by dark, calming hues and a forest setting. It's a satisfying spot for an early evening or post-park snack and sip. The reliable menu has included Wagyu cheeseburgers (with house-made spread and fries), chicken wings, pizza (plain or "charcuterie"), Caesar salad, turkey club sandwiches, and molten chocolate cake (topped with hot fudge, almonds, cherries, and whipped cream). The full-service bar serves up an array of beverages (with or without alcohol), including specialty drinks such as the Make It

NEW

HOT TIP

Looking for a java jolt before a day in the parks? You can secure a satisfying cup o' Joe (and/or a light breakfast) at The Coffee House or Tangaroa Terrace at the Disneyland Hotel, Sketch Pad Café in the Pixar Place Hotel, or at Downtown Disney's Sip & Sonder or Starbucks.

Blue Make It Pink. The Lounge does not accept reservations—seating and service are available on a first-come, first served basis. **DS/$$–$$$$**

NEW

PALM BREEZE BAR: Surround yourself with imaginative decor inspired by the artistry of Disney Legend Mary Blair and indulge in a meal or light bite at this festive alfresco venue. Located at the Disneyland Hotel's new Discovery Tower, the Palm Breeze features art from classic Disney films and Disneyland Park, freshly prepared California cuisine, and hand-crafted cocktails (and mocktails). The table-service eatery serves shareable selections such as cheese fry poutine, ahi tuna tataki, and chicken wings with barbecue bourbon glaze and chile aïoli. The menu's salad section features heirloom beet salad (plain or topped with salmon, grilled steak, or chicken), and Southwest salad (served plain or with any of the aforementioned proteins). There's jumbo lump crab rolls, burgers, and spicy crisp chicken sandwiches—all served with fries. Keep perusing and you will discover avocado & lime hummus dip (with crudité and pita bread), pizza (garden, four-cheese, or "charcuterie"), molten chocolate lava cake, chocolate-chip cookie ice cream sandwiches, and beignets. There's a kids' menu, too—grilled cheese, grilled chicken breast with brown rice and seasonal veggies or fruit, and cheeseburger sliders. The impressive cocktail menu features crafty concoctions known as Blue Bees Knees, Marcie '55, and Nouveau Negroni, plus zero-proof potables: Pineapple Cooler, Citrus Ginger Ale, Virgin Chilly mango, and more. Beer, wine, and soft drinks are also available. The Palm Breeze Bar is located on the ground floor, between the Disneyland Hotel's pool complexes. **LDS/$$$–$$$$**

TANGAROA TERRACE TROPICAL BAR & GRILL: Stop here and travel back in time. The retro-tropical design was inspired by the beloved Tahitian Terrace restaurant— a longtime Adventureland staple. The fare at this casual counter-service eatery, however, is more modern. The breakfast menu has featured Tangaroa Toast (brick toast with citrus custard, guava syrup, whipped cream, and toasted coconut), Japanese pancakes, scrambled egg breakfast platter, loco moco burrito, acai chia bowl, and avocado toast. All-day items include a poke bowl, pork gyoza, panko-crusted long beans, salads, Hawaiian platter, ramen, Hawaiian cheeseburgers, and other tropical specialties. The kids' menu includes teriyaki bowls and cheeseburgers. There is a small grab-and-go selection, too (mostly fruit and assorted pastries). **BLDS/$$–$$$**

PIXAR PLACE HOTEL

The main eatery here—Great Maple—has all the bases covered, from fried chicken and doughnuts to charred cauliflower hummus to maple-pecan-crusted salmon. To make reservations up to 60 days in advance, use the Disneyland mobile app or visit *www.disneyland.com*. Walk-ins may be accepted, based on availablilty. For a more spontaneous bite or beverage, consider Sketch Pad Cafe and/or Small Bytes by the pool.

GREAT MAPLE MODERN AMERICAN EATERY:

NEW

A family-friendly destination, Great Maple serves up classic American fare with a dash of modern flair. The spacious dining room features booth and counter seating, with Pixar touches adorning the walls. Tables spill onto the outdoor patio, with auditory accents courtesy of Pixar Pier in Disney California Adventure park. The all-day menu (yes, you can get breakfast for dinner and vice versa) offers something for just about everyone. Tempting "shareables" come in the form of Parmesan truffle fries, seasonal soup, charred cauliflower hummus, and thick-cut smoked bacon. Brunch fans may choose from fried chicken & doughnuts, Cajun shrimp biscuit Benedict (with shrimp in lieu of ham), buttermilk pancakes, rib eye hash, modern American breakfast platter, or French toast logs (among others). There's no shortage of salads (cheers for the Cobb wedge!) to accompany a hearty main course: maple pecan-crusted salmon, baby back ribs, fettuccine with turkey Bolognese, steak, chicken bowls, sandwiches, burgers, and falafel wraps. You can cap off the modern American meal with beignets or maple bacon doughnuts. A full bar turns out specialty cocktails and "free spirits," as well as beer, wine, coffee, tea, and soft drinks. Reservations are recommended, but walk-ins may be accommodated (pending availability). **BLDS/$$$–$$$$**

A ROOM WITH A CHEW

While dining in a Disneyland Resort restaurant can be delightful, sometimes the perfect remedy for a rumbly in your tumbly is a simple knock on your hotel room door—provided that knock comes from a friendly server on hand to deliver a mouth-watering meal. Fortunately, two of the Disneyland Resort Hotels offer the convenient option of in-room dining—the Disneyland Hotel and Disney's Grand Californian Hotel & Spa. To place an order, simply touch "Room Service" on your in-room phone. Breakfast is usually available from about 5 A.M. until 11 A.M., while dinner is offered from about 5 P.M. till midnight.

THE SKETCH PAD CAFE: A lobby spot, Sketch Pad serves coffee, tea, soft drinks, pastries, and light bites throughout the day. You will find it across from the Store-E shop. **BLDS**/**$$–$$$**

SMALL BYTES: On the pool deck, Small Bytes features bites of all sizes. The alfresco locale serves salads, burgers, nachos, mega pretzels, spirits, and soft drinks. **BLDS**/**$$–$$$**

DISNEY'S GRAND CALIFORNIAN HOTEL & SPA

The restaurants at this resort offer a taste of (and a bit of a twist on) California cuisine. To make reservations visit *disneyland.com*, or use the Disneyland mobile app.

NAPA ROSE: This popular, nationally recognized, award-winning restaurant features a seasonal, upscale menu of market-fresh, wine country–inspired dishes flavored by fruits of the sea and vine (the eatery is named after

HOT TIP

Guests who dine at Napa Rose get five hours of free parking at Disney's Grand Californian Hotel & Spa. Fees apply after the initial 5-hour period. (About $35 for the first hour for self-parking; $65 for the first hour for valet parking. Each hour after that costs $10, with a self-parking maximum of $75 and a $135 maximum for valet).

HOT TIP

Storytellers Cafe offers guests complimentary parking with restaurant validation. After the initial three-hour period (plenty of time to enjoy a meal), hourly parking fees apply.

California's world famous valley of vineyards). A striking, 20-foot, stained-glass window offers views of Disney California Adventure park while the open kitchen gives a view of California cooking. The morning meal, also known as Disney's Princess Breakfast Adventure, invites guests to meet Disney royalty while they enjoy their breakfast.

The offerings evolve as new items are introduced, but favorites have included grilled diver scallop with roasted carrot cloud, portobello mushroom "cappuccino," rabbit and dumplings, filet mignon, and sustainable fish of the day. The dessert menu may offer delectable creations such as tangerine crème brûlée tart, winter pear cake with pomegranate sorbet, and single origin chocolate with hazelnut crunch and praline ice cream. Kid-friendly entrées and desserts are served. The California wine list is one of the most extensive on-property.

The character breakfast is presented Thursday through Monday from 8 A.M. until 11 A.M. The 3-course "Princess Breakfast Adventure" starts at about $135 (plus tax and gratuity) for all guests age 3 and older. This breakfast experience includes a special keepsake. Reservations are suggested. Prices are subject to change. **BD**/**$$$$**

HEARTHSTONE LOUNGE: A great site for a late bite, this lounge offers hearty fare until about midnight each day. The menu has offered chorizo poutine, Cobb salad, shrimp and grits, wings, burgers, cheese & charcuterie, artisanal pizza, desserts, and, of course, an extensive selection of beer, wine, cocktails, and mocktails. It's a great way to cap off a Disneyland day. **LDS**/**$$–$$$**

GCH CRAFTSMAN BAR: The hotel's Arts and Crafts motif extends to this alfresco eatery, located near the Redwood Pool. In fact, the structure of the venue resembles that of the original garage at Pasadena's Gamble House—the landmark building that inspired the design of Disney's Grand Californian Hotel. The signature clinker brick, stone columns, and shady trellis set the stage for outdoor dining amid plush, residential-style patio seating. Dishes of note include poke bowls, burgers, carnitas quesadilla, avocado toast, steak salad, and artisanal pizzas. Oh, they have a hot dog of the month, too! Kid's meals are available, including burgers and Power Packs (yogurt, fruit, carrots, crackers, and more). The dessert menu is simple-but-sweet: classic ice cream sundaes. Beer, wine, specialty cocktails (with or without alcohol), and soft drinks are served. The extensive wine list is quite impressive. Reservations are highly recommended. **LDS**/**$$–$$$**

STORYTELLERS CAFE: It's hard to imagine a time before computers and smartphones (especially for the youngest members of the group), when children were exposed to new cultures and histories only through the stories of others. This eatery salutes tales set in the state of California, like "The Celebrated Jumping Frog of Calaveras County" and *Island of the Blue Dolphins*, through murals that act as backdrops to the chefs at work in the exhibition kitchen. In the morning, the stage is set for a festive, character-hosted buffet known as Mickey's Tales of Adventure Breakfast Buffet. Mickey Mouse and other Disney characters engage guests throughout the meal. The buffet offers a feast of breakfast options, with bagels and smoked salmon, Mickey-shaped waffles, French toast, eggs Benedict, sausage, and a selection of fresh fruit. The brunch buffet, offered daily from 11 A.M. until 1:30 P.M., includes all breakfast offerings, plus artisanal composed salad and beignet bites. The dinner buffet features pastas, salads, flatbreads, carved meats, soups, seafood, and chicken.

Breakfast and brunch cost about $52 per adult; $31 per child; dinner—which does not include character visits—costs about $47 per adult and $26 per child. Prices quoted

PHOTO BY JESSICA WARD

don't include tax or gratuity and are subject to change at any time. **Brunch BD**/**$$$**

GCH CRAFTSMAN GRILL: The splish-splash of the waterfall and kids soaring down the slide at the resort's Redwood Pool set the mood for this elegant casual dining spot. This spot is open for all meals (though hours vary). The snazzy snack bar serves coffee, pastries, and made-to-order breakfast selections in the morning. House-made sandwiches, poke bowls, chicken skewers, steak, Wagyu burgers, artisanal pizza, salad, and hot dog of the month are among lunch and dinner options. Grab-and-go items that may be available throughout the day: Cobb salad, Caesar salad, fresh fruit, yogurt, cereal, chips, dough-nuts, cookies, candy, soft drinks, beer, and wine. Details are subject to change. **BLDS**/**$$–$$$**

HOT TIP

Available especially for the 70th Anniversary celebration, Donald's Tales of Adventure Dinner Buffet serves up a variety of delectable dishes with a side of characters at Storytellers Cafe. Donald, Daisy, Clarabelle, and Goofy or Pluto are in attendance, suited up in their explorer outfits. Dinner costs $62 per adult, $32 per child.

HOT TIP

If you don't have a restaurant reservation, brace yourself for a rather long wait at traditional mealtimes. It's next to impossible to snag a table at Disneyland Resort hotels or Downtown Disney full-service spots with any spontaneity.

Avoid getting caught with a growling stomach—reserve table-service meals far in advance! Restaurants may be bookable up to 60 days ahead. To do so, simply visit *disneyland.com*, or use the (free) Disneyland Resort mobile app.

In Downtown Disney District

TABLE SERVICE

ARTHUR & SONS STEAK AND BOURBON: Occupying the space formerly belonging to Tortilla Jo's, this steak house is the brainchild of Michelin-starred Chef Joe Isidori. The menu promises juicy cuts of beef as well as fresh seafood, salads, and sandwiches. Diners may sit at plush booths or enjoy a bourbon cocktail at the central bar. Note that the restaurant was still being built as this book went to press. For updates, visit *disneyland.com*. **LDS/$$$-$$$$**

BALLAST POINT BREWING COMPANY: Complete with an on-site brewery, Ballast Point pairs its award-winning beers with a menu of SoCal cuisine—pub snacks, salads, wraps, and entrées that feature local, sustainable, and seasonal ingredients. Kids' entrées include grilled cheese, chicken fingers, and corn dogs. In addition to the aforementioned brewery, this sleek space houses a tasting room, kitchen, and outdoor beer garden. Brunch is served until 2 P.M. on Saturdays and Sundays. **Brunch LDS/$$-$$$**

CÉNTRICO: An energetic courtyard bar and restaurant, Céntrico serves upscale Mexican cuisine and specialty cocktails (among other libations). Expect dishes such as fresh guacamole, tacos, quesadillas, pan-seared salmon, Chef Carlos' BBQ ribs, burgers, Mexican street corn, Caesar salad, and much more. **LD/$$-$$$**

DIN TAI FUNG: The world-renowned purveyor of exquisite, hand-crafted soup dumplings has set up shop at the Disneyland Resort. Din's menu offers appetizers such as seaweed salad and hot & sour soup. Entrées include the aforementioned soup dumplings—xiao long bao—as well as steamed dumplings and buns (chicken, veggie, pork & shrimp), pot stickers, wontons, greens (string beans, bok choy, broccoli), noodles, and wok fried rice. A selection of desserts (chocolate and mochi xiao long bao) and teas can provide a sweet finish. **LDS/$$-$$$**

EARL OF SANDWICH: Here you'll find a celebration of the history of the sandwich and the family credited with its creation. The temporary locale has sandwiches, soups, salads, snacks, and drinks. At press time, the Earl's new Downtown Disney headquarters—over by Parkside Market—was a work in progress. For updates, use the Disneyland app or visit *disneyland.com*. **BLDS/$$-$$$**

NAPLES RISTORANTE E BAR: Dine inside or out at this contemporary Italian trattoria. A spacious terrace provides views of the Disney landscape, plus a lovely setting for lunch or dinner. The menu includes wood-fired pizzas, short rib, lasagna, chicken Parmesan, penne pasta, salads, and seared salmon. There's an outdoor bar, too. For reservations, call 714-776-6200. **LD/$$-$$$**

PASEO: A winding wooden staircase leads guests to Paseo's dining room and bar area lined with rich woods, tiles, and accents that celebrate Mexico's craftsmanship culture. (An upper patio offers lovely views of the Downtown Disney District.) Michelin-starred Chef Carlos Gaytán blends his love of Mexico with French culinary style and technique. An extensive menu offers ceviches, empanadas, roasted marinated pork, short rib wraps, lamb barbacoa, oysters, mussels, Caesar salad, guacamole (prepared table-side), creative cocktails, soft drinks, and much more. A children's menu is available. Reservations are highly recommended. **D/$$$-$$$$**

PORTO'S BAKERY & CAFE: The Porto family carries on the culinary traditions of their mom, Rosa, with quality Cuban cakes, pastries, and savory treats. Occupying the space previously graced by La Brea Bakery, Porto's is known for dishes such as guava & cheese strudels, cheese rolls, and their famous potato balls, plus soups, salads, sandwiches, cakes, shakes, and specialty coffees. Note that the eatery was still under construction as this book went to press. For updates, visit *disneyland.com*. **BLDS/$$$-$$$$**

JAZZ KITCHEN COASTAL GRILL & PATIO: This spirited spot—formerly known as Ralph Brennan's Jazz Kitchen—blithely blends California energy with Big Easy flavor. Sample home-style New Orleans specialties at this cafe while you groove to joyful jazz (live music is presented on most evenings). Fried crawfish lettuce wraps, gumbo, salads, po' boy sandwiches, blackened salmon, burgers, BBQ shrimp & grits, and jambalaya dishes have been offered. Reservations are recommended; call 714-776-5200, or visit *disneyland.com*. **LDS/$$$-$$$$**

SPLITSVILLE LUXURY LANES™: Some go expecting just to bowl, not realizing that Splitsville's kitchen turns out impressive fare such as freshly rolled sushi, grilled salmon, chicken Alfredo, steak frites, and sliders. They also have pizzas, cheeseburgers, fish 'n' chips, nachos, fries, chicken tenders, spicy veggie bowls, and chicken fried rice. Desserts include ice cream sundaes and root beer floats. A full bar offers cocktails and zero-proof beverages. Reservations are recommended, but walk-ins may be accommodated. **LDS/$$–$$$**

FAST FOOD & SNACKS

BLACK TAP CRAFT BURGERS & SHAKES: A casual destination, Black Tap has a relaxed atmosphere that's a bit reminiscent of an old-time American luncheonette. Guests may dine in- or outdoors, enjoying burgers, guac and chips, chicken wings, sandwiches, fries, salads, fried pickles, and crispy Brussels sprouts. Shakes (of the classic and "crazy" varieties), beer, wine, and soft drinks round out the menu. **LDS/$$–$$$**

BLACK TAP CRAZYSHAKE WINDOW: If you're in the mood for a mega shake, mosey over to this window for monumental milkshakes and other chilly treats. Some shakes worth noting include Brooklyn Blackout, Bam Bam, and Strawberry Shortcake. **S/$–$$**

BEIGNETS EXPRESSED: This counter spot (at Jazz Kitchen Coastal Grill & Patio) proudly presents freshly made—and deliciously decadent—beignets served in a variety of ways, plus frozen hot chocolate, non-alcoholic mint juleps, coffee, tea, and assorted soft drinks. Beignet dipping sauces are available, too. **LDS/$$**

BLUE RIBBON CORN DOG: Visit this kiosk for tasty hand-dipped corn dogs. Among the dogs from which to choose: classic, kid-size, and pickle. (The latter is a hot dog wrapped in a pickle and fried in cornmeal batter. Yum!) To save ten percent off your Blue Ribbon order, use the coupon at the back of this book. **LDS/$$**

HOT TIP

The East side Earl of Sandwich locations—both quick-service and tavern—will close this year to make way for Porto's. A new, double-decker establishment on the West side will be home to two future Earl eateries: a classic Earl of Sandwich below (quick service) and The Carnaby Tavern above (table service).

CALIFORNIA CHURRO: If you're looking for a place to procure a crispy, crunchy churro, follow your nose to California Churro—a cart that specializes in the crowd-pleasing confection. And if you'd like to stretch your budget, use the coupon at the back of this book. **S/$**

CLYDE'S HOT CHICKEN: Founded in Orange County, CA, in 2019, Clyde now serves savory snacks in the heart of Downtown Disney. Visit this stand for crispy chicken on a stick. Choose from menu selections such as "natural" (no heat whatsoever), "original" (cayenne-based with a sweet finish), or "hot as Cali" (coated with a cayenne-habeñero spice blend that delivers quite a kick). Also served here: waffle fries and bottled soft drinks. **S**/**$**

DIGGITY DOGS: A convenient spot for a portable bite, Diggity Dogs sits across from World of Disney. Do you like the idea of buying a hot dog and getting one free? Use the coupon at the back of this book. Hot dog! **LDS**/**$**

EARL OF SANDWICH QUICK-SERVICE: This ground-floor window offers deli cuisine, sandwiches, salads, snacks, and drinks. At press time, the Earl's two-story Disneyland headquarters was under construction. For updates about the eatery, visit *disneyland.com.* **BLDS**/**$$–$$$**

JAMBA: Craving a cool, tropical smoothie? Perhaps one with pineapple or peanut butter? They've got that and more—including breakfast sandwiches (sausage, egg white, and cheese), Belgian waffles, bowls, pretzels (sweet or savory), cold-brew coffee, etc. **BS**/**$**

KAYLA'S CAKE: Come to this confectious kiosk for handcrafted premium macarons, pastries, and cookies. And get ten percent off your purchase by using the coupon at the back of this book. Sweet! **S**/**$–$$$$**

NAPOLINI PIZZERIA: Adjacent to the popular Naples Ristorante, this pleasant quick-service spot serves freshly prepared pizzas (with an assortment of topping possibilities), sandwiches, salads, fruit cups, and gelato. Soft drinks, beer, wine, and hard seltzer are sold, too. (All alcohol must be consumed on the premises.) **LD**/**$$**

PEARL'S ROADSIDE BBQ: Next-door to the new Arthur & Sons steak house, this quick-service barbecue spot offers pulled pork, smoked turkey, and beef brisket with house-made sauces. The vittles may be accompanied by a craft beer or moonshine cocktail. Note that this eatery was still under construction as this book went to press. All details subject to change. **LDS**/**$$**

GG's CHICKEN SHOP: GG's patrons may choose from a selection of chicken sandwiches (original fried, ranch fried, sweet & spicy fried, or grilled), salads (with or without chicken), sides (Brussels sprouts, waffle fries, broccoli slaw), and sauces (BBQ, garlic ranch, and honey mustard). Dessert could come in the form of chocolate pudding or oatmeal cream pie. The new quick-service eatery—which was named in honor of the founding chef's mom—is located inside Parkside Market. **LDS**/**$**

SEOUL SISTER: The menu at this new casual eatery is inspired by a Korean rice bowl known as *bibimbap.* Choose your entrée from among beef, chicken, pork belly, and tofu (all accompanied by veggies and savory sauces), and then customize it with a base of either rice, noodles, or salad. Dumplings and beverages are also served. Seoul Sister can be found inside Parkside Market. **LDS**/**$**

HOT TIP

Several diverse culinary options come together under one roof at the new Parkside Market. In addition to the tempting cluster of eateries—including GG's Chicken Shop, Seoul Sister, and Sip & Sonder—guests will find a second-story bar called Vista Parkside Market.

SALT & STRAW: The luxurious ice cream served at Salt & Straw is handmade on-site using (when possible) locally sourced ingredients. It is all super yummy, too. What flavors are they serving today? Visit *saltandstraw.com* to find out. Oh and you can also order ice cream from the website and have it shipped to your home. How cool is that?! **S**/**$**

VISTA PARKSIDE MARKET: Guests savor sips while feasting on fabulous views of Downtown Disney at this second-story **NEW** alfresco venue. Selections may include frozen lemonades, frozés, espresso martinis, and zesty zero-proof drinks. **S**/**$–$$**

SIP & SONDER: This inviting java spot is located inside the new Parkside Market. It's known for signature beverages such as **NEW** honey lavender latte and the vanilla dirty chai latte. In addition to hot coffee and tea (customizable with a variety of milks and syrups), expect breakfast sandwiches, cinnamon rolls, slushies, kombucha, and cold brew. **BS**/**$**

STARBUCKS: The familiar, ubiquitous coffeehouse is situated beside Downtown Disney's World of Disney store. In addition to its usual menu of coffee-based drinks, you'll find a selection of teas, pastries, oatmeal, yogurt, breakfast sandwiches, paninis, protein boxes and bowls, and more. It's a popular spot—build in a little extra time to get that java jolt. **BLDS**/**$**

TIENDITA: Mexican street food is the star of this new quick-service neighbor of Céntrico courtyard bar and restaurant. **NEW** Orders (placed via outdoor, self-serve kiosk or inside cashier) may include *esquites* (roasted corn), quesadillas, burritos, tacos, Caesar salad, ceviches, Mexican fritters with orange sauce, and *bebidas* (soft drinks). There's a children's menu, too. **LDS**/**$$**

WETZEL'S PRETZELS: Whether you prefer pretzels salty or sweet, Wetzel's can satisfy. Snackers enjoy the Sinful Cinnamon™, Pepperoni Twist, Cheese Meltdown, and many more. Also served: hot dogs encased in pretzels, fresh lemonade, frozen lemonade, and fountain drinks. Buy one pretzel, get one pretzel free with the coupon at the back of this book! **S**/**$–$$**

Restaurant Roundup

There are more dining choices than ever before at the Disneyland Resort. We've picked some favorites, based on food quality, restaurant atmosphere, and overall value. Use these Birnbaum's Bests to help you decide where to grab a quick bite or have a hearty meal.

BEST RESTAURANTS FOR FAMILIES

TABLE SERVICE:
Goofy's Kitchen . . . . Disneyland Hotel (p. 128)
Blue Bayou . . . . Disneyland Park (p. 119)
Storytellers Cafe . . . . . Grand Californian Hotel (p. 131)
Plaza Inn . . . . Disneyland Park (p. 117)

QUICK SERVICE:
Aunt Cass Cafe . . . . . . Disney California Adventure (p. 125)
Royal Street Veranda . . . . Disneyland Park (p. 119)
Rancho del Zocalo . . . . Disneyland Park (p. 120)
Refreshment Corner Cafe . . . . . Disneyland Park (p. 118)
Flo's V8 Cafe . . . . . . Disney California Adventure (p. 127)

BEST RESTAURANTS FOR ADULTS

Napa Rose . . . . Grand Californian Hotel (p. 130)
Carthay Circle . . . . . Disney California Adventure (p. 123)

RUNNERS-UP:
Lamplight Lounge . . . Disney California Adventure (p. 126)
Din Tai Fung . . . . Downtown Disney (p. 132)
GCH Craftsman Bar . . . Grand Californian Hotel (p. 131)
Jazz Kitchen Coastal Grill & Patio . . . Downtown Disney (p. 132)
Paseo . . . . Downtown Disney (p. 132)
Céntrico . . . . Downtown Disney (p. 132)

BEST CHARACTER MEAL

Goofy's Kitchen . . . . Disneyland Hotel (p. 128)

RUNNERS-UP:
Napa Rose . . . . Grand Californian Hotel (p. 130)
Plaza Inn . . . . Disneyland Park (p. 117)
Storytellers Cafe . . . . . Grand Californian Hotel (p. 131)

BEST SNACKS

Corn Dog Castle . . . . Disney California Adventure (p. 125)
Jolly Holiday Bakery Cafe . . . . . Disneyland Park (p. 116)
Tropical Hideaway . . . . Disneyland Park (p. 118)

BEST LOUNGE

Trader Sam's Enchanted Tiki Bar . . . .
Disneyland Hotel (p. 137)

RUNNERS-UP:
Lamplight Lounge . . . .
Disney California Adventure (p. 126)
Broken Spell Lounge . . . .
Disneyland Hotel (p. 128)

BEST QUICK SERVICE

Bengal Barbecue . . . . Disneyland Park (p. 118)
RUNNER-UP:
Docking Bay 7 Food & Cargo . . . Disneyland Park (p. 122)

BEST ICE CREAM

Salt & Straw . . . . Downtown Disney (p. 135)

BEST PIZZA

Naples Ristorante e Bar . . . . . Downtown Disney (p. 132)

Entertainment
Disney Hotels

The Disneyland Resort has more to offer than theme park attractions. There's plenty to do at Disney's three hotels and in the Downtown Disney dining, shopping, and entertainment district. Whether you're seeking a break from the parks or a place to party the night away, the following options are sure to please.

Note: For more information on theme park entertainment, refer to the *Disneyland Park* and *Disney California Adventure* chapters of this book.

LOUNGES

DISNEYLAND HOTEL: The **Tangaroa Terrace Tropical Bar & Grill**, with its alfresco seating and South Seas vibe provides a pleasant meeting place. The counter-service spot features a full bar, plus a nice selection of nibbles. (Food is available inside, while drinks are served from a window out on the terrace.) **Broken Spell Lounge** (near Goofy's Kitchen), offers elevated pub fare, drinks, and live music (plus an occasional cameo by the Goof himself).

Finally, the always boisterous **Trader Sam's Enchanted Tiki Bar** mixes drinks and light bites with a bit of Disney magic. Indoor seating is limited, so reservations are recommended. They can be made via *disneyland.com,* or with the Disneyland mobile app up to 60 days ahead. Same-day reservations are subject to availability.

F.Y.I.: Trader Sam is the legendary explorer-turned-Lost & Found–operator at Disneyland park's Jungle Cruise attraction. He recently got the bartending bug (which he initially thought was a big mosquito) and began slinging cocktails at this super-immersive drinkery. Kungaloosh!

DISNEY'S GRAND CALIFORNIAN HOTEL & SPA: The lounge adjoining the elegant **Napa Rose** restaurant usually offers an extensive selection of wines by the glass (and bottle) in a soothing atmosphere. Guests may order a savory snack here, too. (The majority of this spot was on "temporary pause" at press time, but the bar itself was open for business.)

Inside the handsome **Hearthstone Lounge**, you can sip a specialty drink or an after-dinner cordial opposite a roaring fireplace. If so inclined, you may even enjoy your beverage on a comfy couch in the majestic lobby.

Guests staying at Disney's Grand Californian hotel may also opt to kick back at the **GCH Craftsman Bar** near the resort's Redwood Pool.

PIXAR PLACE HOTEL: Relax at Small Bytes, a pleasant poolside spot, where you can enjoy nibbles of all sizes, plus a bevy of beverages. Bing Bong greets guests nearby.

SPA SERVICES

DISNEY'S GRAND CALIFORNIAN HOTEL & SPA: A spa escape is as welcome a diversion as they come—especially when it's a visit to the luxurious **Tenaya Stone Spa**. Treatments include all manner of massage, facials, body wraps, manicures, pedicures, and more. There are services tailored for couples and teenaged guests.

For a complete list of Tenaya Stone Spa services or to book an appointment at the spa, go to *Disneyland.com/ TenayaStoneSpa.* To reach the Tenaya Spa by telephone, call 714-635-2300.

LIVE ENTERTAINMENT

DISNEY'S GRAND CALIFORNIAN HOTEL & SPA: A piano player tickles the ivories in the hotel's grand lobby.

HOT TIP

Trader Sam's Enchanted Tiki Bar hosts brave adventurers daily from about 8:00 A.M. until 1 A.M. (or later). Young explorers may enjoy nibbles and "no booze brews" until about 8 P.M. — after that, this lounge is strictly for guests age 21 and older (with valid government-issued photo ID to prove it). After 8 P.M., minors may enjoy some South Seas ambience on the Tangaroa Terrace side of the shared lanai.

Downtown Disney District

Easily accessed by foot (from the Disneyland Resort hotels or parks) or monorail (from Disneyland Park's Tomorrowland), this entertainment district offers a nice break from the theme park hustle and bustle during the day and a busy place to mix and mingle in the evening hours. Many Downtown Disney venues serve double (sometimes triple!) duty as dining, playing, and shopping destinations.

Shops usually open early and don't close until late in the evening. Performers generally hit the stage post-dinner and wrap by midnight.

At press time, Downtown Disney District was in the midst of a major expansion. For details and updates, visit *disneyland.com/DowntownDisney*.

LOUNGES & ENTERTAINMENT

BALLAST POINT BREWING CO.: Featuring a modern, on-site brewery, Ballast Point pairs its award-winning beers with a lineup of Southern California-inspired cuisine—salads, small plates, flatbreads, and entrées featuring local, sustainable, and seasonal ingredients. In addition to the aforementioned brewery, this sleek venue houses a tasting room, kitchen, and patio. You will find Ballast Point between Black Tap Craft Burgers & Shakes and Wetzel's Pretzels. **LDS/$$–$$$**

BLACK TAP CRAFT BURGERS & SHAKES: A colorful burger and beer joint, Black Tap has a casual atmosphere reminiscent of a classic American luncheonette, with a distinctly New York vibe. Guests may sit in- or outdoors, enjoying burgers, chicken wings, sandwiches,

salads, fried pickles, crispy Brussels sprouts, and more. Shakes (classic and "crazy" varieties), beer, wine, and soft drinks round out the menu. **BLDS/$**

DOWNTOWN DISNEY LIVE! STAGE: Downtown Disney District boasts an eclectic lineup of free, live musical entertainment. From calming classical to rousing rhythm and blues, professional musicians create a party-like atmosphere year-round. Entertainment is usually presented on a nightly basis.

JAZZ KITCHEN COASTAL GRILL & PATIO: Soothing sounds of jazz set the tone for the relaxed atmosphere at this refurbished venue, which pays tribute to The Big Easy's legacies of food and music. And it's all served up in a whimsical setting that depicts the charm and hospitality of historic and contemporary New Orleans. For additional information about this spirited spot, visit *rbjazzkitchen.com*, or call 714-776-5200.

SPLITSVILLE KINGPIN STAGE: Step up to Splitsville's patio to enjoy cocktails, dining, and live music (the latter is provided by a rotating lineup of talented local musicians.) Entertainment is usually offered from about 5 P.M. until 9 P.M. Sunday through Thursday and until 10 P.M. on Friday and Saturday.

SHOPPING

NEW

AVENGERS RESERVE: Avengers fans, assemble! A shop has opened in Downtown Disney to meet all of your Marvel fandom needs. Just look for the Hulk bursting through the wall and Spider-Man crouched atop the shop's sign. Inside you'll discover a broad spectrum of wares ranging from Green Goblin masks to X-Men action figures. If you keep your Spidey senses alert, you might even spot some movie props on display such as Loki's Horned Helmet and Dr. Strange's Eye of Agamotto. Hankering for a baby Groot Minnie ears headband? Head here!

HOT TIP

Downtown Disney is undergoing a renaissance at the moment. New shopping, dining, and entertainment opportunities will be added to the scene throughout the next couple of years. Among the latest additions to be announced are lululemon (athletic apparel), Nectar Life (bath and body products), and Bopo Go! (boba tea and snacks). None of these spots had opened when this book went to press. For further details, visit *disneyland.com.*

CURL SURF: You have to figure that anybody who spent not one but 17 years as a champion water skier has to know quite a bit about trends in beachwear and water-sport equipment. See for yourself at this high-end surf shop by Sammy Duvall. Among the assortment of wares you'll find are sunglasses, jewelry, watches, and shoes.

NEW **DISNEY STORYLAND BOUTIQUE:** This shop carries collections of items themed to memorable characters such as Baymax, Lotso, Sulley, Stitch, and the gang from the Hundred Acre Wood. Each collection is unique, but many include clothing, handbags, plush toys, and key chains. There is also a create-your-own-headband display, where guests may customize a headband by choosing mini plush characters to attach. A selection of shoulder plush (mini plush characters that perch on your shoulder with the help of magnets) can also be found here.

DISNEY HOME: If you're like the merry multitudes who would happily call Disneyland home, you're in luck: This shop lets Disney devotees add pixie-dusted touches to their actual homes. Many items vary seasonally, but Disney Home always offers fans a variety of Disney-themed treasures, such as glasswear, linens, kitchen goods, mugs, tumblers, ornaments, and framed art. Here's to the happiest home on earth!

NEW **THE D-LANDER SHOP:** Disneyland fashion meets SoCal boutique in this hip new shopping spot next to Avengers Reserve. Expect clothing with Disney touches (some Mickeys hidden, and others not so hidden) from brands such as lululemon and Her Universe, handbags from Loungefly and Dooney & Bourke, and a Pandora jewelry counter.

DISNEY'S PIN TRADERS: Do we need to spell out what this spot specializes in? Didn't think so.

THE LEGO® STORE: Hundreds of the world's most famous building brick sets and products are for sale here. This is the only store on the West Coast with a Mosaic Maker and a Minifigure Factory, where guests can design and create their own Minifigures. There's also an impressive collection of LEGO models throughout the store to admire and play with. LEGO enthusiasts of all ages can stop in and have fun. You'll find it across from Disney Pin Traders.

LOVEPOP: The eye-popping 3-D cards for sale at this shop are the result of modern technology combined with the ancient art of *kirigami* (a twist on origami in which paper is cut rather than folded). Also on hand are note cards, gift tags, and more. You will find Lovepop next to Pelé Soccer.

NEW **DISNEY WONDERFUL WORLD OF SWEETS:** If you can resist the heavenly aromas wafting out the doors of this sweet-shop, you're made of stronger stuff than we are. In addition to the olfactory enticement, the views of the exhibition kitchen are sure to get your attention. You can watch from the promenade as talented candymakers create Minnie caramel apples (hint: the ears are marshmallows), chocolate-dipped Mickey rice cereal treats, and other delectable desserts. Head inside for cookies, churro toffee squares, chocolate-dipped strawberries, and a wide variety of prepackaged selections.

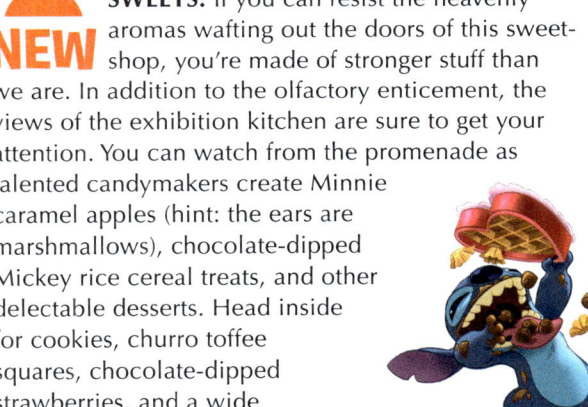

PANDORA JEWELRY: Famous for its customizable bracelets, Pandora also offers contemporary gold and silver necklaces, rings, earrings, and charms—many featuring accents such as gemstones, cultured pearls, Murano glass, and cubic zirconia.

PELÉ SOCCCER: *Fútbol* fans, rejoice! You can gather garb to support your favorite club and load up on gear to tackle the world-popular game yourself—right here at the well-stocked shop named for one of the greatest soccer players of all time. Jerseys can be customized with a name and number (for an additional fee). This spot's goal is to meet all of your soccer needs. Score!

SEPHORA: A black-and-white motif provides the backdrop for the colorful palette of products in this cosmetics mecca. Sephora's own line of makeup is complemented by a selection of beauty products, designer fragrances, and beauty services.

STAR WARS TRADING POST: What do Force-sensitive folks have to say about this destination? "Impressive. Most impressive." Just look for Rey's speeder (from *The Force Awakens*) parked out front. There you'll find a Resistance base stocked with apparel, lightsabers, droids, figurines, costumes, games, and collectibles. Are you in the market for a Mandalorian helmet? This is the way . . . to get one.

SUNGLASS ICON: Stop at this shop for premium peeper protectors—custom-fit shades are the stock-in-trade at this shop. All the big-name designers are represented.

WONDERGROUND GALLERY: Notably distinctive and eclectic, WonderGround is a work of art in and of itself. The venue showcases unique art collections and works from a new generation of artists, interpreted through various mediums, styles, and forms.

WORLD OF DISNEY: The shelves are stacked sky-high at this Disneyland souvenir seeker's go-to. With areas dedicated to plush toys, dolls, clothing, home decor, trading pins and other collectibles, Mickey ears, candy and food items, and more, there's something for just about everyone here. The place is bustling with activity most evenings and weekends—especially after the theme parks close in the evening. Note that some Disneyland Resort annual passes may yield discounts at World of Disney—be sure to ask.

ALL HAIL THE MONORAIL!

If you've got valid Disneyland Park admission, you can take the "Tomorrowland Express" from the west side of Downtown Disney straight to the heart of Disneyland park. The Downtown Disney District Monorail station is conveniently located across from the new Parkside Market (a stone's throw from the Disneyland Hotel and about 1/5 of a mile from Disney's Pixar Place Hotel). Monorail trains depart approximately every 10 minutes and rides are strictly one way (though you're free to reboard and ride again). The monorail does not operate during fireworks performances.

FUN & GAMES

SPLITSVILLE LUXURY LANES™: Boasting bowling, bars, finger food, upscale menu offerings, and more, Splitsville offers something for just about everyone. The two-story venue features 20 bowling lanes, a high-end kitchen, specialty drinks, live music—and billiards! It also hosts parties for the young and the young at heart (advance reservations are required). For additional information about this playful zone, visit *www.splitsvillelanes.com.*

SPORTS & RECREATION

Southern California's combination of warm, sunny weather and invigorating ocean breezes has created a population of outdoor and exercise enthusiasts. Athletes flex their muscles on golf courses and tennis courts; atop surfboards, bikes, and in-line skates; on hiking and jogging trails; or 15 feet underwater, mingling with shimmering schools of fish.

As part of Orange County, California, Anaheim is within easy distance of the county's 35,000-plus acres of parkland and several hundred miles of bike trails. Hiking paths and fishing streams crisscross 460,000 acres of mountain terrain in Cleveland National Forest. Just 15 miles south of Anaheim, prime Pacific Ocean beaches—perfect for basking in the sun or catching the ultimate wave—await the wayfarer. In fact, 42 miles of glistening sand and sleepy seaside communities are within an hour's drive of Anaheim.

Those who delight in spying on Mother Nature can catch glimpses of California's gray whales as they migrate to Mexico for the winter, or ospreys, blue herons, and swallows returning to the area in the spring. A team of Orange County's most entertaining creatures, hockey-playing Ducks, can be spotted from September through April (and later, if they make a run for the Stanley Cup). Even Angels have been sighted, gracing the bases at Angel Stadium, late March through September (and possibly through late October).

No doubt about it, the sporting opportunities in and around the city of Anaheim, California, are quite bountiful indeed.

Anaheim & Orange Counties

Eye on the Ball

GOLF

ANAHEIM HILLS GOLF COURSE: This challenging championship course is a hilly, par-71, 6,245-yard layout nestled in the valleys and slopes of the scenic Anaheim Hills. Greens fees range from about $18 to about $90 based on time of day and demand. Golf clubs are available to rent for about $40 to $60. Reservations are recommended (it's best to call seven days ahead for both weekend and weekday play). Details are subject to change at any time. The Anaheim Hills Golf Course is open for business 365 days a year, from 6 or 6:30 A.M. until sunset. 6501 Nohl Ranch Road, Anaheim; *www.anaheimhillsgc.com*; 714-998-3041.

DAD MILLER GOLF COURSE: "Dad" Miller made a historic hole in one on this course (on the 116-yard 11th hole) when he was 93 years old, and it's still a favorite with older guests, who appreciate the flat, walkable terrain and park-like setting. But if you're a tad on the younger side, don't let that keep you from playing here. This par-71, 5,892-yard golf course is one of the busiest in California—partly because of its convenient location in the northwest corner of the city, but also because it's just right for the strictly recreational golfer. The cost to play changes daily, based on demand, and ranges from about $14 to $58. Golf carts cost about $13 for 18 holes, $8.50 for nine holes.

Reservations are suggested and may be made up to a week in advance. The course is open 365 days each year, from 6 A.M. till 7 P.M. 430 N. Gilbert St., Anaheim; *www.dadmillergc.com*; 714-765-3481 (pro shop and reservations).

TENNIS

ANAHEIM TENNIS CENTER: This public facility has all the perks of a private tennis club—an inviting clubhouse, a well-stocked pro shop, computerized practice machines, lockers, and showers. The staff will make an effort to pair you with a suitable partner, as long as you make your request in advance.

There are 10 fast, hard-surface courts, all lighted for nighttime play. Singles rates cost about $8 to $9 per hour (depending on the time of day). Use of a ball machine is about $30 per hour; they are separated from the courts, but this area is still a good place to practice forehand and backhand strokes.

Playing hours usually begin at 7 A.M. and end at 9 P.M. Monday through Sunday. Racquets are free for those taking lessons. Locker and shower facilities are free of charge (if you want towels, you must supply them yourself). A one-hour private tennis lesson with the resident pro costs about $80 to $110; call for rates for semi-private or group lessons. Drop-in pickleball rates run about $15 per person for two hours. Reservations (which may be booked up to three days in advance for nonmembers) are suggested, especially for court times after 5 P.M. The tennis center is about three miles from the Disneyland Resort. 975 S. State College Blvd., Anaheim; 714-991-9090; *www.anaheimtenniscenter.com*.

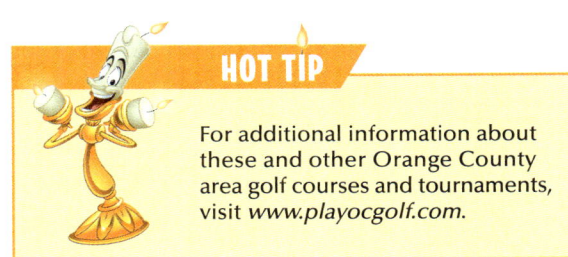

HOT TIP

For additional information about these and other Orange County area golf courses and tournaments, visit *www.playocgolf.com*.

RISE & EXERCISE!

DISNEY'S GRAND CALIFORNIAN HOTEL & SPA: Rise and shine—and exercise! Overnight guests registered at one of the three Disneyland Resort hotels (The Disneyland Hotel, Pixar Place Hotel, and Disney's Grand Californian Hotel & Spa) can enjoy an early morning group workout session (for a fee) at Disney's Grand Californian.

For additional information, or to make a reservation, go to *Disneyland.com/TenayaStoneSpa*. All details are subject to change. Here is a sampling of some recent offerings presented by Tenaya Stone Spa:

Awakening Yoga: Guests (age 14 and over) may wake up with a 45-minute session inside Disney California Adventure park (before it opens). Designed for folks at all levels, the class incorporates various types of yoga meant to improve mental awareness and start the day off right.

Power Walking Workout in Disney California Adventure Park: Kick off the morning with an energetic power walk through Disney California Adventure before the park opens for the day! Each 45-minute session costs $35 and begins at the Grand Californian's private entrance to the park. Participants maintain a 15 to 18 minute per mile pace for two miles—wear comfy shoes. To make a reservation, visit *Disneyland.com/TenayaStoneSpa*.

Paddleboard Fitness: Bathing-suit up for this floating work-out in the Fountain Pool near the Tenaya Stone Spa. It combines cardio, strength, and core exercises—all done on a paddleboard in the pool. Each 30-minute session costs $30 per person.

Paddleboard Yoga: If you've ever thought, "I would love to practice yoga while on a paddleboard floating in a swimming pool," you're in luck: 30-minute sessions are offered on select days. Each Paddleboard Yoga session costs about $30. *Namaste.*

SPECTATOR SPORTS

FOOTBALL

Los Angeles Chargers
(September–January)
SoFi Stadium
1001 Stadium Dr., Inglewood
877-242-7437
www.chargers.com

Los Angeles Rams
(September–January)
SoFi Stadium
1001 Stadium Dr., Inglewood
818-338-0011
www.therams.com

BASEBALL

Los Angeles Angels of Anaheim
(March–September)
Angel Stadium of Anaheim,
2000 E. Gene Autry Way., Anaheim
714-940-2000
www.mlb.com/angels

Los Angeles Dodgers
(March–September)
Dodger Stadium
1000 Vin Scully Ave., Los Angeles
866-363-4377
www.mlb.com/dodgers

HOCKEY

Los Angeles Kings
(September–April)
Crypto.com Arena
1111 S. Figueroa St., Los Angeles
888-546-4752
www.nhl.com/kings

Anaheim Ducks
(September–April)
Honda Center
2695 E. Katella Ave., Anaheim
www.nhl.com/ducks
ticketmaster.com

BASKETBALL

Los Angeles Clippers
(October–April)
Intuit Dome
3930 W. Century Blvd., Inglewood
213-204-2980
www.nba.com/clippers

Los Angeles Lakers
(October–April)
Crypto.com Arena
1111 S. Figueroa St., Los Angeles
www.nba.com/lakers
ticketmaster.com

Los Angeles Sparks
(May–September)
Crypto.com Arena
1111 S. Figueroa St., Los Angeles
213-742-7340
sparks.wnba.com

Surf & Sun

BEACHES

Orange County's public beaches cover 42 miles of coastline—some dramatic, with high cliffs and crashing waves; others tranquil, with sheltered coves and tide pools. In summer, the water temperature averages 64 degrees but can get as high as 70; in winter, it's a nippy 57 to 60 degrees.

Beaches are usually open from around 6 A.M. to 10 P.M., with lifeguards on duty in the summer. Bicycles, in-line skates, and roller skates are available for rent in some locations. Access is free, but there is usually a fee to park. For additional beach information, go to the Surf and Sand section of *www.orangecounty.net.*

BALBOA/NEWPORT BEACH: The Balboa Peninsula juts into the Pacific Ocean, creating lovely beaches—Newport on the mainland, Balboa on the peninsula—that are long and horseshoe-shaped, pleasant and sandy, and popular with families, surfers, and sightseers. Visit *www.ocbeachinfo.com* for water quality and environmental information.

The largest small-craft harbor in the world, Newport Harbor shelters more than 9,000 boats. For a choice view, drive south along the peninsula on Newport Boulevard to Balboa Boulevard; turn right on Palm Street, and you will find parking for the popular Balboa Pier and Fun Zone; *www.balboaferriswheel.com.*

Throughout the fall and winter, the 1,000-acre Upper Newport Bay Nature Preserve and Ecological Reserve teems with great blue herons, ospreys, and many other wild winged creatures. The park's partially subterranean Peter and Mary Muth Interpretive Center, located at 2301 University Drive (at Irvine Avenue), has exhibits on bird life, the watershed, and the history of Newport Bay (open 10 A.M. to 4 P.M.; closed Mondays).

During migratory season (October through March), the Newport Bay Conservancy leads free walking tours, pointing out birds, as well as fossils, marsh plants, and

HOT TIP

For a scenic 45-minute walk, follow the harbor-hugging pathway around Balboa Island. For a mini-expedition, head to Little Balboa Island—it can be completed in about 20 minutes.

fish. On Saturday mornings, year-round, the conservancy also offers a 2-hour guided kayak tour of the Back Bay for $25 per person, ages 8 and up.

The reserve is open daily 7 A.M. to sunset. To obtain updated information about guided tours and various special events year-round, as well as directions to specific parts of the reserve, contact Newport Bay Conservancy: 949-923-2269 or *www.newportbay.org.*

CORONA DEL MAR STATE BEACH: Secluded Corona del Mar State Beach is a favorite for swimming and snorkeling; and the lookout point above the beach is a great place to watch the sun set. There are picnic tables, grills, fire rings, a snack bar, and showers. For information, visit *www.orangecounty.net* (Surf and Sand section), or call 949-644-3151.

HUNTINGTON BEACH: The self-proclaimed "Surf City, U.S.A." (and home to the International Surfing Museum) hosts competitions year-round (winter is best for wave height). Surfboards and wet suits may be rented or purchased; *www.surfcityusa.com.*

Huntington City Beach is a 3.5-mile stretch of sand fronting the town and is a popular place for swimming, bodysurfing, and beach volleyball. The pier provides an ideal spot for fishing and a good vantage point for observing the passing scene. For surf information, call 714-536-9303; *www.surf-forecast.com.*

Bolsa Chica Wetlands, 1,449 acres of Pacific Ocean marshland a mile north of Huntington Beach pier on Pacific Coast Highway, harbors fish and wetland birds. The Interpretive Center is open Monday from 9 A.M. to 1 P.M. and Tuesday through Sunday from 9 A.M. until 4 P.M. with three marine life exhibits. To get there, cross the bridge from the beach parking lot and follow a trail through the marsh; 714-846-1114; *www.bolsachica.org.*

LAGUNA BEACH: More than 20 different beaches and coves line this seven-mile coastline, popular with surfers, kayakers, body boarders, and snorkelers. Laguna is one of the best spots in Orange County to scuba dive, though you need a wet suit year-round.

Beach Cities Scuba (925 N. Coast Hwy.; 949-494-6965; *www.beachcitiesscuba.com*) offers full rentals, guided beach dives, classes, general information, and more; there's a pool on the premises, and it's only two blocks from the beach. Main Beach (which is located in the middle of town) offers basketball and volleyball.

A short walk away, Heisler Park has scenic picnic areas, beaches, cliff-top lookout points, benches, and charcoal grills; stairs lead to tide pools. Serious hikers like to head for the Aliso and Wood Canyons Wilderness Park (*www.ocparks.com*), the Crystal Cove State Park (*www.crystalcovestatepark.org*), or the Laguna Coast Wilderness Park. Watch the sun set from Laguna Art Museum or Laguna Village; *www.visitlagunabeacn.com*.

FISHING

In Orange County, you can cast for bass, catfish, and trout in tranquil lakes; troll the Pacific for bonitos, barracuda, halibut, and more; and hand-scoop grunions (license required) off the beach.

GRUNION ALERT: One scenic place to try your hand—literally—at catching grunion (provided that you have a license) is at Cabrillo Beach in March, July, and August, when the tiny fish come ashore to lay eggs in the sand and then head back out to sea on outgoing waves. (Grunion catching is illegal—even if you have a fishing license—in April, May, and June.)

Grunion are quite slippery, and you are required (by law) to catch them exclusively with your hands; fortunately, they also shimmer in the moonlight, so they're fairly easy to spot. The best time to go grunion fishing is about an hour or two after high tide on the second through fifth nights after a new or full moon. Park gates close at 10:30 P.M. Be sure to observe all parking rules. For more details, visit *wildlife.ca.gov* or *grunion.org*, or call 310-548-7562.

SPORTFISHING: Fishing boats set out from Davey's Locker at Balboa Pavilion in Newport Beach (949-673-1434; *www.daveyslocker.com*) and from Dana Wharf Sportfishing at Dana Point Harbor (*www.danawharf.com*; 888-224-0603). Reservations are suggested. Fishing licenses, which are legally necessary for deep-sea sportfishing, must be purchased in advance via *www.wildlife.ca.gov/Licensing/fishing*. Licenses cost about $20 per day.

PARKS

IRVINE REGIONAL PARK: Located in Santiago Canyon near Irvine Lake, this peaceful place has hiking and equestrian trails that wind through 491 hilly acres and centuries-old sycamores and oaks. The oldest county park in California, it offers bike trails, the Orange County Zoo, playgrounds, a small waterfall, creek, and picnic facilities. Zoo admission is $2 for guests age 3 and up. There is a $3 to $5 parking fee per vehicle year-round (the parking fee is usually about $7 on major holidays). 1 Irvine Park Rd., Orange; 714-973-6835; *www.ocparks.com*.

MILE SQUARE REGIONAL PARK: It's one square mile in area—hence the name. Besides five miles of winding bike trails, the park has a walking course, a nature area, and picnic areas and shelters. Bicycles may be rented here on weekends and holidays. 16801 Euclid Street, Fountain Valley; *www.ocparks.com*; 714-973-6600.

ENC TUCKER WILDLIFE SANCTUARY: This 12-acre sanctuary in the Santa Ana Mountains' Modjeska Canyon is an oasis of diverse flora and fauna. Naturalists can answer questions, and there are hiking trails, a small natural history museum, and a sensory garden. A donation is suggested (and appreciated). 29322 Modjeska Canyon Rd., Modjeska Canyon; *www.encenter.org*; 949-645-8489.

YORBA REGIONAL PARK: These 140 acres in the Santa Ana Canyon cradle four lakes (with connecting streams), picnic areas, playgrounds, hiking trails, equestrian activities, horseshoe pits, model sailboating, volleyball courts, baseball fields, and biking trails (bike rentals are offered on weekend days). Visitors can walk or ride a bicycle into the park without charge; parking costs about $3 to $5 ($7 on holidays). 7600 E. La Palma Ave., Anaheim; *www.ocparks.com*; 714-973-6615.

WHALE WATCHING & DOLPHIN CRUISE

Whale watching and dolphin cruises leave from Newport Beach daily throughout the year. You may see giant blue whales, finback whales, gray whales, humpback whales, minke whales, and dolphins. Birnbaum's readers net a discount on weekday (about $14 per person) and weekend (about $22 per person) cruises with promo code disney18. Other types of cruises are available as well. Call 949-673-1434, or visit *www.daveyslocker.com*.

INDEX

COUPONS

lovepop®

$5 OFF
A PURCHASE OF $50 OR MORE

Subject to terms and conditions on reverse side.

10% OFF

For Birnbaum readers when shopping the greatest selection of designer sunglasses for women, men, and kids at select Sunglass Hut locations! Supplying iconic brands, Sunglass Hut is the perfect way to protect your eyes in style during your Disney Day. See participating locations on reverse side.

Subject to terms and conditions on reverse side.

RECEIVE 10% OFF
ENTIRE PURCHASE

Made to order for that delicious crunchy, crispy bite!

Subject to terms and conditions on reverse side.

RECEIVE 10% OFF
ENTIRE PURCHASE

The most unique churros—you are definitely in for a treat!

Subject to terms and conditions on reverse side.

©Disney

15% OFF RETAIL PURCHASE*

Valid at Ghirardelli® Soda Fountain & Chocolate Shop in Disney California Adventure

Ghirardelli® Chocolate is committed to using high quality and sustainably sourced cocoa beans to ensure a rich and velvety chocolate flavor. Established in 1852, Ghirardelli® Chocolate has been a pioneer in making premium chocolate so delicious it makes life a bite better.

*Offer valid on packaged chocolate gifts only.

Subject to terms and conditions on reverse side.

©Disney

COUPONS

10% OFF
ENTIRE PURCHASE

Offering authentic Disney collectibles, exquisite crystal mementos, and sparkling hand-blown glass gifts.

Subject to terms and conditions on reverse side.

BUY ONE DOG, GET THE SECOND DOG FREE

Subject to terms and conditions on reverse side.

KAYLA'S CAKE
Inspired Artisan Delicacies

10% OFF
ENTIRE PURCHASE

Delectable French macarons and cake in a jar. Visit our kiosk in the Downtown Disney® District near the World of Disney store.

Subject to terms and conditions on reverse side.

Curl SURF

10% OFF
ENTIRE PURCHASE

Premium brand surf apparel, women's fashion, swimwear, accessories, and goods for the entire family!

Subject to terms and conditions on reverse side.

10% OFF
BOWLING

Subject to terms and conditions on reverse side.

BUY ONE PRETZEL, GET THE SECOND PRETZEL FREE

Subject to terms and conditions on reverse side.

TERMS AND CONDITIONS

Redeemable at Downtown Disney® District in Anaheim, California.

Coupon must be surrendered at time of purchase.

Not valid with any other offers or discounts.

Limit one per coupon.

Photocopies will not be accepted.

Non-transferable, non-negotiable.

Offer subject to change without notice.

For information, call 714-535-5994 or 626-432-6900.

Offer valid through 12/31/26

TERMS AND CONDITIONS

Valid at the Arribas Brothers stores at Disneyland® Park at Crystal Arts on Main Street, U.S.A., and at Cristal d'Orleans in New Orleans Square (Park admission is required).

Coupon excludes shipping charges and online purchases. Other restrictions may apply. Discount cannot be combined with any other offers or discounts. No cash value.

Coupon must be presented at time of purchase to receive discount.

Reproductions not accepted.

Offer subject to change without notice.

For more information, visit *www.arribas.com*, or call 714-635-1940.

Offer valid through 12/31/26

TERMS AND CONDITIONS

Valid at the Downtown Disney® District Anaheim location only.

Must present coupon to receive discount.

Discount does not apply to sale items, gift cards, or online purchases. Some product exclusions apply. See store for details.

Terms and conditions subject to change without notice.

Coupon not valid with any other discount.

Coupon cannot be copied or reproduced.

Coupon cannot be redeemed for cash.

For information, call 714-772-2410.

www.curlsurf.com

Offer valid through 12/31/26

TERMS AND CONDITIONS

Valid only at the Downtown Disney® District Anaheim location (near the World of Disney store).

Coupon cannot be combined with any other offers or discounts. Not redeemable for cash in whole or in part. Coupon must be surrendered at time of purchase. Reproductions not accepted.

Offer subject to change without notice.

For information, call 714-869-1522.

www.thekaylascake.com

Offer valid through 12/31/26

TERMS AND CONDITIONS

Redeemable at Downtown Disney® District in Anaheim, California.

Not valid with any other offers or discounts. Offer subject to change without notice. Limit one free pretzel per coupon. Coupon must be surrendered at time of purchase.

For information, call 714-535-5994.

Photocopies will not be accepted.

Non-transferable, non-negotiable.

Offer valid through 12/31/26

TERMS AND CONDITIONS

Offer redeemable at Splitsville Luxury Lanes™. Valid at Downtown Disney® District Anaheim location only.

Must present coupon to receive discount. Reproductions of coupon not accepted. Subject to availability and limited to groups of 10 or less. Cannot be applied to lane reservations or private events.

Limit one coupon per transaction. Coupon cannot be redeemed for cash in whole or in part. Coupon cannot be combined with any other offer or discount. Offer subject to change without notice.

Call 657-276-2440 for reservations.

Offer valid through 12/31/26

THE HAPPIEST PLACE ON EARTH

Disneyland welcomed its first guests on July 17, 1955—which means that it has been the "Happiest Place on Earth" for 70 magical years! The 70th Anniversary Celebration began on May 16, 2025, and runs through the summer of 2026; so if you visit during this happy time, you'll be able to take part in the festivities. You can expect to see new costumes for Mickey, Minnie, and their friends; special entertainment; unique tasty treats; and celebratory touches added to classic attractions. You may even hear the peppy new anniversary theme song, "Celebrate Happy." For entertainment schedules, check a park Tip Board or use the Disneyland mobile app. What follows is a sample of the offerings.

DISNEYLAND PARK

"PAINT THE NIGHT" PARADE: Returning to Main Street, U.S.A., for the first time since its initial run, "Paint the Night" is a nighttime parade that dazzles

HOT TIP

Festive dining opportunities abound during the 70th Anniversary Celebration. At Disneyland Park, Tomorrowland Skyline Terrace offers a dinner package paired with exclusive views of Wondrous Journeys. At DCA, the World of Color Dessert Party includes reserved seating for the show as well as a variety of tasty treats. Visit *disneyland.com* for a complete list of dining packages.

with more than a million LED lights. Look out for floats inspired by *Beauty and the Beast*; *The Little Mermaid*; *Cars*; *Monsters, Inc.*; and *Toy Story*. Don't forget to wave hello to Anna and Elsa on the Frozen float!

WONDROUS JOURNEYS: Watch as Sleeping Beauty Castle, the Rivers of America, and the façade of "it's a small world" become canvases for this stirring nighttime projection show. Over a century of Walt Disney Animation Studios storytelling is celebrated through images, music, and—on select nights—fireworks. You'll see moments come to life from films such as *Hercules*, *The Princess and the Frog*, *Peter Pan*, *Frozen*, *Big Hero 6*, *Moana*, and *Encanto*.

CELEBRATE HAPPY CAVALCADE: Wearing their special new 70th Anniversary costumes, Mickey, Minnie, and many of their friends dance their way

THE LAST VERSE

Inside the Main Street Cinema, you can watch a short film about the Sherman brothers called *The Last Verse*. Robert and Richard M. Sherman were a famous songwriting duo. Their many credits include "it's a small world," songs for *Mary Poppins* such as "A Spoonful of Sugar," as well as music for *The Jungle Book* ("I Wanna Be Like You") and *Bedknobs and Broomsticks* ("Substitutiary Locomotion").

down Main Street in this celebratory cavalcade. Princesses, heroes, and even those adorable stuffed bears, Duffy and ShellieMay, join Mickey in the procession.

TAPESTRY OF HAPPINESS: If you wove together 70 years of happy memories created at the "Happiest Place on Earth," what would you get? A Tapestry of Happiness, of course! This projection show, featuring images inspired by artist Mary Blair and music from Disneyland attractions, can be seen on select nights on the façade of "it's a small world."

DISNEY CALIFORNIA ADVENTURE

BETTER TOGETHER PARADE: Returning to DCA for a limited time in honor of the 70th Anniversary Celebra-

tion, Better Together: A Pixar Pals Celebration! Parade is a panoply of favorite characters rarely seen at the parks. Red Panda Mei and friends from *Turning Red* throw a dance party; Luca, Alberto, and Giulia wave *ciao* to passersby; and Joe Gardner brings some soul to the streets in this Pixar parade.

WORLD OF COLOR HAPPINESS!: If you close your eyes and think of happiness, what color do you see? Hosted by Joy and the other emotions from *Inside Out*, this new World of Color show answers that question in brilliant fashion. Fountains, lasers, fog, flame, and music come together to evince moments from films including *Tangled*, *Encanto*, *The Incredibles*, *Turning Red*, and *A Goofy Movie*. You will surely feel joy— and a slew of other powerful emotions!

HOT TIP

When you ride the attraction "it's a small world," look for a couple new singers in Mexico. Miguel and Dante from the Pixar film *Coco* have joined the chorus!

AUTOGRAPHS

AUTOGRAPHS